Explore the World

NELLES

SWEDEN

Authors:
*Gerhard Lemmer, Birgit Krämer,
Otto Steiger*

*An Up-to-date travel guide
with 127 color photos
and 19 maps*

Dear Reader: Being up-to-date is the main goal of the Nelles series. Our correspondents help keep us abreast of the latest developments in the travel scene, while our cartographers see to it that maps are also kept completely current. However, as the travel world is constantly changing, we cannot guarantee that all the information contained in our books is always valid. Should you come across a discrepancy, please contact us at: Nelles Verlag, Schleissheimer Str. 371 b, 80935 Munich, Germany, tel. (089) 3571940, fax (089) 35719430, e-mail: Nelles.Verlag@t-online.de

Note: Distances and measurements, including temperatures, used in this guide are metric. For conversion information, please see the *Guidelines* section of this book.

LEGEND

★★ ★★	Main Attraction *(on map) (in text)*	
★ ★	Worth Seeing *(on map) (in text)*	
❽	Orientation Number in Text and on Map	
▪	Public or Significant Building	
—•—	Metro	
🚹	Tourist-Information	
✝ ✡	Church, Synagogue	
※	View-Point	

Örebro *(Town)* Tanum *(Sight)*	Places Highlighted in Yellow Appear in Text	
✈ ✈	International Airport / National Airport	
Kebnekaise (2111)	Mountain (altitude in meters)	
13	Distance in Kilometers	
∴	Ancient Site	
🅢🅢🅢 🅢🅢 🅢	Luxury Hotel Category Moderate Hotel Category Budget Hotel Category *(for price information see "Accomodation" in Guidelines section)*	

▨	Line of Demarcation
▬	Provincial Border
═══	Expressway
▬▬	Principal Highway
──	Main Road
──	Provincial Road
──	Secondary Road
E18 2	Route Number
━━	Ferry
∩	Cave
⚐	Castle

SWEDEN
© Nelles Verlag GmbH, 80935 München
 All rights reserved

First Edition 2000
ISBN 3-88618-103-0
Printed in Slovenia

Publisher:	Günter Nelles	**Photo Editor:**	K. Bärmann-Thümmel
Managing Editor:	Berthold Schwarz	**Translator:**	Kent Lyon
Project Editor:	Gerhard Lemmer	**Cartography:**	Nelles Verlag GmbH
English Edition		**Lithos:**	Priegnitz, Munich
Editor:	Chase Stewart	**Printed By:**	Gorenjski Tisk

TABLE OF CONTENTS

TRAVEL INFORMATION

LIST OF MAPS

HISTORY
AND CULTURE

Prehistory

Flatly describing the Swedes as descendants of the Vikings is certainly not inaccurate, however, it leaves out the important parts of the country's long history in which the legendary Viking Age represents only a relatively short period.

The beginnings of the settlement of Sweden go back approximately 10,000 years. Immediately after the last Ice Age, the first hunters and gatherers arrived and spread out into what is now central Sweden in the course of the following centuries. Permanent farmsteads were established as early as the 3rd century B.C., while the oldest burial mounds and chamber tombs also appeared at that time. Bronze reached southern Sweden in the middle of the 2nd century B.C., and numerous rock carvings date from this period, such as the ones found near Tanum. The first iron weapons and tools were obtained through trade with the Celts, the undisputed iron-working specialists of the time. For this reason, from 500 B.C. onward, the period is referred to as the Celtic Iron Age.

With the Romans' triumph over its competitors for power, the Celtic influence dwindled in northern Europe; upon adopting a new calendar, the Celtic Iron Age was taken over by that of the Romans. This lasted until the end of the Roman Empire in the 5th century A.D. The advanced cultures of the Mediterranean evinced only little interest in the northern edge of the empire at that time. Pliny the Elder knew of an "Island of

Preceding pages: Dandelion field in Väster-götland. Finally summer vacation! Left: Stone picture fragment from the Viking Age, found in Gotland (in the Statens Historiska Museum, Stockholm).

Scatinavia" only from hearsay, and had presumably Latinized a Nordic name.

The great migrations (A.D. 400-550) did not pass by Sweden unnoticed. The Goths living in the south fled to the mouth of the Weichsel River to escape the northward immigration wave as the first Teutons arrived in the country. The fact that their intrusion certainly can not have been a peaceful one is witnessed by the numerous fortifications and refuges dating from this time.

The following period (ca. A.D. 500-800), named the Vendel Age for a location of findings near Uppsala, is one of the most noteworthy phases of Sweden's history. First attempts of a state organization developed in the form of loose coalitions of small kingships; art and trade also experienced a flourishing unknown until that time. Because of the many gold-plated burial findings, the Vendel Age is also known as Sweden's Golden Age. The Vendel people, possibly Celts who had fled to the north, called themselves *Svear*. They had taken on the leading role in the southern region; their empire, *Svea rike,* gave the Sweden of today its name: *Sverige*. The Svear were gradually driven out by the advancing Teutons, who were later called *Vikinger* due to their settlements in protected bays *(vik)*. It is certain that the Vikings overran the Svear, whether they were totally annihilated remains unknown. At any rate, the Vikings did pick up many art and craft elements from their predecessors.

The Viking Age

The first known date of the Viking's rule in Scandinavia is A.D. 793, when the Lindsisfarne monastery on the west coast of England was attacked, pillaged and completely destroyed. This was the beginning of an unprecedented spree of violence. In rapid succession, the Vikings appeared at the mouths of the Seine and Thames Rivers, as well as the Rhine, and

later on did not spare the European Atlantic coast and the Mediterranean in their series of cruel raids either. Even Charlemagne paid protection money to remain immune to attacks. No one in Europe was prepared for the onslaught of the "North Men," and in the medieval way of thinking, they were soon seen as the apocalyptic disaster. The acts of cruelty associated with the raids – without exception in survivors' accounts – led them to be depicted as heathen devils. How deeply the fear was rooted can be seen by the fact that the request to be spared was still an integral part of all religious masses in France up until the 18th century.

What drove the Vikings to conduct their raids was certainly not a purely destructive urge. The food supply in the sparsely populated Scandinavia was par-

Above: Bird mask from the late Bronze Age, found in Glasbacke, Halland, southern Sweden (Statens Historiska Museum). Right: Varangians as traders crossing the Baltic Sea (painting by N. K. Roerich, 1901).

tially catastrophic and virtually forced them to obtain their food by rapacious acts. Salt could not be mined in the north, but the Vikings needed it for the preservation of their foodstuffs, for instance, fish; what they needed were goods they could use for trade. If there were none to be found, stealing them was the only alternative. This is certainly where the Vikings profited from their nautical expertise. They had inevitably developed it on their long voyages: water passageways were practically the only transportation routes in Sweden.

It will probably never be clear whether it was coincidence or desperation that led them to the western coast of England. The rich booty that fell into their hands allowed them to continue trading easily for valuable goods. Their success was helped rather than hindered due to their religion, with its warrior gods Odin, Thor and Frey, based on an eternal battle and an honorable hero's death.

As casually as we refer to "the Vikings," the label is also problematic. They could be classified as two groups early on. The West Vikings in Denmark, who also settled on the west coast of Norway, used the North Sea and the Atlantic almost exclusively as their domain – and the Mediterranean Sea later on. The East Vikings, called "Varangians," concentrated on the Baltic Sea and the adjacent East European regions. There are few reports of raids; they traded rather extensively, which took them to Byzantium and Baghdad – thereby leading them to the western end of the legendary Silk Road. They used the large East European rivers as transport routes where they set up trading posts. They dragged their light boats and goods across land when they encountered watersheds and rapids.

Although the individual Varangian groups operated relatively independently, there was a capital of sorts for their empire: Birka, on the island of Björko in Lake Mälaren, 30 kilometers west of

present-day Stockholm. According to the bishop Ansgar of Bremen, an unsuccessful missionary in the 9th century, it was a rich, fortified city with a harbor, refuge fort and some 1,000 inhabitants. Birka's heyday came to an end about 150 years later. In addition to native arts and crafts, the archeological findings there, consisting of Chinese silk cloths, Arabian coins and Franconian glass as burial objects, are testimony to the former extensive trade links of the Varangians. These expanded even farther when the East Vikings conquered Haithabu (Schleswig-Holstein) in the 9th century, thus enabling them to control trade between the North and Baltic Seas.

This was the beginning of the first frontier between the Danish West Vikings and the Swedish East Vikings which was followed up by the differentiation in the development of the formerly uniform language. Religious beliefs were also affected. While the East Vikings had nearly all been converted to Christianity in the 10th century, the Varangians still believed

in their gods for the most part. Adam of Bremen reported about a sizable Viking shrine near Uppsala with curious sacrificial rites. Nine male specimens of every species, including human beings, are said to have been sacrificed to the gods every nine years there – using the blood to calm the rage of the gods. Afterwards, they hung the halved cadavers in a nearby sacred grove.

Not until the Viking chief Olof Eriksson had himself baptized in 1008 did Christianity gradually begin to triumph. This also ended the pirating crusades of the Vikings and marks the beginning of the medieval period in Sweden.

The Middle Ages

While the Viking Age was marked by tribal and chief rule, a bitter internal power struggle for supremacy arose in the region after Christianization. The monotheistic religious concept of "only one ruler" was certainly significant here. An electoral kingdom was founded after long and bloody battles; with elections taking place near Uppsala. A legal administrator *(Jarl)* was placed at the side of the king, who was intended to serve as liaison between the king and the nobility. In reality, however, he often actually wielded power himself.

By the middle of the 12th century, the Erik dynasty had become the most powerful house in the country, and its lineage produced Swedish kings for over a century. The most well-known, Erik IX (1156-60), known as "The Saint" after a conquering crusade through Finland, is still considered to be the patron saint of Sweden. It was under his reign that the first Swedish bishopric was founded in which his successor designated the town of Uppsala as an archbishopric in the year 1164. The last representative of the Erik dynasty on the throne, Erik Eriksson, had his kingdom governed by Birger Jarl (1248-66) and died childless. This moved Birger Jarl to have his own son (a minor at the time) crowned to carry out the tutelage himself.

Sweden experienced a revival under Birger Jarl: laws were standardized, the role of the church was strengthened, and in 1252 he transformed the strategically important Stockholm into a powerful harbor city. In the following period, the privileges of the nobility and clergy were more precisely defined; this was intended to reward the fulfillment of duties with tax exemption. The farmers were liable to tax, but were not subjected to submit taxes to land owners.

In the 13th century, Sweden also sided with the German Hanseatic League, which not only provided funds and specialists for the initial construction of a mine, but also sent administrative experts and businessmen to the north. In return, Sweden had to accept that by the end of the 13th century already half of all city residents and councilmen in the country were German.

In the 14th century, Sweden experienced its largest expansion under the Norwegian king Magnus Eriksson (1319-64), who had inherited the Swedish throne. His empire stretched from the area between the mouth of the Neva River and the Norwegian fjords to as far as Skagerrak in the south. It collapsed when the Danes conquered Gotland in 1361. Magnus' successor, Albrecht of Mecklenburg, had a falling out with the Swedish nobility, but joined forces with Queen Margaret of Denmark and swept King Albrecht from the throne.

The Kalmar Union

The great Scandinavian union to solve the conflict that followed was named the "Kalmar Union" after the location of its founding; it united the states of Denmark, Sweden and Norway in 1397. The initiator was Margaret of Denmark; until her death in 1412, she understood well how to tactfully balance the diverging interests of the Scandinavian states, a skill her successor and grandnephew Erik of Pomerania (1412-39) hardly possessed.

Contrary to the contractual agreements, Erik used Danish protectors in Sweden and attempted to undermine the political trade domination of the Hanseatic League. A revolt in 1434 led by the Swedish land and mine owner Engelbrekt Engelbrektsson was just the first sign of bitterness which saturated all classes, including the farmers, who made their organized debut at the so-called First Parliament, or national assembly *(Riksdag)*, in 1435.

When Karl Knutsson was named king, thus placing him in opposition to Christian I of Denmark, the dispute escalated. This resulted in all foreigners losing some of their many privileges and the loss of all their seats in the Riksdag.

Right: The Castle of Kalmar, the city which gave the "Kalmar Union" (the Scandinavian states in the Middle Ages) its name.

While the Kalmar Union continued to exist officially, a deep rift opened up straight through the nobility. One group stood on the side of the Swedish regent Sten Sture, who, at the same time, was allied to the Hanseatic League. The other part remained loyal to King Christian II of Denmark, who had ruled Norway and Denmark since 1513. Gustav Trolle, the archbishop in Uppsala, was a powerful advocate of this party. After the death of Sten Sture in 1520, the Danish king and the archbishop were successful in winning the loyalty of the Sture supporters of crowing the Swedish king by promising them extensive rights as well as a general amnesty.

None of the promises were kept and worse was yet to come: shortly after the coronation of Christian II, Trolle declared all Sture supporters heretics and promptly had them sentenced; 82 of the most influential were executed in front of Stockholm's City Hall. This "Stockholm Bloodbath" marked the end of the Kalmar Union. The following revolts resulted in

Gustavus Vasa, an in-law of Sten Sture, coming to power. He became regent in 1521 and was elected king in 1523. One of his first official duties was to declare Sweden's withdrawal from the Kalmar Union. And as an advocate of Lutheran church reform, he ordered the secularization of church property in 1527, economically anticipating the Reformation, but the process, carried out without bloodshed, still took until 1593. From that point on, only Protestants were allowed to hold public office.

The Vasa Period

King Gustavus I Vasa is considered to be, and rightly so, the king who led Sweden out of the confusion of the Middle Ages into becoming a strong and modern state. In doing so, he acted very much in the same tradition as his predecessors had, not only keeping an eye on the welfare of the community, but especially on the interests of his own extended family. When the king died in 1560, approxi-

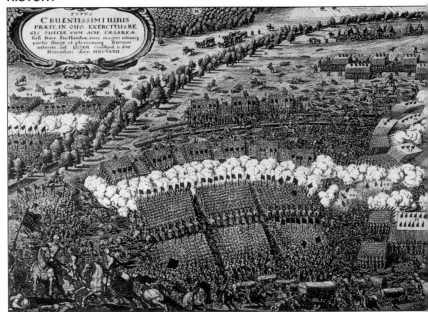

mately 60 percent of the land was in the hands of his clan. Gustavus Vasa had achieved an ancestral monarchy in 1544, so not only did his successors wage numerous wars for power in the Baltic Sea region, but they also wrangled amongst themselves for the throne.

Not until Gustavus Vasa's youngest son Charles IX was crowned in 1604 did a certain stability begin to prevail in Sweden. With his tremendous foresight, he had the harbor town of Gothenburg designed when he noticed the role of the Baltic Sea region had begun to wane with the development of Atlantic trade and the discovery of the Arctic Sea Passage to Russia. Charles' politics were directed towards making Sweden the dominating power in all of Scandinavia and the entire Baltic Sea region. When he suffered a stroke in 1611 he was far from realizing his plans, but his 16-year-old son Gus-

Above: The Battle at Lützen, 1632, where Gustavus II Adolphus found his death (copperplate etching by Merian the Elder, 1637).

tavus Adolphus was standing ready as a successor who was second to none in his energetic ability to achieve.

The Rise of a Superpower

Shortly after his coronation in 1611, Gustavus II Adolphus called a cease fire, thus ending the war that had just broken out with Denmark. Poland had planned to put pressure on the young king; Gustavus, however, beat them to to the draw with an attack of his own. Gustavus Adolphus profited by having Axel Oxenstierna (1583-1654) standing at his side as chancellor, field marshal, advisor and friend throughout his entire reign.

After the successful offensive against Poland, Sweden gained control over the entire length of the Polish Baltic Sea coast between Pomerania and the Baltic states. In Sweden itself, the king and his chancellor had carried out an army reform which resulted in some 20,000 ready troops. They were self-sufficient and armed with products of Swedish ar-

mories. When the Catholic Polish king laid claim to the throne in 1617, the right to residency in Sweden for non-Protestants was abolished. Beginning in 1618, the Habsburgs attempted to win back the Protestant provinces of Germany for Catholicism in the wake of the Counter-Reformation; they made the same attempt for the Swedish possessions in Germany. The conflict with the Habsburgs was predetermined; the Thirty Years' War had begun.

Sweden could not remain neutral with the new distribution of power in Europe it was now facing. German Protestant princes used Sweden's support to protect them from being run over by the Habsburgs. The Swedes feared a Madrid-Vienna-Warsaw axis, which would have threatened their dominance in the Baltic region, and the Hanseatic League made a pact with the Swedes for fear of losing their privileges. The Protestant Gustavus Adolphus also allied himself with Cardinal Richelieu; it was in both of their interests to prevent the formation of a German nation-state. The French cardinal promised support for everyone who contributed to weakening the position of the Habsburgs in the War of the Spanish Succession. In short, the religious differences that were to be settled peacefully in the Conciliations of Trent were popularly used as a pretext for pure power-political struggles. However, in political propaganda, the question of faith stood in the forefront, splendidly allowing itself to be used for condemnation of the respective opposition. This reactivated the long-forgotten fear of the Vikings, now transferred to the Swedes. They were credited with such perfidious atrocities as "laughing oneself to death" and the lethal "Swedish drink," both being methods of torture. The following popular nursery rhyme vividly illustrates how the Swedes were feared:

> *Pray children pray,*
> *The Swede will come today,*
> *Tomorrow comes the "Oxen star,"*
> *He'll teach you children how to pray.*

19

After Sweden had entered the war events quickly developed in favor of the Protestant camp. The Habsburg general Tilly was overwhelmingly defeated in the battle of Breitenfeld in 1631. Gustavus II Adolphus conquered Pomerania and Magdeburg, held court in Frankfurt the following winter and continued pushing southward before reaching Nuremberg and Munich in the spring. His kingdom then extended from Lapland to the foothills of the Alps.

The imperialist Habsburgs were able to retaliate in a desperate offensive led by Wallenstein in November 1632 at Lützen. Gustavus II Adolphus died in this battle after falling from his horse. The successor to the throne was his six-year-old daughter Christina, for whom an imperial official under Oxenstierna carried out business until 1644. The Swedish-Danish War flamed up again in 1643, and Swe-

den triumphed in 1658 once and for all: the Treaty of Roskilde granted Sweden the provinces of Skåne, Blekinge, Halland and Bohuslän, as well as parts of Härjedalen and Jämtland. The ancient Swedish dream of controlling the Öresund and access to the North Sea had finally come true.

The Treaty of Westphalia, the general settlement which ended the Thirty Years' War in 1648, stipulated that Sweden would be granted Pomerania, Stettin and the island of Rügen, as well as the archbishopric (but not the city) of Bremen and the adjoining bishopric of Verde. This restructuring of Europe confirmed the superpower status of Sweden. The queen, however, became more and more an element of uncertainty. When she ascended the throne she declared her intention never to marry; she joined the Catholic Church in 1654, announced her abdication and, in doing so, was forced to leave Sweden as her father had decreed in 1617. As successor she named her cousin Charles Gustavus of Palatine-Zweibrück-

Above: The end of the Thirty Years' War was sealed with these documents at the Treaty of Westphalia on October 24,1648.

en, who replaced her on the throne as Charles X Gustavus.

The End of the Superpower Period

The immense costs of war had forced the Crown to lease or sell the Church's land, secularized under Gustavus Vasa, and all its tax privileges to the nobility. This meant that the nobility of Charles X's reign ruled over a good 70 percent of the land and intended to introduce a central European type of manorial system, while the tax-paying farmers were pushing for a new distribution of their land and its return. The king, already dependent upon the farmers for military reasons, reacted in a contact-eschewing manner. He did transfer the proceeds of the estates to the Crown, but refrained from officially touching the actual ownership situation. This was not achieved until his successor Charles XI, who had decreased the acreage of the nobility-owned land so much that in the end, the state, the nobility and the farmers each owned one third of the country's arable land. This "reduction in nobility" was also accompanied by a military reform, the so-called *Indelningsverk*. This stipulated that the precisely measured districts now be required to provide a given number of soldiers and officers and to sustain them. This then gave Sweden a self-sufficient army of farmers ready for battle at any time.

This reform put the public finances back on an even keel while producing an independent farming community, which successfully resisted all attempts of serfdom or feudalism. The following years of peace until the death of the king gave the country enormous economical growth, allowing the population to grow to one and a half million.

His son, Charles XII, was just as traditional as the absolutist monarchies of central Europe and was not at all averse to warlike adventures. The Swedish king overwhelmingly defeated the alliance of Russia, Saxony/Poland and Denmark in the Great Northern War at Narva (1700-1721); his Russian campaign against Peter the Great, on the other hand, was a fiasco. The peace treaties that followed resulted in the country being reduced to its mother country, large portions of Finland and a few possessions in Pomerania.

The Era of Liberty

During the century of the Enlightenment, Sweden was ruled more by the Riksdag than by the king himself; this was due to the constitutional reform of 1734, in which the monarch's rights were cut back considerably. The state administration at the time consisted of an upper chamber with 16 representatives, some of whom were farmers. It was divided into two parties: the "Hats" (mercantile nobles), who strove for a foreign alliance with France, and the "Caps" (liberal commoners), who preferred an alliance with England and often acted inconsistently and totally haplessly. Despite this, the foundations of Swedish democracy were laid during this period, and are still present in the constitution of today. It is for this reason that the period is often dubbed the "Era of Liberty."

Independent Swedish creative arts began to develop in the 17th and 18th centuries. Until that time, German scientists and artists had predominated, but now the French influence began to grow. Queen Christina had already had the philosopher and mathematician Descartes brought to Sweden, as well as the statesman Grotius and the theologian Comenius. The Swedish philosopher Olof Rudbeck was so inspired by them that he transposed the birthplace of the Indo-Germanic peoples to Scandinavia, thus giving an entire ideology his name.

During this peaceful period, the universities of Åbo (Turku) and Lund were founded, as was the Academy of Sciences, where great thinkers such as Carl

von Linné and Anders Celsius worked and carried out their research.

Gustavus III

Gustavus III's fame outside the borders of Sweden is almost completely limited to the fact that he was assassinated in 1792 (after a 20-year reign) while attending a masked ball at Stockholm's Opera House, a bloody deed that became a part of music history through Verdi. But not only was his death extraordinary: the absolutist, enlightened monarch was just as strict a ruler as he was disposed towards the arts and sciences. He seized the governing powers by cutting back the rights of the parliament, and patronized science and literature and paid homage to the fine arts by building an academy of the same name. It was also Gustavus III's initiative which is responsible for the Swedish

Above: Gustavus III is assassinated at a masked ball in Stockholm's Opera House in 1792 (wood engraving, 19th century).

Academy of Language and Science (1786); Alfred Nobel named this academy in his testament to administer the awarding of his prize. In addition to distinguishing himself by having the Opera House in Stockholm built, Gustavus' signature is on the founding documents of the Academy of Music, as well as those of the Theater of Drama. Tragically, though, not only did Gustavus III find fulfillment as an actor and playwright there, but also his death.

All in all, the assassination of Gustavus III was a perhaps inevitable result of his often inconsistent politics drifting between liberalism and despotism. Furthermore, his particular way of holding court was a thorn in the side of his subjects. In the end, the group of nobles behind the conspiracy responsible for his assassination was never prosecuted.

Initially succeeding under his uncle, later King Charles XIII, Gustavus IV officially ascended the throne in 1796; he was a stark opposite to his father as far as politics were concerned. Pedantically, and with extreme budget cuts, he attempted to return the country's finances to order. The so-called *Enskifte* (pooling), the redistribution of farmland in the villages, is attributed to him. Until its implementation, each farmer had a certain share of each field belonging to the village. This had led to a steady division of the fields and forced cooperative farming whose yield left much to be desired. Now the land of the entire country was redistributed in such a way that the emergence of economically independent farmsteads was possible, which quickly increased agricultural production. Another consequence, however, was that the poorest farmers lost their independence. In addition, this measure caused villages to dissolve and favored widely scattered individual farms. Still today, many lone churches mark the location of these old abandoned villages.

As far as foreign affairs are concerned, Gustavus IV was far less successful. His flat out disapproval of the country's acquisitions during the French Revolution, and trade policies with England, led him to find a way around Napoleon's continental blockade and to keep Gothenburg and other seaports open for trade with England. Napoleon, however, took revenge in the Treaty of Tilsit in 1807, where he gave Russia a free hand in Finland. This led to the incorporation of Sweden and Finland, and even Umeå in northern Sweden, into the Russian Empire for a short time. This was an enormous defeat, and it had dire consequences for the king: not only was he removed from the throne and expelled from the country, his descendants were excluded from the line of succession – forever.

When his uncle Charles XIII, who was to share power with the Riksdag, ascended the throne in 1809, a constitutional committee was introduced as a corrective measure. The more mature English parliamentary government, as well as the ideas of the French jurist and political philosopher Montesquieu, influenced the new constitution laid down by the Riksdag. This brought forth a very democratic institution: the *Ombudsman* – the citizens' representative protecting them from arbitrary bureaucracy is still valid today in modified form.

The House of Bernadotte

Due to the aging Charles XIII being childless, the choice of his successor became a significant political signal for the future of the country. To bring about closer ties to France and to gain a military expert at the same time, the Swedish government's choice as heir to the crown eventually fell on Jean Baptiste Bernadotte (1763-1844), a French revolutionary general. Before setting foot on Swedish soil, however, he had first joined the Lutheran Church and was adopted by the king as Crown Prince Charles John in accordance with a resolution of the Riksdag in Örebro (1810). This choice also won the support of Napoleon, who had hoped for a weakening of England and forced Sweden into war with England, but only on paper. As Napoleon's defeat in the wars of liberation became increasingly apparent, Sweden again turned more and more towards England. The continental blockade was evaded and the English-Swedish War officially ended immediately following the French invasion of Swedish Pomerania.

A move towards Russia confirmed its annexation of Finland, and in response, Russia supported the monarchical union of Norway and Sweden under a single king as it had been agreed to in the Treaty of Kiel (1814). This ruling was confirmed at the Congress of Vienna; Sweden had been ordered to cede its Pomeranian possessions.

The wars of liberation were the last battles which Sweden ever engaged in. The French marshal Bernadotte, crowned as Charles XIV in 1818, maintained peace throughout his reign, thus becoming the first Swedish king to have been on the throne without having needed to lead a war. Instead, his reign was most notably marked by a reform of the school system and the completion of the Göta Canal.

Heading for the Modern Age

As far as foreign affairs are concerned, the 19th century was a peaceful period and presented Sweden with the opportunity to recover economically, compared to the other European nations. The infrastructure was improved, the first railway line was built and the Göta Canal between Gothenburg and the Baltic Sea was opened. With the invention of the steam saw, the construction of the first industrial complexes was made possible. This is where the Swedish forests were simply "sawed up." Whenever the timber supply had been depleted, the sawmill owners just bought up the nearest farms, whose value was based on the amount of forest ownership. The newly unemployed farmers turned to the sawmills for employment; the workers then formed an early industrial proletariat which gradually became organized.

A second pillar of the industrialization of Sweden was iron mining and processing, which experienced unprecedented growth after the railway for transporting ore from Kiruna to Narvik was completed in 1903. The early industrial companies had patriarchal organizations, but in spite of paying low wages, they offered the workers a degree of job security that was, until then, unheard of in the rest of Europe. The population had actually grown so quickly that food supplies were practically depleted. Therefore, nearly one quarter of the five million Swedes sought

Right: Sawmill workers and loggers – Sweden's first industrial proletariat at the end of the 19th century.

their salvation in America as part of the massive waves of emigration in the 19th century.

Politically speaking, under Charles John's son, Oscar I (1844-59) and his grandson, Charles XV (1859-72), Sweden developed an early form of parliamentary democracy. It was a period of progressive liberalization in government and of industrial development. Freedom of the press was established (1844), the privileges of the nobility were annulled, the guild obligation was lifted, extensive freedom of religion was permitted and the influence the church had on the school system was reduced. Communal reform produced an electoral system based on class which only granted voting rights to those (including women) who had paid a certain amount of taxes. In addition, these individuals enjoyed unlimited freedom of trade and admission to the country's universities.

The four-class parliament (*Riksdag*) was replaced by a system based on the organization of the English parliament. Freedom of trade was granted (1864), and the protective tariffs were lifted which in turn resulted in cut-price imports ruining trade and farming. For this reason, the tariffs were reintroduced in 1888. At that time, King Oscar II (1872-1907) was already in power; he saw himself more as an artist, writer and musician than a politician, and transferred the business of the day to a state minister in 1876, a post that still exists today and is nearly equivalent to that of a chancellor. The Norwegian Crown was relinquished during Oscar's reign. The union with Norway, which had existed since 1814, was completely severed in 1905 by a referendum after a ten-year struggle over the consular representation of the Norwegians.

Sweden's industrial development of the late 19th century was accompanied by the establishment of the Social Democratic Workers' Party; it was to become a formative political power in the 20th

century. Job protection laws were being put into effect, and an unprecedented universal pension was granted shortly before the outbreak of World War I. Universal suffrage was then introduced in two stages in the years 1908 and 1919. Ultimately, Sweden became a parliamentary democracy during the reign of Gustavus V (1907-50), the longest reigning of all Swedish kings. He helped improve economic prosperity and avoided involvement in two world wars. To the rest of Europe he was still better known as the tennis player who played in major tournaments under the pseudonym of Mr. G.

The Era of the World Wars

As far as foreign affairs were concerned, Sweden's foremost objective was to maintain its neutrality. The Baltic Sea Treaty of 1908, in which the countries of Russia, Denmark, Germany and Sweden guaranteed the inviolability of their respective territories, was an extremely important step toward this goal. Sweden did,

along with Norway, remain neutral throughout World War I, although Germany had offered to give Sweden the Åland Islands in return for becoming war allies. The debates between the bourgeois parties and the Social Democrats had been put on ice for the duration of the war and did not flare up again until after it had ended. The elections of 1917 had already given the leftists so much strength that they were officially able to become part of the government; four years later the Social Democrats provided the state minister for the first time ever. Until 1932, the power frequently alternated between the bourgeois parties and the Social Democrats, while the governments themselves were usually of short duration and quite unstable.

The stock market crash of 1928 and the ensuing world economic crisis took Sweden by surprise. The rate of unemployment rose dramatically when the empire of the "King of Matches," Ivar Kreuger, collapsed, thereby ruining numerous other businesses as well. Since Kreuger

25

had secretly donated substantial sums of money to the bourgeois parties, the Social Democrats emerged as winners in the 1932 election; they remained uninterruptedly in power until 1976.

Sweden maintained a firm hold on its foreign policy of neutrality between the world wars. In hopes of a peaceful world order, they were also active in disarmament and allowed, for the first time, conscientious objectors to do community service in lieu of military service.

However, the pacifist position changed with the German National Socialists' aggressive seizure of power, especially when the first Jewish pogroms became known. When, at the onset of World War II, Soviet troops occupied Finland in accordance with Stalin's pact with Hitler, Sweden did support Finnish resistance by granting them transit permits, but refused any sort of direct partisanship. Sweden also remained neutral with Germany, but after Germany's attack on the Soviet Union, Sweden allowed German troops to march from Norway to Finland, thus traversing Sweden.

With the German war machine dependent on Sweden's ore, along with the fact that Sweden was producing weapons factories for Germany, trade with Nazi Germany soon grew to enormous proportions. Not until massive threats were received from the Allies in 1944 did Sweden terminate these lucrative trade relations. Early on, however, Sweden granted asylum to victims of the National Socialist regime and offered Germany, even if in vain, to take in all of the Danish and Norwegian Jews.

In domestic politics, the "Swedish Welfare State" *(folkhem)*, that particular Swedish society model, was developed under King Gustavus V and his state min-

Right: Olof Palme (center), Sweden's Prime Minister in the 1970s and '80s, made Sweden world famous through his strong stance against Apartheid.

ister Per Albin Hansson between 1932 and 1946; it views the citizens not as competitors of interests, but rather as members of one and the same family, sharing the same goals, supporting each other and joining in. (For more on the "Swedish Model," see p. 236.)

The Postwar Period

Following the death of Per Albin Hansson (1946), Tage Erlander continued with the politics of the *folkhem*, which had become the consensus of all parties in the meantime. Matters also proceeded smoothly when Gustavus V handed over the crown to Gustavus VI Adolphus. The policy of neutrality has remained unchanged, but has been anchored by considerable defense efforts which also involve protecting the civilian population. Sweden still does not belong to any military alliance, but does participate in international organizations such as the United Nations Organization, of which it is actually a founding member.

With its economic policy, Sweden has, on the other hand, only been able to remain moderately independent. In 1951/52 the Nordic Council was founded with Denmark, Norway and Finland, which led to a customs and passport union seven years later. In 1960, Sweden was a founding member of the European Free Trade Association (EFTA).

When the difficulties of the 1970s, such as the oil crisis, shook the world's economy, Sweden's Social Democrats under Olof Palme had to, for the first time, make way for a center-right coalition government which did not touch the *folkhem*. After his return to power in 1982, Palme increasingly used Sweden as a mouthpiece for independence movements around the world, and distinguished himself especially in the fight against Apartheid. Presumably, this strong and open commitment was the reason for the assassination of Olof Palme in

1986. The last constitutional reform in Sweden was carried out during his term, which introduced a unicameral system annulling the bicameral system, thereby leaving the king with exclusively representative rights and responsibilities. In addition, the succession to the throne for females was also introduced.

Charles XVI Gustavus, the successor of his grandfather, has worn the crown since 1973. His marriage to the middle-class Sylvia Sommerlath did not harm his popularity as some thought it might; it did, however, put the Royal Family in the headlines of some scandal sheets, although they are not responsible for any "Windsor-like" scandals.

Ingvar Carlsson, a member of the *Sveriges social-demokrattiska arbetar parti (SAP)*, former minister of several posts and Deputy Prime Minister, was named Prime Minister on February 28, 1986 – thus becoming Sweden's first Prime Minister. In March of the same year he also became chairman of the SAP. Between 1991 and 1994, however, he had to turn over power to the middle class before being reelected. Not only did he lead Sweden to the EU in 1995, but he also initiated a certain movement away from the "Swedish Model." This meant the introduction of rest days and paying a percentage of medical expenses; food at schools and child care would no longer be free of charge, and the universal pension returned to the basic minimum level of income. With additional cuts in social services, Sweden has been able to stabilize the employment rate, a feat unparalleled in any European country of equal size. Göran Persson has carried on Carlsson's politics as Prime Minister since 1996.

Incidentally, the high organizational level of the Swedish workers' trade unions has prevented the existence of an America-like low-wage job situation. In this respect, Sweden recognized the problems of globalization earlier on and solved them better than the so-called "classical industrial countries," such as France and Germany.

GEOGRAPHY

Sweden is, with an area of some 450,000 square kilometers, the fourth-largest country in Europe – after Russia, France and Spain. Nearly nine percent of its area is covered with rivers or lakes, of which there are about a hundred thousand. The north-south extension reaches from the 56th parallel to the 69th parallel latitude, stretching almost 1,600 kilometers. From west to east, on the other hand, it is only about 500 kilometers wide. Sweden shares its borders with two countries, the 1,700-kilometer Norwegian border is nearly three times as long as that of the one with Finland. Figures concerning the length of the coastline vary from 2,500 kilometers to 7,500 kilometers, depending on whether it is a straight measurement or the numerous bays and inlets are included. In addition, there are the rocky islets, or skerries, off the coast of Stockholm, Kalmar and Gothenburg, exceeding 40,000 in number.

Sweden's high mountains are only in the north. Mount Kebnekaise, in the Skanden *(Kölen)* Mountains at the border to Norway, reaches an elevation of 2,111 meters, making it the highest peak in Sweden. Additionally, there are four others higher than 2,000 meters in the Lapland of northern Sweden. The mountain region farther south is just 1,200 meters high, with peaks of over 1,700 meters. The northern area of Sweden is marked by a slightly hilly plate sloping southeastward from the northwest. It is for this reason that most of the rivers flow from the *Kölen* to the Gulf of Bothnia and are between 200 and 400 kilometers long. The valley in central Sweden begins south of Lake Siljan and extends from the province of Dalarna to the lakes of Vänern and Vättern. The adjacent Småland is a region of rolling hills that in some places barely

Right: One of nature's geomorphological works of art.

reach elevations of 370 meters. The countryside of southern Sweden has a morainic character, with gentle rolling hills extending as far south as Skåne; they are a result of the last Ice Age, which also caused comparable landscapes in Denmark and the lowlands of northern Germany.

The climate of Sweden is highly determined by its geographical location. Due to maritime influences from the west it is temperate and humid, on the other hand, it is subject to Eurasian continental influences which consist of dry weather and extreme temperatures. On the whole, it is a much milder climate than other comparable areas of the world, such as Siberia or Alaska. Due to the great length of the country from north to south, one can expect a wide diversity of temperatures; while the annual average summer temperatures vary only 5°C, the winter temperatures between Malmö and Kiruna differ by 17°C. One of the reasons for this is that Kiruna is located north of the Arctic Circle. It is light from late May to mid-July, and dark from late November to mid-January. The Arctic Circle, 150 kilometers to the south at 66.33° latitude, is the line where one doesn't see the sun set on Midsummer Day.

Thanks to the continental influences, the summers are generally warm, sunny and dry; the average annual amount of sunshine, at 300 hours, is a good 100 hours more than in central Europe. By contrast, the winters in Sweden are generally snowy and cold, whereby it differs from east to west; in Stockholm you can count on approximately 120 winter days with temperatures not exceeding -2°C, while in Gothenburg there are only 70 such days each year. Precipitation varies greatly: 800 mm in the south and west, significantly more than in the north and east (400 mm).

As far as administration is concerned, the country is divided into 24 provinces *(län)*, which are relatively equivalent to

the respective historical, cultural and linguistic regions. The administrative duties of the *län* are similar to those of other governmental districts in democratic countries, but in addition they are responsible for health and traffic.

Geology

Sweden's oldest rocks are 2.8 billion years old. They can be found on the Precambrian landmass of the Baltic Shield, which also consists of heavily eroded, 1.7 to two-billion-year-old fold mountains of gneiss and granite. Young Precambrian rock, such as the sandstone in Dalarna, porphyry in central Sweden or in the mining regions of northern Sweden, spreads as far south as Schonen in southern Sweden. Toward the end of the Precambrian and in the subsequent Cambrian and Silurian periods (600-440 million years ago), The Skanden were folded upward and pushed west-easterly like a blanket across parts of the Baltic Shield. They lie as long crests resembling a keel (*Kölen* = keel)

along the border area of Norway and Sweden, and consist of mica, limestone and gneiss, as well as magmatic rocks. In the region linking the Skanden to the Baltic Shield there are layers of rock from the Cambrian to the late Tertiary periods: sandstone, slate and limestone. Due to erosion they have disappeared from many places, but have remained in especially good condition on the islands of Öland and Gotland, and in parts of Schonen.

The characteristic rolling terrain dominating in Sweden originates from several ice ages over the course of less than two million years. Massive ice layers with thicknesses of up to 3,000 meters covered Scandinavia several times. The glaciers, on the one hand, planed down the soil while advancing and regressing, on the other hand, they deposited this material as mires as soon as the ice melted.

Free from the burden of the ice, Scandinavia has been rising for 10,000 years. The northern end of the Gulf of Bothnia rises about one centimeter per year. The interplay between the land lifting and the increasing sea level due to ice melt has caused the Baltic Sea to change from a continental lake to an open sea several times in the last ten thousand years.

The People of Sweden

Sweden presently has nearly nine million inhabitants. Statistically speaking, every 19 inhabitants could share one square kilometer of land, but the population density varies greatly. It is much more sparsely populated in the north than in the south, where the cities attract the population more strongly. Today, 85 percent of all Swedes live south of the Gävle-Mora line, whereby three million of them are concentrated in urban centers, such as Stockholm, Gothenburg and Malmö. Seventeen percent of the population live in the metropolitan area of Stockholm alone. Conversely, the population density in the northern provinces of Lapland and Norrbotten amounts to only three inhabitants per square kilometer. This is also the area where the 15,000 native Sami settled, as well as being the home of the Finnish minority, which includes a quarter of a million people. Besides this group, there is a Danish minority in the south, which, similar to the Finns, is slowly assimilating into the Swedish population. Relevant statistically are also the many civil war refugees Sweden has taken in since World War II; they represent a good majority of the one million foreigners living in Sweden.

Since an economic alliance of the Scandinavian labor market was created in 1954, many Danes, Norwegians, Finns and Icelanders had been drawn to work in the former welfare state of Sweden, where the highest wages were paid. Meanwhile, Sweden has handed over this

Right: When the cloudberries are ripe (they turn yellow), they are processed into a jam called hjortronsylt – an expensive, but popular souvenir.

role to oil-abundant Norway, which has since hired many Swedish workers. When Sweden became a member of the EU in 1995, this allowed all EU foreigners to settle in Sweden. For example, there are a good 20,000 Germans living in Sweden today. Sweden's population growth is mainly attributed to immigration and not to a birth surplus. Sweden has the highest percentage of foreigners of all European countries.

This, however, has consequences for religious affiliations. Although 90 percent of the population belong to the Lutheran Church of Sweden, of which one automatically becomes a member unless otherwise stipulated, the percentage of Catholics, Moslems and Hindus has risen considerably since World War II. Taking in many refugees automatically led to Islam becoming the second-largest religious denomination in Sweden.

Flora

Most central Europeans first think of cloudberries *(hjortron)* and elk when considering Swedish flora and fauna. Vegetation and the animal world vary greatly due to the country's great extension in length. Generally speaking, it has been determined that the northern timberline is continuously dropping. At the 62nd parallel latitude – about the latitude of Gävle – it is 900 meters; in Kiruna, north of the Arctic Circle, it is already below 400 meters. The forests are mainly coniferous, and they spread extremely far to the north; in the forests there is an astonishing variety of lichens and mosses – also above the timberline. The vegetation in southern Sweden is similar to that of central Europe. The northern line of beech runs approximately along the Kalmar-Borås line, while oak, maple and linden flourish 400 kilometers farther north. Up to this line there are also apple, pear, plum and cherry orchards in protected areas. Islands of vegetation, con-

sisting of dwarf birch and gray alder, which usually appear farther north, have developed in some areas with a less suitable climate. The vegetational period becomes shorter the farther north one goes: it lasts 250 days in southern Sweden, but only 120 in the north. For this reason, the forests of the north need twice as much growth time before they can be felled, which in turn means that the wood in the north is more valuable because it is harder than that of the south.

The amply growing birch trees have their own special status; because they are so abundant, they are considered to be a type of "weed," and everyone is free to help themselves and stock up their woodpile with birchwood.

The Baltic Sea islands of Öland and Gotland are also botanically interesting; chestnut and walnut trees as well as rare orchid variations flourish on the small islands, despite little precipitation.

The famous cloudberry grows best north of the 62nd parallel. The fruit, resembling a blackberry, is red when unripe and then turns to yellow. This ripening process, however, can take over two years in cold summers. The berries are usually processed into jam, *hjortronsylt*, which is available in many stores. It is a popular souvenir, though not a cheap one. The jam is usually eaten on waffles or pancakes *(plättar)*.

Besides the cloudberry, many other berries and varieties of mushroom grow in the Swedish woods and in the numerous moors, and there are many people eager to pick them.

Fauna

The Swedish fauna resembles that of central Europe to a large degree. Deer, roe deer, hares and foxes are found in southern Sweden and almost everywhere in the central regions. Bears, wolves, beavers, polar foxes and European wolverines have practically been annihilated by humans, but those that remain have found refuge in some of Sweden's 25 national parks (ranging from 28 to 50,000 hectares

in area), where their populations are actually increasing. The elk, the largest of the deer species, has become Sweden's "heraldic animal." Once roaming all over Europe, today elk outside of Scandinavia can only be found in the former East Prussia. The population of these animals is estimated at around 350,000, and most of them live in the more nutritious southern and central regions of Sweden. They also press north and roam beyond the Arctic Circle in summer. Despite the high number of 100,000 elk hunting permits issued every year, their numbers have remained stable; and even the so-called "elk plague" didn't have a long-term effect on the herd's population.

The elk is a very shy animal possessing an extraordinary sense of smell and hearing, which makes spotting one a feat in itself. The best places for elk watching are clearings amidst young birch trees and along lake shores, where they stand with the water up to their bellies while feeding on the tender plants. The best time for observation is at twilight. During the day, the chances of seeing an elk in the wild are best just after a good rain. As is the case with all hoofed game, elk rather dislike the rain and tend to withdraw from open areas and retreat to the forests. Not until after the rain has stopped do they leave their forest refuge to avoid the dripping leaf cover. In spite of everything, one's first real encounter with a free-roaming elk is a rare and unforgettable experience, and also well worth the patience invested.

Particularly for forest landowners and motorists, elk present a risk that should not at all be underestimated. The damage the elk do to young trees is sometimes quite devastating, while, fortunately, high fences line most of Sweden's larger highways to prevent elk from wandering onto them. Luckily, collisions with one of these animals (they can weigh in excess of 1,000 kilos) do not occur very often,

Above: Snowy owls – Nyctea scandiaca – a protected species. Right: Salmon – the delicious king of the northern waters.

but when they do they have severe consequences for all those involved. Nowadays, even trucks are equipped with massive elk catchers, since the sound of a running engine or an approaching vehicle is no longer a sufficient deterrent.

In severe winters it can happen that the animals dare to go to into cities where they plunder garbage containers in search of food. There was once an elk that strayed into Stockholm's *Tunnelbana* – there was unfortunately no alternative but to kill the panic-stricken animal.

In the vast solitude of the far north, where old animals wander off to die, elk pose quite a threat to the natural food supply of the reindeer. Due to the sparse vegetation existing north of the Arctic Circle, the elk are practically forced to radically graze large areas of land to cover their nourishment needs. Reindeer, on the other hand, have the intrinsic ability to use the available food supply for only so long, without harming the vegetation. This way, there will be enough for the herds to eat upon returning from their mi-

grations. There are well over a million reindeer in Sweden; approximately 2,500 Sami still live exclusively off their herds. There are no longer wild reindeer in Sweden. Instead, the herds live half wild, i.e., they migrate between their fixed winter site and their summer treks. All the animals are branded, which shows who owns them. Meanwhile, there is a trend to breed reindeer on enclosed farms where they are fattened, leaving them with too little energy to waste on migrations.

Swedish rivers and lakes have no lack of fish, in fact, they have quite a lot to offer: varieties of salmon, trout, pike and perch – everything a fisherman's heart could desire. A fishing license is required everywhere except on the North and Baltic Seas and on large continental lakes.

The bird population also offers quite a wide variety: more than 350 species can be found here in the summer; 250 of these bear their young here in the land. These include such rare breeds as the snow grouse, snow bunting and snowy owl, which are all protected species.

Ödmjukast jag Er ber
Fast rösten är nog matt,
Kom lägg en penning ner
Men lyften uppå min hatt
Säll är den, som låter sig
wårda om den fattige

Kon. Dav. 41:2.

SCHONEN – THE SWEDISH SOUTH COAST

HELSINGBORG
SCHONEN'S SOUTHWEST
MALMÖ
LUND
SCHONEN'S BALTIC SEA COAST
BLEKINGE

Schonen

*HELSINGBORG
The Gateway to Sweden

Schonen, the collective name outside of Sweden for the two southern regions of **Skåne** and **Blekinge**, is next to Stockholm the most densely populated area of the country. This extremely fertile region, called "Sweden's Garden" – and rightly so – was a bone of contention between Denmark and Sweden for centuries, until it was eventually granted to Sweden in the 17th century. In spite of this, the Danish influence is still very noticeable – even the Swedish language has a slight Danish touch here.

Schonen lies directly adjacent to the regions of Halland and Småland to the north, the Baltic Sea to the south and east, and **Öresund** to the west. At its narrowest point, between Helsingør in Denmark and **Helsingborg ❶** in Sweden, the sound (*sund*) is only four kilometers wide. This is where the majority of import/export business is conducted. In addition, most of the tourists come and go via the so-called "as-the-crow-flies" line,

Preceding pages: A giant Finn has been supporting the vaulted ceiling for 1,000 years in the crypt of Lund. Serene coasts near Kristianopel. Left: "Old Rosenbom" collects donations in Karlskrona.

which requires only two short trips by ferry for the Germany-Denmark-Sweden connection.

Helsingborg is still the gateway to the Swedish kingdom, just as it was two centuries ago when Jean Baptiste Bernadotte ferried across. The 120,000 inhabitants live primarily from the trade links to Denmark. The processing industry, however, is expanding constantly, and as soon as the Öresund connection between Malmö and Copenhagen is completed, Helsingborg will lose its long-time dominant role on the sound as a mediator.

The Sights of the City

The long dispute for control of the Öresund resulted in the fact that there are only two buildings remaining from the pre-Swedish period, the *Kärnan (defensive tower) and the Sankta Maria kyrka. The Kärnan was the fortified tower with living quarters of a 14th-century fortress which was razed in 1680. The 35-meter-high tower with its 4.5-meter-thick walls still looms over the city today. Originally, it could be entered by a separate staircase tower, whereby access required the use of ladders. Today, a wide staircase leads up to the terrace (you can also take an elevator). A small museum displays models of the former fortress complex,

which has now become a public park. From the rooftop of the museum you can enjoy a beautiful view of the harbor, the Öresund and the Old Town below. To get there from the ferry terminal, just head inland on Hamntorget. After passing Carl Milles' **seafaring monument** and the Neo-Gothic **Rådhuset** with its 65-meter-high tower, follow Stortorget, which leads to the Kärnan.

Approximately 150 meters behind the City Hall is where the Norra and Södra Storgatan branch off from Stortorget. Many of the old streets are now pedestrian zones, including the **Kullagatan**, Sweden's oldest auto-free zone, which is located here. The carefully renovated **Jakob Hansens hus**, a half-timbered brick building from the 17th century and the city's oldest private house, is on Norra Storgatan. The **fountain monument** standing in front of it is from 1927 and commemorates the most prominent as-

tronomer of the 16th century, Tycho Brahe (1546-1601), who was born here in Schonen (then Scania, Denmark). The **Sankta Maria kyrka** is situated on the Södra Storgatan. Originally a Romanesque sandstone church from the 12th century, it was rebuilt in the 14th and 15th centuries as a two-aisled brick basilica based on designs from northern Germany. The Virgin Mary altar, a work from Stralsund, bears a Low German inscription. Noteworthy, modern buildings are located in the immediate vicinity of the port on **Drottninggatan**: the **Konserthuset** (Concert Hall) from 1932 and the **Teatern**, which upon completion in 1978 was considered to be Europe's most modern theater.

It is also worth visiting the open-air museum of ***Fredriksdalen**: its expanses cover an area of 36 hectares, including a village typical of the Schonen region and a number of interesting gardens (herbs, orchards and roses); it is located just two kilometers northeast of the Kärnan. From there, Route 111 (called Strandvägen)

Above: The cityscape of Helsingborg is dominated by the tower of the Neo-Gothic City Hall.

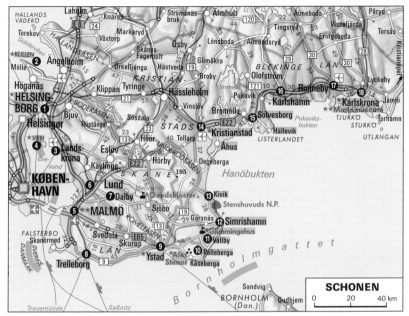

will take you to the peninsula of **★Kullen ❷**. Around the many seaside resorts promising tranquility and hospitality, you will also discover a few castles. The most famous of them, **★Sofiero** (Sophie's Silence), was built by Oscar II for his wife in 1864. Today, it belongs to the city of Helsingborg and is a favorite destination for outings; it is especially popular every year in June when its rhododendron garden is in full bloom. The Kullen peninsula ends with a promontory of gneiss, a formation 15 kilometers long and up to 180 meters high; this was created during the last Ice Age. Here, in the middle of a nature reserve, Sweden's highest lighthouse is to be found.

SCHONEN'S SOUTHWEST

Nowhere in Sweden is the density of bicycle paths as high as it is here in Skåne. The **Skånespåret** is an elaborate network of bicycle paths some 800 kilometers long, which takes in the entire coast of Schonen while deliberately shun-

ning busy roads. Heading south a few kilometers on the E6, you'll come to **Ramlösa**, a health resort, which owes its existence to a mineral-water spring. Beautiful villas and hotels adorn the resort whose name has become synonymous with mineral water in Sweden.

Landskrona ❸, 20 kilometers farther south, was founded during the Kalmar Union (15th century). Traces of that epoch can no longer be found in the city, however. The mighty **Landskrona slott**, built in the 16th century under Christian III of Denmark, is surrounded by a moat and ramparts of red brick; it also served as a prison until 1940.

The city's variable history is documented in the old **Landskrona museet** on Rådhustorget. It is worth taking the time to visit the **Sofia Albertina kyrka** with its glass paintings. Directly behind the church in **Haijska huset** was Selma Lagerlöf's apartment, where she lived at the end of the 19th century while teaching at a boarding school for girls and writing *Gösta Berling's Saga*.

It is worth taking a trip to the island of ⋆**Ven ④**, five kilometers off the coast. This is the remaining part of the former land connection between Skåne and the Danish shoreline. The Danish king Frederick II presented the island to the astronomer Tycho Brahe as a feudal tenure. He lived and carried out his research here in the now run-down castle of **Uranienborg**. Brahe's **Observatorium Stjärneborg** has been restored; the castle gardens have also been replanted. A small museum commemorates the scientist who was one of the first in Europe to pursue astronomy without astrological tangents. When he fell out of favor with King Christian IV in 1598, he went to Prague in exile, where he died three years later.

⋆⋆MALMÖ

The most important city of southern Sweden is **Malmö ⑤**; with 250,000 in-

Above: Radiant dog roses decorate numerous houses on the Kullen peninsula (Arild).

habitants it is also the third-largest city in the country. Flourishing trade with the Danish islands and the Hanseatic League made the city so rich in the 14th century that it was able to build a church like Sankt Petri. Erik of Pomerania, the Union King of the 15th century, took advantage of the city's position and had Malmöhus built as a fortification against the Hanseatic League.

In the 16th century, Malmö was granted the right to mint coins for all of Denmark, thus making it Copenhagen's economic equal. The union between Skånes and Sweden put a stop to Malmö's growth in the 17th century, and it took a good hundred years until the city was able to free itself from its one-sided orientation toward the south and west. But then a new period of prosperity began for the city, as the unfavorable peripheral location at the southern extremity of the Swedish kingdom was transformed into a distinct advantage thanks to the completion of the railroad link between Copenhagen and Stockholm.

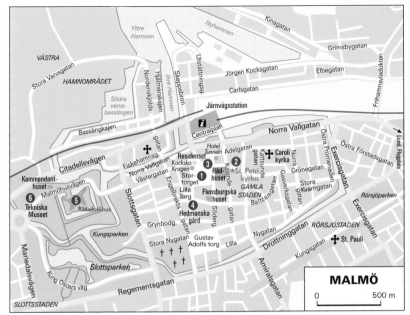

The Heart of the City

The Old Town of Malmö is still surrounded by a canal belt which originated at the beginning of the last century when the fortifications were razed and the moats were filled. The center of the Old Town is **Stortorget ❶**, the largest market square, where you should begin your walking tour of the city.

The Stortorget was considered to be the largest market square in Scandinavia as early as the 16th century. Since the end of the 19th century it has been dominated by the **equestrian statue of Charles X Gustavus**, the monarch who fought to provide the groundwork for handing Malmö over to Sweden (1658). The **fountain** on the northeast corner of the square is from the 1960s. Stig Blomberg placed it where its medieval predecessor stood and marked its shape with white stones. The most dominating building on Stortorget is the **Rådhuset** (City Hall), which didn't receive its present Dutch Renaissance look until the 19th century. Ori-

ginally, Jörgen Kock, a progressive mayor of the 16th century, had a plain stone building erected, of which only the vaulted cellar remains. This cellar now serves as the *Rådhuskällaren* restaurant. The **Knutsal**, the former meeting place of the most influential guild of the city, and the **Landstingsal**, the courtroom of the province's parliament, located on the second floor, are worth seeing.

*Sankt Petri kyrka

The oldest, and in terms of art history most valuable, structure in Malmö is the **Sankt Petri kyrka ❷**, located diagonally behind the City Hall. Although it has a long and eventful construction history. Construction of the church began around 1300 on the site of where a Romanesque chapel once stood. The two-aisled basilica with an ambulatory and a transept was nearly complete by the end of the 14th century. However, the church tower was not finished until 1450. The Gothic murals in the church were badly damaged by unruly Protestants in 1529, who totally destroyed the church furnishings. The murals were then whitewashed in 1555. Shortly afterwards, the initial plans for the restoration of the church interior were drawn up. The **pulpit** as well as the **Renaissance epitaph** were completed around 1600. The **high altar**, one of the largest in northern Europe, was completed in 1611.

As early as the 15th century the church had three annexes: **St. Anne's Chapel** to the south, today housing a beautiful alabaster altar from the 16th century, a **Chapel of the Virgin Mary** to the north, and an **armory** – the latter two being used as sacristies today.

The German merchants were permitted to build their own chapel, the **Krämer Chapel**. Since it had been separated from the Petri church in the last century and had its own entrance, its frescoes and sculptures escaped the radical church restoration of 1850 and convey a clear picture of the original condition. Today, the Krämer Chapel is connected to the church and serves as a baptistery. The **font** with a baldachin is from the 17th century, while the **font basin** is a replica of an older silver one.

City Residences and Fortifications

Diagonally opposite the City Hall, at the northeast corner of the Stortorget, is the **Residenset ❸**, the governor's residence. Two older buildings were connected to this residence in the 18th century. On the northwest corner of the square is the early-16th-century **Jörgen Kocks gård**; today it is the gourmet restaurant **Kockska Krogen**. The originally significantly larger estate was commensurate to the position of its owner as the royal coin master, later the mayor.

Right: Shops in the carefully restored houses on Lilla Torget in Malmö invite you to do a little casual shopping.

Lilla Torget, the small market square, is located south of the Stortorget. When the large market square was redesigned in the 16th century, small businesses were forced to relocate. The creation of this small square gave them their own market with direct access to the main market. The low houses around the Lilla Torget from the 18th and 19th centuries have been carefully renovated. The numerous bars and restaurants in the area, often with live music, provide the square with an almost Mediterranean character in the summertime.

The **Form Design Center**, located in **Hedmanska gård ❹** (Skomakaregatan), has an interesting exhibition of Scandinavian-style home décor.

If you follow Skomakaregatan to Södergatan you will find the **Flensburgska huset**, a handsome manor house in the Dutch Renaissance style.

Two additional buildings are also worth mentioning: the **Hotel Tunneln**, an enclosed ensemble constructed above five cellars from the 14th century which serve as restaurants today (corner of Södergatan and Adelsgatan), and the remains of **Dringenbergska gård** at Norra Vallgatan 65, once owned by another royal coin master.

Heading westward on Norra Vallgatan you will reach **Slottsparken**, a spacious park with canals cutting through it, and a moated fortification, ***Malmöhus ❺**, located in the center. The four-winged fortress dates back to the city's retaining wall built by Erik of Pomerania. It was, however, modified in the 16th century and rebuilt after a fire in the 17th century. Malmöhus has served as a **museum** since 1932. The ground floor has exhibits on the fauna of southern Scandinavia, the basement level houses an aquarium and a collection of nocturnal animals, and the collection of arts and crafts is located on the second floor.

Upon leaving the fortress, the Malmöhusvägen takes you past the former

Schonen

Kommendanthuset (now the Military and Toy Museum) to the **Tekniska Museet** ❻, where aircraft, rail and road vehicles as well as boats are on display.

The nightlife in Malmö is modest to say the least, since amusement seekers tend to take the more interesting "party ferries" which shuttle between Malmö and Rostock or Travemünde and offer affordable drinks and all-night dancing.

✱✱LUND
The Old Capital

Before Malmö became the most important city in southern Sweden, ✱✱**Lund** ❻ held this prominent status. Lund is located just 20 kilometers north of Malmö, and is easily accessible via the E22 (to Kalmar) and the Royal Highway 23 (to Hässleholm).

Lund is over a thousand years old and was founded by the Danish king Sven Gabelbart in 990. The city soon became rich and powerful after the Danish king Knut the Great (1118-35) granted the city

minting rights in the year 1020. It was just 40 years later that the city became a Danish diocese, and after an additional 43 years even the see of the Danish archbishop. This honor meant that Lund had essentially obtained the rank of being the most important religious metropolis of northern Europe. The city's importance decreased, however, with the Reformation in 1536, but the lasting affiliation to Denmark saved Lund from Gustavus Vasa's reduction of the number of churches. The church properties were not secularized until after the Treaty of Roskilde (1658), and a significant amount of the proceeds was used for the founding of the university (1666). Today, Lund has a population of 90,000, including about 20,000 students.

The ✱Cathedral

The most prominent sight of the city is the Romanesque ✱**Domkyrka**, the oldest and most important of its kind in all of Sweden. Saint Knut (1080-86) founded

the first church here, but it had to be re-placed by a larger one by the next century.

The oldest part of the church is the **krypta**, which was consecrated as early as 1123. The vaults of the crypt rest on massive decorated columns, and it contains a well which for a long time was the city's only one – an indication of the fortification role the previous church had. The life-sized depictions of a man and woman on the north and west columns are said to represent a strong, giant Finn and his wife, who, according to legend, substantially contributed to the construc-tion of the cathedral.

The actual church grew from the apse to the choir, to the nave with two aisles and then to the twin towers and, until the great fire of 1234, was outfitted with a wood joist ceiling which was replaced by Gothic ribbed vaults. The first major ren-ovation was necessary at the beginning of

Above: The Romanesque cathedral of Lund was given Gothic ribbed vaults after the fire of 1234.

the 16th century; it was overseen by the German Adam von Düren. He was not only a fine architect but a gifted stone-mason as well. He completed the **well head of the crypt** and the **Virgin Mary relief** in the south transept. Around 1860, the church was once again extensively re-stored, so that today it is only a partial representation of the original 13th-century structure.

The **Romanesque capitals** of the nave, the **altarpiece** (one of the oldest in Swe-den) with its many figurines from the 14th century, the **astronomical clock** from the 15th century at the west end of the northern aisle, and the **marble-alabaster pulpit** from 1599 are all worth seeing.

In the Bourgeois Center

The cathedral is situated on the edge of a small park, the **Lundagård**. The arch-bishop's castle once stood here. The small building behind the cathedral, the so-called "Laurentius Chapel," served as a library (**Libreriet**). The **Kungshuset** at the east end of the park was the residence of the Danish king Frederick II (16th century) and was later taken over by the university. Most of the university buildings are from the 19th century and adjoin the Lundagård to the north. Located east of the park, the **Tegnérplatsen** was named for a bishop from the 19th century who made a name for himself as both a poet and a scientist. The **Kulturen**, the art history museum, is located here, part of a large open-air section with 30 buildings. Here you can learn about styles of cultivated living from diverse eras and various classes of society.

The **Skissernas Museum** (Archive for Decorative Art), located at Finngatan 2, is packed with over 20,000 designs of artworks – both sketches and models – on display.

Mårtens Torg, 200 meters south of the cathedral, is home to a colorful and busy flower and vegetable market which takes place in the mornings.

In addition to all of the culture, it is also worth going for a stroll through the charming cobblestoned streets of the Old Town east of the *torg*, with their many little shops and cafés (e.g., Magle Lilla Kyrkogatan). Young students like gathering at Lundagård when the weather is favorable, and meeting at the cafés of the Old Town in inclement weather or during the long winter. Here, too, the nightlife is quite modest, and since going to a discotheque is rather expensive; many prefer to take turns hosting parties. In the summer, especially in Lundagård Park, parties often start up spontaneously, and anyone who contributes a bottle is more than welcome to join in.

Excursions from Lund

The small national park of **Dalby Söderskog** is located north of Route 16 (Lund-Simrishamn), two kilometers outside Dalby. Its carpet of flowers in the gradually overgrowing forest meadows in Söderskog and Norreskog are especially inviting in the spring for walks or even a full day's hike.

The church in the town of **Dalby** ❼ (13 kilometers from Lund), in which the remains of Sweden's oldest stone church (11th century) were integrated, is worth a visit. The baptistery on the lower level of the entrance is particularly interesting; it is the only preserved subterranean church in the entire country.

★Övedskloster, Sweden's most beautiful Rococo palace with its fabulous park and café, is located on **Lake Vombsjön** (30 kilometers east of Lund).

The **Bosjö Convent**, situated on a peninsula in the middle of **Lake Ringsjön**, is a good 30 kilometers from Lund. A Benedictine convent before the Reformation, it was privatized in the 18th century and then restored. Not only are the rose and herb gardens worth a visit, but the restaurant, serving delicious Swedish specialties, is as well.

SCHONEN'S BALTIC SEA COAST

Trelleborg ❽ was affluent as early as the Middle Ages – that is, until the shoals of herring, the basis of the city's richness, suddenly failed to appear. In the 17th century, a fire not only totally destroyed the city, but also forced it to lose its town charter. Not until the arrival of ferry lines in the 20th century did the city experience a new upswing. Today, Trelleborg is the second most important gateway to southern Sweden. Train ferries have been running to Sassnitz on the German island of Rügen since 1929, and also to Travemünde since the end of World War II. Since the end of the Cold War, the number of connections to Poland and the Baltic republics has also increased. The expanding docks dominate the cityscape. Although Trelleborg lacks any particular sights worth seeing, just looking at the old picturesque houses at **Gamla Torget**

Schonen

(Old Market) while waiting to board the ferries is a pleasant way to pass the time.

Nature lovers get their money's worth 20 kilometers west of Trelleborg: **Falsterbo**, a peninsula with moors, meadows, dunes and extensive beaches, is also a birdwatcher's paradise during the annual migrations.

Leaving Trelleborg heading east, Route 9 takes you through sandy moraine landscapes with a nice view of the pine forests and the sea before reaching ***Ystad ❾**. The town of 25,000 inhabitants has an almost museum-like character: nearly all of its well-preserved half-timbered houses from the 18th century (around 300 of them) have been renovated with great care and are therefore first-rate tourist attractions. From the tower of the **Sankta Maria kyrka**, a church which has been remodeled many

Above: Quaint little pastel-colored fishermen's houses line the streets of Simrishamn. Right: Sunbathing on the beaches of Stenshuvud National Park.

times since the 13th century, a trumpeter blows his horn every quarter of the hour at night. This all-clear signal dating from the 17th century means "no fire in sight!"

In the immediate vicinity you will find the **Latinskola**, Sweden's oldest school house, and the **Pilgrändshuset**, the oldest half-timbered building (1480) far and wide. **Gråbrödraklostret**, originally a Franciscan monastery, became a hospital after the Reformation, and then a liquor distillery before it was given its new task – to house the museum of local history. There are ships running daily from the ferry port to the Danish island of Bornholm and to the Polish harbor of Swinoujscie.

For those interested in swimming, there are many possibilities on the coast between Ystad and Simrishamn, with a few little gems along the way. For example, Skåne's only round church, located near **Valleberga ❿**, is comparable to the churches in Bornholm. Heading south towards the coast, located on a hill above the sea near **Kåseberga**, you will discover Sweden's largest stone composition stemming from the Bronze or Iron Age: ***Ales Stenar**, 59 huge pieces of rock set up vertically in the shape of a ship. The stones at the bow and stern of the "ship" mark the points of sunrise and sunset at midsummer and midwinter.

The path to ***Glimmingehus**, Skåne's best-preserved castle from the late Middle Ages (15th century), is marked from **Vallby ⓫** on. It owes its warehouse-type appearance to Queen Margaret, who expressly forbade the construction of castles during the Kalmar Union. For this reason, "castles" were built in the style of residential and storage buildings to get around the ordinance. **Simrishamn ⓬**, located five kilometers north, is an old herring fishing town and still an important fishing port on the Swedish Baltic Sea coast. Little houses adorned with rosebushes line the lanes of this town of 20,000 inhabitants.

Fifteen kilometers further north, you will come to the edge of the **Stenshuvud National Park** (390 hectares in area), which extends all the way to the coast. The **Naturum** provides information about the park's abundant animal and plant life, hiking trails lead throughout the woods and bushes, sunbathing on the beach is permitted, and there are tables and benches for a picnic.

The small town of **Kivik ⓭**, the country's cider producing center, is located just a few kilometers to the north. Sweden's largest **chambered tomb** from the Bronze Age is situated amidst the apple orchards. Discovered in the 18th century, the royal grave was long used as a source for stone until its restoration in 1930. On the inside of the huge grave chamber numerous stone plates with symbolic depictions point the way to the kingdom of the dead.

Åhus and Vä on routes 118 and 10 toward Kristianstad were once Danish market towns on the border to Sweden. Their prosperity enabled the construction of elaborately decorated churches, but it was also the reason for numerous Swedish attacks. At one point the city wall of **Åhus** was totally destroyed; remains from the Middle Ages can be seen at the town church. The **Sankta Maria kyrka** of **Vä**, on the other hand, remained intact. It still has the most impressive Romanesque **mural series** north of the Alps.

In 1614, Christian IV had the inhabitants of both cities relocated to the newly fortified **⋆Kristianstad ⓮**. Still remaining are the Trefaldighetskyrkan, the largest Renaissance church in northern Europe, and an arsenal, where the **Länsmuseum** (Provincial Museum) has exhibits concerning the city's history and regional arts and crafts. Nowadays, the military as well as the wood and furniture industries characterize the city of 70,000.

BLEKINGE

Having an area of around 3,000 square kilometers, **Blekinge** is the second smallest of the Swedish districts. In *The Won-*

derful Adventures of Nils, Selma Lagerlöf described the landscape as three stair steps: the skerry belt lies in the south, north of that is the agricultural countryside and then the woodlands.

Blekinge kept experiencing waves of destruction until the Treaty of Roskilde in 1658, and with the eventual annexation to Sweden, despite the founding of cities by Charles XI, the city seems to have dozed off economically and did not begin to slowly wake up until its connection to railway traffic.

Coming from Skåne, the E22 crosses the border to Blekinge at **Sölvesborg** ⓯. This formerly rich, small Danish market town lost much, including its inhabitants, after Karlshamn was founded and they were forced to move there. Only the **ruins of the Danish castle** and those of the **Sant Nicolai kyrka** are reminiscent of the grand past of the oldest city in

Above: Salmon fishing near Mörrum. Right: The evening sun bathes the skerries in an almost mystical light.

Blekinge. From Sölvesborg you can take an excursion to the **Listerlandet** peninsula (Route 123), with its beautiful beaches and the picturesque fishing village of **Hällevik**.

Heading toward Karlshamn (E22), the salmon hatchery of **Mörrum**, on the river of the same name, is worth a visit. An aquarium was built in the **Laxens hus** where you can look through a window under the river's surface and watch the salmon swimming by.

Karlshamn ⓰, designed by Erik Dahlberg, is a planned city from the 17th century. The strategically favorable location for a naval port against Denmark was chosen by Charles XI; its harbor basin at Karlshamn is the deepest of the Baltic Sea. Many emigrants to America began their voyage to the New World from here.

The town of **Ronneby** ⓱, 30 kilometers farther east, is a former health resort. It was closed down in 1939 when the iron-bearing springs dried up, but the facilities and the beautiful park have been preserved.

Schonen

*Karlskrona , founded by Charles XI in 1680, is still Sweden's most important naval base on the Baltic Sea. In 1998, its harbor was even included on UNESCO's World Heritage List. The Swedish military had tried for years to track down Soviet submarines among the skerries hereabouts. They were never successful in this endeavor, though, and made themselves look rather silly – especially when a submarine carrying nuclear warheads was caught by a fishing boat. Amateur sailors should always inquire about any restrictions in the coastal area between Karlshamn and Karlskrona. The new **Naval Museum** on the pier of Stumholmen brings to life the history of the Swedish navy, the shipyard in Karlskrona and life at sea.

Karlskrona, consisting of several islands, was also designed by Erik Dahlberg. The city center is on **Trossö** at **Stortoget**, where, in addition to the **Rådhuset** and **Fredrikskyrkan**, the **Trefaldighetskyrkan** is located. It was built for the many German-speaking sailors in

the navy from Pomerania, which belonged to Sweden until the 18th century. There are still a few beautiful old wooden houses on **Drottninggatan**.

The oldest building in the city is the *Ulrica Pia kyrka (Admiralty Church), the largest timber-built church in Sweden, which miraculously survived the devastating fire of 1790. *Nils Holgersson* hid from the angry Swedish king – in a dream – under the hat of the wooden donation-collecting figure **Gubben Rosenbom** (Old Rosenbom).

The **Dreimastbark Jarramas** at the harbor is an inviting location for a cup of coffee while enjoying the view of the old **Bastion Aurora**.

Kristianopel, located at the level of the southern tip of Öland, was founded by the Danish king Christian IV in the 16th century, whereby its name was an indication of the plans for the cosmopolitan city. Conflicts between Denmark and Sweden swept away these dreams, however. Today, Kristianopel is a paradise for sailors and surfers.

HELSINGBORG (☎ 042)

ℹ️ Kungstorget, 25278 Helsingborg, tel. 120310.

🛏️ 😊😊😊 **Marina Plaza Hotel**, Kungstorget 6, tel. 192100, fax 149616, directly at the harbor and train station. **Radisson SAS Grand Hotel**, Stortorget 8, tel. 120170, fax 218833, centrally located 😊😊 **Hotell Linnéa**, Prästgatan 4, tel. 114660, fax 141655, small, cozy hotel, 16 rooms. **Hotel Nouveau**, Gasverksgatan 11, tel. 185390, fax 140885. 😊 **Villa Thalassa Rumsuthyrning**, Dag Hammarskjölds Väg, tel. 110384, fax 128792, nice *YOUTH HOSTEL* with *CABINS* for 2-6 people, tel. 110284.

❌ **Blomberg and Co.**, Ålgränden 1, tel. 114330, popular meeting point, central, bar and outdoor seating, good lunch menu. **Brasserie Mollberg**, Storgatan 18, tel. 120270, good food, large servings, nice atmosphere.

🏛️ **Kärnan** (castle tower), May-Aug 9 am-8 pm daily, Sept 9 am-6 pm daily, Oct-March 9 am-3 pm daily. **Sankta Maria kyrka**, Mon-Fri 1-2 pm. **Jakob Hansens hus**, can only be viewed from the outside.

🎫 August: **Festival of the Helsingborg Symphony Orchestra**

KULLEN PENINSULA (☎ 042)

ℹ️ Storgatan 67, 26331 Höganäs, tel. 349793.

🛏️ 😊😊😊 **Grand Hotel Mölle**, Bökebolsvägen 11, Mölle, tel. 347280, fax 347144. **Rusthållargården**, Utsikten 1, Arild, tel. 346530, fax 346793, both hotels have excellent restaurants, the fish is especially recommendable. 😊😊 **Mölle Touristhotell**, Kullabergsvägen 32, Mölle, tel. 347084, fax 347484.
CABINS: Also **Mölle Turisthotell**.

❌ **Flickorna Landgren**, Skäret, on the road to Landgren, tel. 346044, local cuisine, large garden. **Tunneberga Gästgivargård**, Jonstorpvägen 16, Jonstorp, tel. 367481, seafood smörgåsbord.

🏛️ **Sofiero slott**, May 1-15, Sept 10 am-6 pm daily.

LANDSKRONA (☎ 0418)

ℹ️ Rådhusgatan 3, 26131 Landskrona, tel. 16980.

🛏️ 😊😊 **Hotel Chaplin**, Östergatan 108, tel. 16335, 70 rooms, town center.

🏛️ **Landskrona Museum** at the Adolf Frederiks Casern and **Landskrona slott**, June 15-Sept 15, Sat-Thu 1 pm-5 pm. **Sofia Albertina kyrka**, Mon-Fri 10 am-5 pm. **Haijska Huset** can only be viewed from the outside.

🚢 **Ven Island**, crossing from: Ven Trafiken, Kungsgatan 9, tel. 79823.

VEN ISLAND (☎ 0418)

🏛️ **Brahe's Observatory**, June7-Aug 29, 10 am-1 pm and 2-5 pm daily.

🏠 *YOUTH HOSTEL* and *BICYCLE RENTALS,* tel. 72555 and 72550.

MALMÖ (☎ 040)

ℹ️ Skeppsbron 1, 21120 Malmö, tel. 300150, e-mail: info@tourism.malmo.com. The tourist information office also sells the **Malmö Card**, which entitles you to free parking, free entrance to a few museums and discounts in a few stores and restaurants. It is part of the **Malmö Package** and includes up to three nights in a hotel with breakfast in various price categories.

🛏️ 😊😊😊 **Provobis Hotel Kramer**, Stortorget 7, tel. 208800, fax 126941, classic luxury hotel in the city center. **Radisson SAS Hotel**, Östergatan 10, tel. 239200, fax 6112840, large hotel. 😊😊 **City Hotel Anglais**, Stortorget 15, tel. 71450, fax 6699559, nice hotel of the Salvation Army. **Garden Hotel**, Baltzarsgatan 20, tel. 104000, fax 6116808. **Residens Hotel**, Adelgatan 7, tel. 6112530, fax 300960. 😊 **Prinze Hotel**, Carlsgatan 10 C, tel. 6112511, fax 6112310. **Hotel Tunneln**, Adelgatan 4, tel. 101620, fax 101625.

❌ **Kockska Krogen**, in Jörgen Kocks Gård, Stortorget, tel. 70320, best restaurant in Malmö, fish specialties. **Radhuskällaren**, beer and wine restaurant in the ratskeller, small meals, outdoor seating in the summer, Stortorget, tel. 79020. **Tunneln**, cellar restaurant in the hotel of the same name. **Restaurang Johan P.**, Market Hall Lilla Torget, tel. 971818, specializes in fish. **Market Hall** (Saluhallen), Lilla Torget, many other restaurants and fast food. **Årstiderna**, Grynbodgatan 9, tel. 230910, first-class Swedish cuisine.
CAFÉS: **Mäster Hans**, Stortorget, tel. 15900, best homemade pastries. **Dockhuset** at Lilla Torg, tel. 70481, often live music. **Surfers' Paradise**, Internet café, www.surfersparadise.com.

🎷 Nightclub in the Scandic Hotel Konserthus, Amiralsgatan 19, tel. 100730, **party liner**, departure information available from the tourist office or TT-Line, Trelleborg, tel. 0410-5622, after hours 56163.

🏛️ **Council Chambers**, Tue-Sat 10 am-3 pm, Sun 10 am-2 pm. **Sankt Petri kyrka**, 10 am-6 pm daily, except during services. **Residenset**, Jörgen Kocks Gård, **Hedmanska Gården** and **Flensburgska Huset** can only be viewed from the outside. **Form Design Center**, Tue, Wed and Fri 10 am-5 pm, Thu 11 am-6 pm, Sat 10 am-4 pm, Sun 12-4 pm. **Museum of Malmöhus** (natural history museum, aquarium, arts and crafts collection) and **Military Governor's House and Museums** (military and toy museum), Tue-Sun 10 am-4 pm, June-August, also Mon 10 am-4 pm .

🎪 August: **Crayfish Festival** all over town with Kräftskiva (crayfish feast) on the Stortorget, theater and longboat races.

🚌 **City Tours**: Bus line 20, every 10 minutes from the main train station (circular line).

By bicycle to the beaches of **Skanör** and **Falsterbo**.

By **hovercraft** to **Copenhagen. Canal trips:** June 16-Aug 15 11 am-4 pm daily, on the full hour from the docks at the main train station.

🛫 *PLANE:* To **Gothenburg** and **Stockholm** from the regional airport 30 km away. There is a shuttle bus (line 104) from the main train station to the **Copenhagen-Kastrup International Airport.**

TRAIN: Connections to **Helsingborg, Trelleborg, Lund** and **Stockholm.**

BUS: Connections to **Ystad, Copenhagen** and **Jönköping.**

LUND (☎ 046)

ℹ️ Kyrkogatan 11, 22100 Lund, tel. 355040; region Skåne: Skiffervägen 38, 22478 Lund, tel. 124350.

🛏️ 🌟🌟🌟 **Grand Hotel**, Bantorget 1, tel. 2117010, fax 147301. **Star Hotel**, Glimmervägen 5, tel. 2112000, fax 2115000. 🌟🌟 **Best Western Hotel Djingis Khan**, Margaretavägen 7, tel. 140060, fax 143626. 🌟 **Good Morning Hotels**, Förhandlingsvägen 4, tel. 303120, fax 307684.

❌ The **Grand Hotel** as well as the **Star Hotel** have good restaurants with typical Swedish cuisine. **Petri Pumpa**, Kyrkogatan 7, tel. 135515, also a hotel. **Café Mejeriet**, Södergatan 64, tel. 114700, live music on weekends, Saturday jazz brunch.

🏛️ **Domkyrkan**, 10 am-6 pm daily, the astronomical clock moves: Mon-Sat 12 and 2:15 pm, Sun 1 pm and 3 pm. **Historiska Museum, Skissernas Museum,** Mon-Wed and Fri-Sat 12-4 pm, Thu and Sun 1-5 pm. **Kulturen,** May-Sept Fri-Wed 11 am-5 pm, Thu 11 am-9 pm.

🚶 **Church** of **Dalby,** May 1-Aug 15 10 am-4 pm **Övedskloster,** May 15-Sept 15 11 am-4 pm daily, tel. 63001. **Bosjökloster,** April-Sept 10 am-8 pm daily.

TRELLEBORG (☎ 0410)

ℹ️ Hamngatan 4, 23142 Trelleborg, tel. 41220.

🛏️ 🌟🌟 **Dannegården Hotell & Restaurang**, Strandgatan 32, tel. 711120, Internet: www.dannagarden.se. 🌟 **Pensionat & Café Dalköpinge**, Strandvägen 7, 23162 Trelleborg, tel. 42100, fax 43580.

YSTAD (☎ 0411)

ℹ️ Stora Kungstorg, 27142 Ystad, tel. 77681.

🛏️ 🌟🌟🌟 **Ystads Saltsjöbad**, Saltsjöbadvägen 6, tel. 13630, fax 555835. 🌟🌟 **Hotell Continental**, Hamngatan 13, tel. 13700, fax 12570, the hotel's bar is the most popular one in town. 🌟 **Hotel Tornväktaren**, Stora Östergatan 33, tel. 78480, fax 72927.

❌ **Pilgränds Värdshus**, Pilgränd 6, tel. 14731, pretty terrace in the courtyard. **Rådhuskällaren**, in the cellar of the Gamla Rådhus, tel. 18510.

🏛️ **Sankta Maria kyrka** open Mon-Sat 10 am-4 pm, **Gråbrödraklostret** and all other museums June-Aug Mon-Fri noon-5 pm, Sat-Sun 12 pm-4 pm.

🚶 **Church** of **Valleberga**, Mon-Fri 10 am-4 pm **Glimmingehus**, April-Sept 9 am-5 pm daily. **Stenshuvud National Park**, information: Länsstyrelsen Kristianstads Län, tel. 044-131700. **Ales Stenar**, always open.

KRISTIANSTAD (☎ 044)

ℹ️ Stora Torg, 29132 Kristianstad, tel. 121988.

🛏️ 🌟🌟🌟 **First Hotel Christian IV**, Västra Boulevarden 15, tel. 126300, fax 124140. 🌟🌟 **Hotel Turisten**, **Sweden Hotels**, Västra Storgatan 17, tel. 126150, fax 103099. 🌟 **STF Vandrarhem Haväng**, Skepparpsgården, Kivik, tel. 0414-74071.

🏛️ **Trefaldighetskyrkan** Mon-Sat 10 am-4 pm, **Länsmuseum**, open June-Aug daily 10 am-4 pm, Sept-May Tue-Sun noon-5 pm.

🚶 **Sankta Maria kyrka** of **Vä**, Mon-Sat 10 am-4 pm **Chambered Tomb of Kivik**, May-Sept 10 am-6 pm daily.

MÖRRUM (☎ 0454)

🏛️ **Laxens Hus**, **Laxakvariet**, tel. 50123, Feb-Sept 9 am-5 pm daily, in October to 4 pm.

KARLSKRONA (☎ 0455)

ℹ️ Stortorget, 37183 Karlskrona, tel. 83490.

🛏️ 🌟🌟 **Hotel Carlskrona**, Skeppsbrokajen, tel. 19630, fax 12700. **First Hotel Statt**, Ronnebygatan 37-39, tel. 19250, fax 16909. 🌟 **Dragsö Bad and Camping**, Karlskrona beach, tel. 15354, rents *CABINS,* also *BICYCLE* and *BOOT RENTALS.*

🏛️ **Tyska Kyrkan**, **Ulrica Pia kyrka**, open Mon-Sat 10 am-4 pm. **Bastion Aurora**, always open to the public. **Marine Museum**, Stumholmen, June and August open daily 10 am-4 pm, in July until 6 pm, otherwise Tue-Sun 12-4 pm.

SMÅLAND AND ÖSTERGÖTLAND

SMÅLAND
JÖNKÖPING
LAKE VÄTTERN
VADSTENA
LINKÖPING
NORRKÖPING
VÄXJÖ / KALMAR

Småland

SMÅLAND

The name **Småland** is based on the history of this Swedish region, which developed from small (*små*), formerly independent estates (*land*). Including the northern province of **Östergötland**, the area encompasses some 40,000 square kilometers. The borders of the entire region are the Ljungby-Kalmar line to the south, the E4 to the west and the eastern parts of Lake Vättern; the northernmost city is Norrköping, and the eastern border is the Baltic Sea.

The landscape was formed during the last Ice Age, when massive sheets of ice created smoothly polished rock knolls and melt water produced countless lakes. Millions of boulders left behind by the glaciers, some of them as big as houses, impart the impression of a primeval world. Nearly a third of the region is covered by pine forests inhabited by a large population of elk. Lakes and moors comprise an additional third – areas suitable to farming are therefore very limited. For the very reason that this region has

Preceding pages: For many the quintessence of a vacation in Sweden – tranquil days on a secluded lake (near Växjo). Left: Children from all over the world enjoy Pippi Longstocking at "Astrid Lindgren's Värld."

largely been left to itself without much human encroachment, extraordinary natural landscapes remain unchanged, lending charm to the area and allowing it to be accepted for its true value.

The ever-increasing shortage of farmland for a rapidly growing population led to the great waves of emigration of the 19th century. Only after the development of the iron, wood, leather and glass industries could the inhabitants begin to make ends meet and the population begin to stabilize.

Until the Treaty of Roskilde in 1658, Småland was the southernmost region in the Swedish realm. Constant wars and internal turmoil hindered a continuity in development so that not until modern times could at least the cities of Växjö and Kalmar attain some sort of significance outside the region. The infrastructure also remained undeveloped for quite a long time. The major traffic artery in the west consists of the E4 and the railway, both following the old trade routes between Helsingborg and Stockholm. Secondary train routes lead to Kalmar, Oskarshamn and Västervik. The recently completed E22, following the Baltic coast, is a rapid connection between Kalmar and Norrköping. The region's inland area, on the other hand, is served only by a system of royal highways.

SMÅLAND

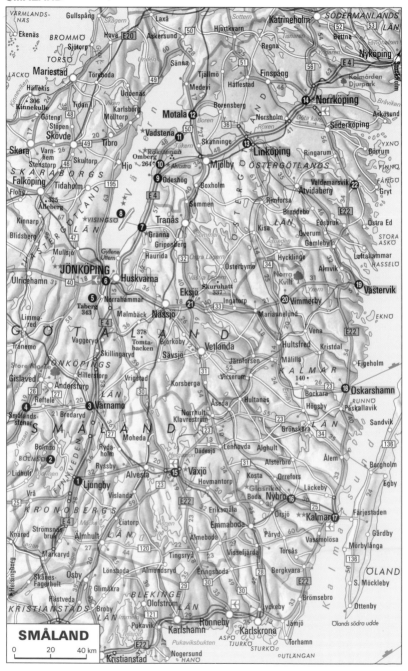

In the Forests of Småland

Travelers from the south heading for central or northern Sweden usually take the E4. The 560-kilometer stretch between Helsingborg and Stockholm can be covered in six to eight hours by car or rail. This leads to the temptation to forgo the small detours leading to many sites which are well worth visiting.

Shortly before reaching **Ljungby ❶**, the first town after crossing Småland's provincial border, signs direct you to a road leading to the burial site of **Kånna**, with numerous burial mounds, stone settings and other relics from the Bronze Age and the Vikings. Ljungby's picturesque marketplace is an inviting place for a coffee break. Those in search of peace and tranquility can make an excursion to nearby **Lake Bolmen**, where the island of **Bolmsö ❷** is home to other archeological findings; the Pikesborg for instance. On the northern route, along the E4, you will become acquainted with the vast forests of the Småland highlands, having an elevation of only 100 meters above sea level.

From **Värnamo ❸**, a westbound detour leads via routes 27 and 153 to **Smålandsstenar ❹** 40 kilometers away; five huge circles of stones from the Iron Age lend the city its name. Taking Route 27 or 151, you will reach the **Store Mosse** (Great Moor) **National Park**, with a unique population of birds you can watch from observation towers. Hiking trails lead through the park: they must be strictly followed in order not to disturb the flora and fauna.

Shortly before reaching Jönköping, two detours are worth taking: to **Taberg ❺** (towards Norrahammar) and to the country estate of **Riddersberg** (towards Nässjö). The Taberg (343 meters) is a large hill of stone containing iron, titanium and vanadium ores. Mining was carried on here from the 15th century until World War II. In 1986, the Swedish government purchased the mountain to stop the proposed construction of a ski resort, thereby protecting the last remains of a unique ecosystem. From the mountain peak, you have a beautiful view over the forests of Småland, and of **Lake Vättern** a hundred meters below. The country estate of Riddersberg boasts an exhibition of contemporary wooden sculpture executed in the naive style by Calle Örnemark. Especially due to the massive dimensions of the work, the sculptures have drawn interest even from abroad.

**JÖNKÖPING

Jönköping ❻, with over 100,000 inhabitants, is the largest city in Småland. **Huskvarna**, once a city of its own, has been absorbed in the meantime by its encroaching neighbor. The twin cities are located on the southern end of Lake Vättern – the second-largest lake in Sweden, measuring 130 kilometers in length and up to 30 kilometers in width, with an area of 1,800 square kilometers.

Economically speaking, Jönköping has had quite an eventful history. Favorably located at the crossing of the important east-west and north-south trade routes, the city was granted a charter in the 13th century and soon gained renown as a trading center. During Sweden's period as a superpower, Jönköping became the most important armorer in the country, and in the 19th century the city became the kingdom's chief manufacturer of snuff. The safety match was invented here, and the first sewing machine was made in Huskvarna. The two cities maintained their monopolies for these products up into this century. Today, not much remains of the original buildings; the city, which was built from wood, periodically suffered from catastrophic fires.

The most interesting in town site is the **Stadsparken**. In addition to animal enclosures, there is also an ornithological museum displaying over 500 stuffed specimens of our feathered friends.

Småland

In the city center, the City Hall and the courthouse are reminders of the 17th century. Not far from here is the ***Tändsticksmuseet** (Match Museum), inside a factory from 1848, where you can marvel at the old machines used for producing the "Swedish match." In the **Länsmuseet** there are sections dedicated to iron working, Småländ art and missionary work: Jönköping is the headquarters for many free churches that are busily spreading the faith, when necessary even among themselves. This has given the city the nickname of "Småland's Jerusalem." The moral severity of the Protestant religion can be felt here even today.

****LAKE VÄTTERN**

When you leave Jönköping on the E4 heading north, on the right-hand side you can see the monumental sculpture of the

Above: Vist the Giant, a sculpture of refuse wood. Right: Candy canes and peppermint sticks are the main industry in Gränna.

giant **Jätten Vist**, made of refuse wood by Calle Örnemark.

The E4 follows the eastern shore of Lake Vättern for a good 60 kilometers and offers a multitude of beautiful lookout points. A special treat is to take the highway exit to the **Gyllene Uttern** (Golden Otter) hotel, and then enjoy the view of the lake and the island of Visingsö from the picturesque turf-roofed building. Take the old road directly along the lake to reach the small idyllic settlement of ***Gränna ❼**. This town of 3,000 inhabitants was founded in the 17th century by Count Per Brahe, who laid out the main street, Brahegetan. The beautiful wooden houses, most of which are yellow, fortunately never fell victim to a fire. Here you can watch the locals make *polkagrisar* (candy sticks), the main product of the town. The city also offers artisans' shops and cafés. The town's **museum** is dedicated to the arctic explorer Andrée, a native son of the city who was lost in an attempt to reach the North Pole in a hot air balloon in 1897.

A boat ride to the island of ***Visingsö ❽** is a very rewarding excursion. In the summer shuttle boats leave for the island every half hour. You can tour the island by bicycle or by horse and carriage; there is hardly any automobile traffic. The magnificent **Brahekyrka** contains Count Brahe's tomb and a statue of St. Birgitta in Ecstasy. In addition, Visingsö offers plenty of opportunities for relaxing walks along the beaches; unfortunately, the water in Lake Vättern is too cold for swimming (the warmest it gets is 15 °C).

If you leave Gränna on the old road going north, you will get back to the E4 at the modern highway rest stop of Brahehus. Here are the ruins of **Brahehus Castle**, which burned down in the 18th century. Per Brahe built it for his young wife should she become his widow, but she died and he used it as a hunting lodge. The ruins can be reached via a tunnel from the parking lot at the rest stop.

At **Ödeshög** ❾ you cross the border-line between Småland and Östergötland. It is recommended that you leave the E4 here and take Route 50. Along the almost 50 kilometers to Motala there are several small treasures very close to one another – all nestled somewhere in the marvelous landscapes around the shores of Lake Vättern.

Route 50 takes you to **Omberg**, an "eagle's nest" made of primary rock tow-ering 175 meters over the lake: it was left standing when the remaining part of the surrounding landscape collapsed during geological unrest. The ten-kilometer-long and three-kilometer-wide rock knoll is covered with lush vegetation and is its own nature reserve. Numerous hiking trails are posted, and there is a lookout tower on the highest point.

*VADSTENA
The Realm of St. Birgitta

On the southern outskirts of Omberg lies *Alvastra ❿, the oldest cloister in Sweden. Founded by French Cistercians in 1143, it adhered to the cloister regula-tions of Bernhard von Clairvaux: it was laid out on land the monks had cleared themselves, and the buildings were con-structed in the modest tradition of the or-der. Alvastra was the most powerful cloister in the country with more than 900 farms during its heyday in the 14th cen-tury. It was abandoned after the Reforma-tion, fell into ruin and was later used as a source of stone for construction of the castle at Vadstena. The extensive land holdings and forests were used by Gustavus Vasa as hunting grounds.

Between Alvastra and **Lake Tåkern** is Sweden's most famous rune stone: *Rökstenen, the Rök Stone. The stone, standing over three meters tall, is located in front of the church and has more than 800 inscriptions in different runic writ-ings. The 9th-century text has not been completely deciphered. Even Theodoric the Great is mentioned in the writings; the chart next to the stone includes a transla-tion of the inscriptions.

Located 12 kilometers north of Alvastra is ***Vadstena ⓫**, the cloister of St. Birgitta, the patron saint of Sweden. Birgitta Birgersdotter, her maiden name, was a niece of Birger Jarl and lived with her husband at the court of King Magnus Eriksson. When the mother of eight became a widow at the age of 41, she retreated to the Alvastra cloister in 1344. Here she had her first visions: the visions told her to establish a completely different type of cloister in Vadstena. It should be a cloister for monks and nuns with a shared cloister church as its center and have an abbess as head of the cloister hierarchy. King Magnus – she was in his good graces anyway – gave her an abandoned mansion for the nunnery and another building for the monks' lodgings. Construction of the cloister church began immediately. The Pope's permission was the only thing missing for the novel regulations of the order. In 1349, Birgitta set off to visit the Holy Father. In those confusing times – at that time the popes resided in Avignon – it wasn't until 1370 that she was finally granted permission. Sick and weak after a pilgrimage to the Holy Land, the founder of the order never returned to Sweden; she died in Rome in 1373. Her remains were brought here to Vadstena and provisionally buried.

St. Birgitta had also looked after the construction of her cloister from abroad. In addition, she fastidiously wrote down her visions and translated countless theological works into Swedish or had them translated. This was the foundation of the cloister library in Vadstena. After she was canonized in 1391, an unprecedented "Birgitta Cult" started, which led to the establishment of another 80 "Birgitta cloisters" throughout Europe.

Even after the Reformation the common people still revered the saint and they prevented the destruction of her cloister, although the cloister buildings were used for secular purposes. In 1935, the convent was granted papal permission to reopen, and nuns have been seen in the city of Vadstena ever since – an unusual sight in Sweden.

It's best to start your tour through the city at the harbor, where the **castle** of Gustavus Vasa stands. It is a typical mixture of fortress and living quarters from the 16th century. The castle was abandoned in 1716. It has been open to the public since it was restored in 1957. They have also renewed the tradition of holding regular opera performances in the castle, a tradition dating from 1654.

Walk past the **convent**, where the nuns run a nice **guesthouse**, to get to the **cloister church**. The modest two-aisled hall church has little exterior ornamentation and is also called *Blåkyrkan*, because of the blue-gray stones used to build it. The interior design became more and more elegant with the progression of the "Birgitta Cult" and the pilgrimages. The saint's shrine is in the west sanctuary; Charles IX had the silver coat melted down when he yet again needed money. There are two sculptures of the saint in the nave. Both are from the 15th century, as are the rest of the ornaments. There is a hotel with an exceptionally good restaurant in the **monastery** on the other side of the church.

Along the **Göta Canal

If you follow Route 50 for 16 kilometers northwards, at **Motala ⓬** you will cross the ****Göta Canal** (see p. 230), which starts at Lake Vättern. From there you can take an excursion by boat through five locks to reach **Lake Boren**. Between the first and second locks is the **Canal Museum**, which documents the history and route of the almost 400-kilometer-long Göta Canal. The builder of the canal, Baltazar von Platen, was buried di-

Right: The Göta Canal, an ambitious 19th-century transportation project, is only a tourist attraction today.

Småland

rectly adjacent to the museum in 1829. Today the waterway is a highlight for tourists, who can take a four-day boat tour on it from Gothenburg to Mem via lakes Vänern and Vättern, and then continue on the Baltic Sea to Stockholm. In Motala, Route 36 runs along the canal to Linköping, where it meets up with the E4.

★LINKÖPING
The Old Cathedral City

Towards the end of the 11th century, ★**Linköping** ⓭ was promoted to a cathedral town; in 1152, a council of bishops agreed here to put Sweden directly under the Roman Catholic Curia. At this time they started the construction of the **Domkyrkan**. The cathedral, however, did not reach completion in the "Flamboyant Gothic" style until a good 300 years later. The different designs of the pillars in the nave and the two aisles, as well as the stone masonry done by over 60 architects, are testimony to its long construction period. The cathedral, how-

ever, has a homogeneous appearance. The great fire of 1700 razed the city of Linköping. Only a small number of the houses built afterward still stand; today they are the open-air museum of ★**Gamla Linköping**, the city's chief attraction. The district, with 60 wooden houses, is always open; the many small museums, mom-and-pop stores and workshops have fixed opening hours. The center of the modern city is the **Stortorget** with the **Folkunga Fountain** by Carl Milles. The subject of this fountain has to do with an old Swedish saga of a king.

The prime economic force in Linköping is the SAAB aircraft factory; located on an airbase in the Malmslätt quarter, the **Flygvapenmuseum** (Swedish Air Force Museum) has a collection of military aircraft on display.

★NORRKÖPING
Sweden's Manchester

Only 14 kilometers to the northeast is the industrial city of ★**Norrköping** ⓮.

The 1,600 **rock carvings** (*Hällristningar*) near the bathhouse at the southern end of the city testify to the fact that this area was already settled in the Bronze Age

Norrköping is the Swedish synonym for the early Industrial Age. The numerous textile factories and spinning mills were able to use the rapids of the Motala River as a free source of energy and gave the city an enormous boom in the 19th century. The Europe-wide crisis in the 1960s and '70s brought about the end of the textile industry in Norrköping as well. Numerous factory buildings were left standing, and they are now used to house the **Museums of Industry**.

On the island of Laxholm, in the middle of the Motala, the old ironing shop of a weaving mill was added onto and converted into the **Arbetets Museum**, where exhibitions show the working conditions of the early industrial society. You have a

Above: The Museum of Labor in Norrköping is worth a visit. Right: Inside a glassworks in Kosta.

good view of the old industrial quarter from the restaurant on the sixth floor. Nowadays, rubber, paper and synthetics factories are the economic lifeline of Norrköping.

Just 20 kilometers north of Norrköping is the **Kolmården Djurpark**, the largest animal and safari park in Europe, which you can ride through on a three-kilometer-long cable railway. In addition to the indigenous fauna kept here, there are also exotic animals, a dolphin center and an adventure park.

⋆VÄXJÖ
The Heartland of Småland

Back to the E4 in Ljungby: head East and after 55 kilometers on Royal Highway 25 you will arrive at the heartland of Småland; ⋆**Växjö** ⑮ on **Helgasjön** (Lake Helga). Two old trade routes intersected here; their modern successors are routes 23 and 30. Today, Växjö has 70,000 inhabitants and is the center of education and administration for a large surrounding area. Following several disastrous fires, particularly in the 19th century, the only remnant of the Baroque period is the right-angled system of streets. The **Domkyrkan** on the Stortorget was not spared by the fires either. The cathedral, originally from the 12th century, was rebuilt from 1956 to 1960 based on the original plans. Next to the cathedral is Växjo's old **secondary school** (*Gamla gymnasiet*), at which the botanist Carl von Linné was once a pupil. On the south side of the train station you will find the **Smålands Museum**, with a huge collection of drinking glasses and other glassware. This glass museum not only collects glassware from the *Glasriket* (Glass Realm), east of the city, but also has glassware from other countries.

The **Utvandrarnas hus** (Emigrant Museum) next to the Smålands Museum recalls the 200,000 Småländ citizens who were forced to leave the country by the

Småland

sheer poverty of the 19th century. The study of Vilhelm Moberg, who wrote a five-volume novel about this exodus, "The Emigrants," can also be seen here.

Two short excursions from Växjö can be made: only five kilometers north of the city there is a peninsula on Lake Helgasjön with the ruins of **Kronoberg Castle**, which was built in the 14th century as a border fortification against Denmark. The Vasa kings converted it into a residential complex with defense installations 200 years later. After the Treaty of Roskilde in 1658, the complex became superfluous, and it was left to go to ruin.

Twenty-five kilometers to the east of Växjö (routes 23 and 31) you will find an architectural jewel, the church of **Dädesjö**. It was abandoned in the 18th century and was later used as a granary. When they rediscovered the painted wooden ceiling in 1905 it was still in relatively good condition. There are no other late-Romanesque paintings from the 13th century in Sweden that are comparable to these. The 30 panels depict scenes and various legends from the gospel concerning the Nativity.

The area surrounding Växjö fulfills every dream of an uncomplicated vacation: lakes, islands, wooden houses with boats and piers, fishing and tranquillity await stressed-out people from the big city.

In the Realm of the Glass Herring

In the eastern region of Småland, between Växjö and **Nybro** ⓰, is the Swedish ★**Glasriket**. In the 16th century Gustavus Vasa brought a Venetian glassblower to Sweden who made his art known quickly. The huge supply of firewood in the forests and, for those times, the good transportation routes for the fragile product meant Småland was an ideal production site for glass. **Kosta**, **Boda** and **Orrefors** are the oldest glassworks. From designs by modern artists to classical designs to pure kitsch, everything sellable is produced here. Most of the renowned glass factories also have a small museum with exhibits featuring

their wares and/or glassblowers' tools from the past. Even a look inside a glass furnace is often possible, and sometimes you will be invited to have a "glass herring." In the past, the glassblowers brought raw herrings with them for their meals and roasted them in the glass ovens – a tasty as well as an inexpensive snack.

**KALMAR
The City of the Union

Only one single event was enough to place **Kalmar ❼ in the world's spotlight: the union between Denmark, Norway and Sweden in 1397; it henceforth bore the name of its founding location and officially lasted until 1523. Kalmar, now the provincial capital, is located on the Kalmar Sound.

The proximity to the Danish border at that time, however, had catastrophic consequences for the city, as it was destroyed

Above: In Norra Kvill National Park near Vimmerby.

during virtually every conflict between the Danes and the Swedes. Not until 1658, after the Treaty of Roskilde, did the city experience peace and quiet.

In the 13th century the city was on the mainland, only a few meters from its fortified castle on an island in the Baltic Sea. The oldest houses (17th century) are in **Gamla Staden**; they survived the great fire which led to the relocation of the city. The new city was built on the island of **Kvarnholmen** (Mill Island), northeast of the castle, because the city could be defended better from here. The new design adhered to the regulations of urban development of that time: right-angled streets with a large market (Stortorget) in the center. Here you will find the **Domkyrkan**, consecrated in 1682.

Nicodemus Tessin the Elder designed the cathedral as a Baroque cruciform church. It rises from its granite foundation and was constructed of limestone and covered with white plaster. Only the decorative elements, such as the pilasters, alcoves and volutes, were not plastered.

Worth mentioning in the interior of the austere Protestant church are the pulpit (late Renaissance), the Baroque altar by Tessin, and the numerous gravestones embedded in the floor.

On the opposite side of the Stortorget is the City Hall, which has undergone drastic changes since the 17th century.

The new **Länsmuseet** was built just two blocks away from the yacht harbor. Its central theme is a warship, the **Kronan**, which exploded off the coast of Öland in 1676 before it could be employed against the Danish-Dutch fleet. With 2,200 gross tons it was almost twice as large as the famous Vasa; and it also had 220 tons of cannons, three times as many as the Vasa. They never raised the Kronan, but a lot of the salvaged equipment is on display here. In conjunction with the ongoing salvage operation, the museum also has an exhibition on underwater archeology.

On the shores of Kvarnholmen there are still remains of the former fortifications. The houses on the island are all from the 18th and 19th centuries. The only thing comparable in terms of appearance is the Old Town in Stockholm or the one in Visby.

The **castle** dates from the 12th century and was used as a fortress; it owes its present-day look to the Vasa kings, who built, among other things, the round towers on the corners. After having been used as a prison and liquor distillery in the 17th century, it was later restored. The rooms on the second floor were recreated at this time.

Pippi Longstocking's Homeland

Along the 130-kilometer stretch between Kalmar and Västervik there are not many places of interest.

Oskarshamn ⓲ is dominated by its harbor and its industry. **Västervik** ⓳ has a beautiful collection of old wooden houses, nicely grouped around the harbor.

There are still the so-called seamen's houses here; today they serve as tourist lodgings. The coast north of Kalmarsund is a paradise for sailors: Västervik's real treasure is the 5,000 islands of the archipelago, where you can find a Robinson Crusoe on almost every island on a warm summer day.

An absolute "must" for families with young children is an excursion to the town of **Vimmerby** ⓴, 40 kilometers from Västervik, where **Astrid Lindgren's Värld** (see p. 232) beckons young and old alike with the locations from Lindgren's stories recreated in miniature. **Lönneberga** and the **Kattult Farm** (30 kilometers from Vimmerby) really do exist, but don't lose time looking for Bullerby, which is actually Svedentorp, the birthplace of the famous author of children's books.

Eksjö ㉑, a small town between Vimmerby and Jönköping with cozy-looking wooden houses, is an ideal starting point for exploring the wilderness of Småland's many lakes and forests. The most exciting day trip on foot is a hike through the Skurugata, a gorge 50 meters deep and 550 meters long; the 337-meter-high **Skuruhatt** offers the best view. Breathtaking canoe and hiking trails (for example, the 350-kilometer-long *Höglandsleden* or the *Kalmarsundsleden*) make this sparsely-populated woodland with countless lakes and rivers easily accessible.

Mighty stands of pine trees are protected in the small national park of **Norra Kvill** (18 kilometers northeast of Vimmerby); a path leads through the miniature primeval forest. Sweden's oldest oak tree, with a circumference of 14 meters, is also here.

If you take the E22 from Västervik north to Norrköping, it pays to stop in **Valdemarsvik** ㉒. At the old harbor, cut off from the sea during geological upheavals in the 17th century, there are several pretty wooden houses.

Småland

LJUNGBY (☎ 0372)

i Stora Torget 3, 34130 Ljungby, tel. 83333.
🛏️ 😊😊 **Hotel Terraza**, Stora Torget 1, tel. 13560, fax 83978.
🏛️ **Burial Mounds of Kånna**.
▦ **Pikesborg Castle**, information: tourist office.
🏕️ **Store Mosse National Park**, info: Länsstyrelsen Jönköpings Län, Hamngatan 4, tel. 036-157000.

JÖNKÖPING (☎ 036)

i Djurläkartorget 2, 55189 Jönköping, tel. 105050.
🛏️ 😊😊😊 **Scandic Hotel Elmia**, Elmiavägen 8, tel. 719160, fax 712868. 😊😊 **Provobis Stora Hotellet**, Hotellplan, tel. 100000, fax 719320. **Grand Hotel**, Hovrättstorget, tel. 719600, fax 719605. **John Bauer Hotel**, Södra Strandgatan 15, tel. 100500, fax 712788. **Comfort Home Hotel Victoria**, Elmgrens Gate 5, tel. 715050, fax 712800. 😊 **Good Morning Hotels**, Strömsnäsgatan 3, tel. 164100, fax 164103. **Sjöåkra Gården**, Sjöåkravägen, Bankeryd, tel. 378035, fax 378422, directly on Lake Vättern.
🅰️ **Roselunds Camping**, tel. 122863, fax 126687.
❌ Restaurant in **Stora Hotellet**, fish specialties from Lake Vättern. **Krogen Svarta Börsen**, Kyrkogatan 4, tel. 712222, very good, reasonably-priced lunch.
🏛️ **Fågelmuseet** (**Ornithological Museum**) in the city park, May-Aug 11 am-5 pm daily. **Tändsticksmuseet** (Match Museum), Tändsticksgränd 27, June-Aug Mon-Fri 10 am-5 pm, Sat-Sun 10 am-3 pm, Sept-May Tue-Thu 12-4 pm, Sat 11 am-3 pm. **Länsmuseum**, Slottgate 2, Thu-Tue 11 am-5 pm, Wed to 8 pm.
🏕️ The country estate of **Riddersberg**, June-Sept 10 am-4 pm daily.

GRÄNNA (☎ 0390)

i In the Andréemuseet, 56322 Gränna, tel. 41010.
🛏️ 😊😊 **Gyllene Uttern**, tel. 10800, fax 11880, rooms in an old manor house with a wedding chapel. **Hotel Västanå Slott**, Västanå, tel. 10700, fax 41875. 😊 **Smålandsgården**, Öserum, tel. 30014, fax 30417.
🅰️ **Getingaryds Familjecamping**, tel. 21015. **Grän-nastrandens Familijecamping**, tel. 10706.
🏛️ **Andréemuseet**, May 15-Aug 31, 10 am-5 pm daily, Sept 1-May 15, 12-4 pm daily.
📷 August 11 (weather permitting): **Hot-air balloon day**.

VISINGSÖ (☎ 0390)

🛏️ The tourist information office in Gränna arranges **private accommodations** on the island of Visingsö.

📷 Year-round ferry traffic between Gränna and Vis-ingsö, in summer up to 10 times daily
❌ **Strandgården**, tel. 40359, meals according to Peter Brahe's recipes, the Royal Family's chef.
🏛️ **Brahehus** and **Brahekyrka**, 10 am-4 pm daily.

VADSTENA (☎ 0143)

i Vasaslottet, 59280 Vadstena, tel. 15125.
🛏️ 😊😊 **Vadstena Klosterhotel**, Klosterområdet, tel. 31530, fax 13648, occasional opera music in the court-yard. **Starby Kungsgård**, Ödenshögsvägen, tel. 75100, fax 75170.
🅰️ **Vättervikbadets Camping**, tel. 12730, fax 4148, 2 km north also *CABIN RENTALS*.
❌ **Munkeklosteret** in the monastery hotel, tel. 13000, excellent. **Guesthouse** in the women's religious institution, tel. 11488.
🏛️ **Blå Kyrkan** (Blue Church), May and Sept 10 am- 5 pm daily, June and Aug 10 am-6 pm daily, July 10 am- 7 pm daily. **Castle**, May 12 pm-4 pm daily, June and Aug 12 pm-5 pm daily, July 11 am-5 pm daily.
📷 July-August: **Opera** performances in the castle, in-formation: Sept-May tel. 08-6526180, otherwise tel. 12229, advance ticket sales: Wetterheds Bokhandel, tel. 10094.
Boat trips on **Lake Vättern** and the **Göta Canal**, infor-mation: tourist office Vadstena or Motala.

MOTALA (☎ 0141)

i Folkets Hus, 59129 Motala, tel. 225254.
🛏️ 😊😊 **Motala Stadshotell**, Stora Torget, tel. 216400, fax 214605. 😊 **Hotell Urban Hjärne**, Bispmotalagatan 11, tel. 235200, fax 217545.
🅰️ **Z-Parkens Camping Veramon**, tel. 211142, fax 217042, with a wonderful beach directly on the lake.
🏛️ **Canal Museum**, May 11-June 11 and Aug 3-27, 9 am-noon and 1-4 pm daily, June 12-Aug 2, Mon-Fri 9 am-8 pm, Sat-Sun 9 am-2 pm and 3-7 pm, tel. 53510.
📷 **Bicycle Tours** along the Göta Canal.
BICYCLE AND BOAT RENTALS: Tourist office, also arranges rides to other cities.
Mid-June: **Bicycle race** around Lake Vättern.

LINKÖPING (☎ 013)

i Klostergatan 68, 58223 Linköping, tel. 206835.
🛏️ 😊😊😊 **Hotell Ekoxen**, Klostergatan 68, tel. 146070, fax 121903, special weekend rates, great quality for the money.
😊😊 **First Hotel Linköping**, Storgatan 70-76, tel. 130200, fax 132785.

Good Evening Hotel, Hantverkergatan 1 and Stora Torget 9, tel. 129000, fax 138850.

Le Bistro, Nya Tanneforsvägen 43 A, tel. 123837, French cuisine. **Restaurang Krouthén**, Klostergatan 26, tel. 146070. **Restaurang Stora Hotell**, Stora Torget 9, tel. 129630, with a nightclub and piano bar.

Domkyrkan, Mon-Sat 9 am-6 pm. **Gamla Linköping**, stores and workshops, Mon-Fri 10 am-5:30 pm, Sat-Sun 11 am-4 pm, Mon no craftwork presentations. **Flygvapen** daily 11 am-4 pm.

NORRKÖPING (☎ 011)

i Drottninggatan 11, 60181 Norrköping, tel. 151500.

Grand Hotel, Tyska Torget 2, tel. 197100, fax 181183. **First Express**, Skomakargatan 8, tel. 197220, fax 126506. **Alosa Hotel**, Norra Grytsgatan 10, tel. 182211, fax 239895. **Hotel Centric**, Rådhusgatan 18-20, tel. 129030, fax 180728. **Södra Hotellet**, Södra Promenaden 142, tel. 253500, fax 124696. **Hotel Kneippen**, Kneippgatan 7, tel. 133060, fax 167773.

Kolmårdens Canoeing, tel. 398250, fax 397081, 22 km north of Norrköping on the Bråviken.

Palace, Bråddgatan 15, tel. 189600, various restaurants, dancing, café, nightclub and the excellent **Palace Gourmet**. **Guskelov**, Dalsgatan 13, tel. 186004, Swedish home-style cooking. **Värdshuset Löfstad slott**, tel. 335165, rustic atmosphere, generous servings of Swedish home-style cooking.

Industrimuseet Färgaregården (dyeing works), St. Petersgatan 3, 12-4 pm daily, **Stadsmuseet** (old looms), Västgötagatan 19-21, Mon-Fri 11 am-5 pm, Sat-Sun 12-4 pm. **Arbetets Museet** (Museum of Labor) daily 11 am-5 pm, restaurant on the 6th floor.

Kolmården Animal Park, 20 km north, April 29-Sept 3, 10 am-7 pm daily, tel. 249000. **Dolphin show** April 8-Nov 5 daily.

VÄXJÖ (☎ 0470)

i Kronobergsgatan 8, 35112 Växjö, tel. 41410.

Cardinal Hotel & Restaurang, Bäckgatan 10, tel. 13430, fax 16964.

Hotel Statt i Växjö, Kungsgatan 6, tel. 13400, fax 44837. **Hotel Teaterparken**, Västra Esplanaden 10-12, tel. 39900, fax 47477.

Hotell Esplanad, Norra Esplanaden 21, tel. 22580, ideal for a long stay. **Tofta Strand Hotell & Konditorei**, Lenhovdavägen, tel. 65290, fax 61402, small hotel on a lake, good rates, bakery, rents cabins. *YOUTH HOSTELS:* **STF Vandrarhem Växjö**, Evedals Brunn, tel. 63070, fax 63122, am Helgasjön.

With *CANOE RENTALS*, tel. 63034.

Restaurant in **Statt Hotel**, tel. 13400 good food. **Evendals Värdshus**, directly on the Helgasjön, tel. 63003, country guesthouse with home-style cooking.

Småland's Museum (glass museum), Södra Järnvägsgatan 2, Mon-Fri 9 am-4 pm, June-Aug Mon-Fri 5 pm, Sat 11 am-3 pm, Sun 1 pm-5 pm. **Utvandrarnas Hus** (Emigrant Museum), Strandvägen, same opening hours as above.

Church of Dädesjö, June-Aug 10 am-5 pm daily.

BICYCLE AND CANOE RENTALS: Tourist office, also organizes guided hiking tours.

GLASRIKET (☎ 0481)

i Glasriketinformation, 38280 Nybro, tel. 45215.

Stora Hotellet, Melangatan 11, 38230 Nybro, tel. 51935, fax 10835. **SFT Vandrarhem**, Nybro, tel. 12117.

Glassworks: Kosta, tel. 0478-34500. **Boda**, tel. 24030. **Orrefors**, tel. 34195, all open Mon-Fri 9 am-6 pm, Sat 10 am-4 pm, Sun 12 pm-4 pm. Glass blowing: Mon-Fri 9 am-3 pm.

Glass Herring Feast: June 2-Aug 29 from 7 pm daily in alternating glassworks. Menu: Glass herring, baked potatoes, cranberries, cheesecake. Reservations through Bergdala, tel. 0478-31650, Kosta, tel. 50835, and Orrefors, tel. 30059.

KALMAR (☎ 0480)

i Larmgatan 6, 39120 Kalmar, tel. 15350.

Slottshotellet, Slottsvägen 7, tel. 88260, fax 88266. **Calmar Stadshotell**, Stortorget 14, tel. 15180, fax 15847, nice, old hotel in the center of town. **Frimurarehotellet**, Larmtorget 2, tel. 15230, fax 85887. **First Hotel Witt**, Södra Långgatan 42, tel. 15250, fax 15265.

Hotel Witt good food. **Calmar Hamnkrog**, Skeppsbrogatan 30, tel. 18100. **Ernesto**, Larmtorget 4, tel. 20050, steaks, pizza, spaghetti, cocktail bar.

Länsmuseum, Skeppsbrogatan 51, June 15-Aug 15, Mon-Sat 10 am-6 pm, Sun 12-4 pm, June 16-Aug 14, Mon-Tue and Thu-Fri 10 am-4 pm, Wed 10 am-8 pm, Sat-Sun 12-4 pm. **Palace**, June 15-Aug 15, Mon-Sat 6 am-6 pm, Sun 12 pm-6 pm.

VIMMERBY (☎ 0492)

Astrid Lindgrens Värld, tel. 15950, open May 3-June 8 and Aug 11-31, 10 am-5 pm daily (admission is 35 percent cheaper at these times), June 9-Aug 10, 10 am-6 pm daily.

Småland

69

GRAND ISLANDS OF THE BALTIC SEA

ÖLAND

GOTLAND

**ÖLAND

As a vacation island, **Öland offers a lot of what you would expect to find in more southern climes; miles of sandy beaches, deciduous forests and windmills are not exactly typical of Sweden. The little precipitation in the summer months can even lead to water shortages. The island is a large, half-submerged mountain ridge 137 kilometers long and no more than 16 kilometers wide. It precipitously drops away in the west while gently sloping into the sea in the east; the ridge is only thinly covered with deposits from the Ice Age. The vegetation, so different from that of the mainland, is due to its chalky sandstone subsoil.

Öland was already inhabited in the Stone Age; the Vikings and their successors built refuge forts here. The windmills – once numbering 1,300 – are signs of bountiful grain yields.

The Barren South: **Stora Alvaret

Öland can be reached by a six-kilometer-long bridge built in 1972, which spans

Preceding pages: Relive a week in the Middle Ages (Visby, early August during the Medeltidsveckan). Left: Öland's 350 windmills are under historical preservation.

the sound between Kalmar and the island. You will arrive at **Färjestaden ❶**, the former ferry station. The tourist information office is located here and will assist you in finding last-minute accommodations or campgrounds in the high season.

Heading south from Färjestaden (Route 136), you should switch over to Route 946 in **Skogsby**, which runs parallel to the main road near the coast. After five kilometers, you will arrive at **Karlevistenen**; it is considered to be the most beautiful rune stone on the island. The stone, still standing at its original location, was erected by a Danish king more than a thousand years ago. Altogether there are more than a dozen such stones scattered about the island, many others, though, are likely to have ended up as building material for churches.

The **Stora Alvaret**, a vast limestone steppe covering most of the southern part of the island, begins near **Vickleby ❷**, where a 12th-century fortified church still stands. At first glance the grassy heath countryside looks rather sparse, but actually, quite a variety of plant life thrives here. Some 35 types of orchids, rare grasses and herbs flourish here in the mild, dry climate.

There is a good view of the countryside from the gentle hills of the burial mounds of **Mysinge**, south of Resmo. Ornitholo-

gists also prize these hills, especially for watching the resting swarms of cranes on their southward migration, for instance. A narrow road that winds through the Stora Alvaret and leads to the east coast begins at the Ice Age refuge fort of **Bårby borg**.

If you continue driving farther south, you will pass through the Iron Age burial grounds of **Gettlinge ❸** and arrive at the **Wall of Charles X** on the other side of Grönhögen. The king, an avid hunting enthusiast, had the five-kilometer-long wall built from coast to coast in 1653 to prevent his royal deer on the southern tip from leaving their territory, thereby protecting the farmers' fields.

The 18th-century **Långe Jan ❹**, Sweden's tallest lighthouse, is located on the southern cape of Öland. The 42-meter tower is open in summer to visitors.

Above: Stones laid out during the Iron Age in the form of ships, as seen here in a burial field at Gettlinge, can be found in many places in Sweden.

The East Coast

For the return trip from the "Tall Jan," you should take the road on the east coast. After a few kilometers you will come to the refuge fort of *Eketorp ❺, which was built and used in three phases between 300 and 1300 A.D. Following careful excavations, the refuge was partially reconstructed as an open-air museum and creates a vivid impression of the lifestyle of the 200 people and their livestock within the ramparts. An additional example of 19 such refuges is located 30 kilometers farther inland near **Möckleby**: the **Gråborg ❻**, whose circular ramparts, once up to six meters high, measure 640 meters in circumference. This is the largest refuge fort on the island. Presumably, the fort was used from the days of the great migrations up into the Middle Ages. The remains of Knut's chapel, a pilgrimage chapel from the 13th century, are located in front of the fort. An attempt is being made to restore the original vegetation of the surrounding meadows.

The Stormy North

The five old windmills near **Lerkaka** ❼, like the other 350 on the island, are under historic preservation. In the little town of **Himmelsberga**, two old Öland farmhouses were joined to establish an open-air museum whose main collection displays the island's beautiful country furnishings. The best-preserved church on the island is from the 12th century and is located in Gårdslösa. **Kapelludden** ❽ is where the remains of Saint Birgitta first reached Swedish soil after being brought from Rome and taken to Vadstena in 1374.

The northernmost part of Öland consists of the **Böda kronopark**, an extensive forest whose pines in the east have been twisted into bizarre shapes by the wind; hence the name **Trollskogen** (Troll Forest). A grove of arborvitae (thuja pine) lines the sandy beach of **Böda** ❾. Ferries run from the port of **Grankullavik** to the island of Gotland in the summer. There is also a lighthouse on the northern tip of the island: **Långe Erik** ❿, whose tower can be climbed, is open to visitors.

On the way back south, it is worth stopping at **Neptuni åkrar**, "Neptune's Fields," as Carl von Linné dubbed the area: between the scree embankments in June and July, the sea-blue blossoms of viper's bugloss (blue thistle) sway here in great numbers. The beautiful bathing cove of **Byerums Sandvik** is also worth the detour; its *raukar*, oddly shaped freestanding lime- and sandstone formations, are unparalleled on Öland.

Blå Jungfrun – The Island of Witches

The island of **Blå Jungfrun**, located in Kalmar Sound, can be reached in summer by boats running from **Byxelkrok** (weather permitting). The island has been a national park since 1925. Blå Jungfrun is popularly referred to as the legendary *blåkulla*, where witches dance through

ÖLAND

0   20 km

The Grand Islands

the night on Maundy Thursday. Unlike Öland, the island (86 meters above sea level and 66 hectares in area) is composed of granite, similar to the mainland. The island served as a quarry for many years, which unfortunately caused the destruction of numerous grottos.

The Royal Residences of the West Coast

Borgholm ⓫, the capital of the island of Öland, has 3,000 inhabitants and lies at the foot of a 40-meter-high cliff called a "land castle." The imposing ruins of the ***Borgholm slott** tower over the little town. There have been fortresses here since the 12th century – constantly fought over by the Swedes, the Danes and the Hanseatic League. Using the ruins of the Renaissance castle as a tremendous stage setting, open-air events take place here in summer.

Not far from Borgholm is **Solliden**, the summer residence of the Swedish king. The magnificent ***Royal Park**, encom-

passing an Italian-style villa built in 1905, is open a few hours daily to the public even when the Royal Family is present. This is an extraordinary opportunity for royalty enthusiasts to catch a glimpse of the crowned leaders.

Probably more worthwhile is a stop in **Halltorps Hage**, a grove of thousand-year-old oaks, hornbeams and many other deciduous trees. The cozy country inn **Halltorps Kro**, the only one in the village, offers a setting for a nice break.

*Ismantorps borg, the romantic refuge fort from the Iron and Viking Ages, is the last sight before returning via the Öland bridge.

****GOTLAND**

Large modern ferries provide the transportation between ****Gotland** and the Swedish mainland. During the high season from June to mid-August they shuttle

Above: Chamber music in the special atmosphere of the ruins of St. Nicolai, Visby.

throngs of "summer Gotlanders" – as often as twice a day – on the Nynäshamn-Visby route (for central and northern Sweden; 5-6 hours) and Oskarshamn-Visby (for southern Sweden; 4-6 hours). Approximately 350,000 travelers visit Sweden's most popular vacation island annually.

The steep western coastline starts becoming discernable during the crossing to the largest Baltic Sea island (3,142 square kilometers in area; 125 kilometers long; 50 kilometers wide; 57,000 inhabitants). Only little forest land is visible, and the countryside is quite flat. It rains little in summer; the subsoil of limestone and sandstone blesses the island with unique vegetation and exotic white beaches, which rank with those of Öland. Unlike Öland, however, Gotland can look back on a brilliant past: bountiful harvests and exceptional trade relations in the Baltic Sea region have determined Gotland's fortunes since the Bronze Age.

German settlers and Hanseatic merchants, mainly from Lübeck, first began using Visby as a lucrative trading center. They left their distinctive mark on the culture and politics of the flourishing city. With their favorable relations to central Europe, they gradually drove the Gotlanders out of the island's back woods. The locals had not only subsisted on farming, sheep raising and fishing, but they were experienced mariners and merchants as well. Their competition, the town dwellers of Visby, recognized envy and unrest developing in the back country; they therefore protected their valuable possessions with the city wall still visible today. The wall had to undergo its first use for defense when the farmers revolted against the townsfolk in 1288. In 1361, Visby citizens had no choice but to passively watch from the battlements while the Danish king Valdemar IV Atterdag laid waste to the farmland.

Afterwards, the city and its surroundings were weakened by attacks from the Swedes, the Danes, Hanseatic merchants and pirates, as well as through the government changing hands. In addition, the European trade routes moved westwards from the Baltic Sea area: Gotland had lost the importance it once enjoyed – that is, until tourists discovered "The Pearl of the Baltic Sea" in the 19th century.

★Visby: Roses and Ruins

The ferry terminal in ★Visby ⑫ lies just a few kilometers from the southern part of the 3.5-kilometer-long ★town wall. Standing meters high and made of light-colored limestone with 44 towers, the wall encircling the city can be seen from afar. Located near the harbor, the city wall to the south also functioned as the outer wall of the fortress of Visborg until into the 17th century. Construction of the fortress began in 1414, and it was blown up by the Danes in 1679. A symbol of foreign rule to the Gotlanders, the unpopular ruin served as a source of building material for a long time.

The historic docks were located a few hundred meters north of the present **Almedalen**, a popular park, spreading from the seaward **Kruttornet** (Powder Tower) to a section of the city wall curing inland. The large number of gates at this very location reveals one thing: Almedalen is an old dried-up harbor. Entering the city through one of the gates on the east side of the park, you find yourself on the square **Packhusplan** – clearly indicating that the goods were carried from the ships to the multi-leveled warehouses along the streets and squares protected by the city wall. Stretched out between Packhusplan and **Donners plats** is the **Strandgata**, exhibiting numerous medieval houses with crow-stepped gables, e.g., **Gamla apoteket** and **Liljehornska huset**, parts of the **Gotlands fornsal** complex (Museum of Antiquities – a must for those interested in the history of Gotland), and the block of houses where the **Visby Hotell** has spread out. Two elaborate buildings on Donners plats date back to the days of the German mer-

The Grand Islands

chants: the **Burmeisterska huset** on the north side, a half-timbered house, and the **Donnerska huset** diagonally opposite, where the tourist information office is located.

You will find more houses from the Middle Ages along **Mellangata** and **Sankt Hans gata**, streets running parallel to Strandgata on the upward slope. You will also encounter the most impressive remains of Visby's great past: the ivy-covered medieval **church ruins** surrounded by wildly growing trees and bushes, while roses adorn the quiet squares of the town.

Each of the 11 churches in ruins scattered about the city has its own charm and, to some extent, is being used for another purpose: **Sankt Hans**, a construction united with **Sankt Per**, houses a cozy café, the Franciscan monastery church of **Sankta Karin** displays an exhibit of old

Above: Hustle and bustle on the streets of Visby in the summer. Right: A nice jug anyone? Renaissance week in Visby.

churches. Annual concerts and a lyrical drama are preformed above the first priory of the Dominican monastery, which is part of the massive skeleton-like stonework of **Sankt Nicolai**.

Only one church remains from Visby's heyday, **Sankta Maria**; it had been the place of worship for the German immigrants since 1225 and then, in 1572, became the **Domkyrkan**, the city's cathedral. It is striking in several ways. Located on a limestone plateau in the northeastern part of the city, the light-colored Gothic walls and three prominent towers capped with dark Baroque domes are visible from a distance. The high nave leads one to assume the presence of a basilica, but a hoist on the east wall reveals how goods were once raised to the spacious loft.

Nowadays, instead of the busily working merchants of the Middle Ages, you see the nostalgically inclined tourists walking along the cobblestoned streets marveling at the carefully restored houses adorned with rosebushes. The present inhabitants are experts at upholding tradition. Their city, included on UNESCO's World Heritage List, relives the Middle Ages every year in early August. During the *Medeltidsveckan* they transform Visby into one giant theatrical stage.

Gotland's North

From Visby's **Norderport** (North Gate), Route 149 runs north almost parallel to the striking cliffs on the west coast. While on the east side of the road open plains such as the airport grounds, fields and meadows dominate, the view of the sea on the west is often obstructed by the thick forests.

Located in the dense forest near the steep coast five kilometers south of the village, the popular **dripstone caves** (*grottorna*) of **Lummelunda** – 2.6 kilometers in length – are among Sweden's longest cave systems. Miles of pebble

The Grand Islands

beaches have evolved at the foot of the high cliffs. Sandy beaches, like on the small cove directly adjacent to the harbor of **Lickershamn** ⓭, are more of an exception in the northwestern areas of Gotland. Here, on the other hand, are the dramatic wind- and water-beaten remains of a limestone cliff, the only preserved *rauk*. The **Jungfrun** *rauk* is the tallest (27 meters) of these peculiar rock towers and can be reached after a 600-meter walk from the harbor. Hiking trails along the steep coast *(klint)* lead to beautiful panoramas or additional *raukar* near **Hallshuk**, the northern tip of the island.

The villages in the protected inland area are part of the long tradition of the Gotlandic farming community – still visible due to their churches. The houses of worship of Lummelunda and **Stenkyrka** ⓮ (Stone Church) are just two examples of approximately 90 churches from Gotland's heyday prior to the 15th century that are still in use today. Stenkyrka, formally a *tingstäd* (council and court town), presumably had the first wooden

church on the island (11th century). The inhabitants built a new church in the 12th century; this time of stone, thus giving the town a new name.

Despite their dissimilar appearances, the rural Gotlandic churches actually do have a similar history. After Christianization – according to legend, Saint Olav converted the inhabitants of Gotland to the new faith during a visit to the island in 1029 – wooden churches were built in the *tingstäde,* or council and court towns; Stenkyrka in the north, Atlingbo in central Gotland and Fardhem in the south. However, the widely traveled and wealthy farmers soon replaced the old wooden constructions with solid Romanesque stone churches exhibiting elaborate furnishings.

The churches were continually undergoing modifications in accordance with the latest style. However, after the demise of the farmers' culture in the 14th century, the resources for further restoration and additions were lacking dreadfully. For this reason, these beautiful churches have been handed down to us as heirlooms in relatively original Gothic and Romanesque styles.

The murals have been preserved in most of the churches, and in some, even valuable glass windows from the Roman Era still remain. The names of the architects are largely unknown, however, stylistic peculiarities of the artists have inspired art historians to assign names: a "Byzantios," for example, refers to Byzantine models, or a "Calcarius" used limestone for baptismal fonts instead of the customary sandstone.

In some cases, the community eventually disappeared, whereas the solid stone church endured, at least as a ruin. Five kilometers east of Stenkyrka, the side walls of **Elinghems ödekyrka** were restored around 1924 so that it could be used for open-air productions. The vaulted ceiling and roof no longer remain. **Ganns ödekyrka**, four kilometers north of **Lärbro** ⑮, has also been preserved in its ruined state.

Routes 147, 148 and 149 converge in Lärbro. While constructing their church in the 13th century, the citizens of this town spared neither labor nor expense: the interior decoration and furnishings are of excellent quality, and the church tower has a rather unusual octagonal base. The *kastal,* or fortified tower, directly adjacent to it is a reminder of the tumultuous times towards the end of the Middle Ages.

Today limestone is quarried on Gotland, mainly for the production of cement. The most important industrial town is **Slite** ⑯, nine kilometers south of Lärbro. There are numerous abandoned quarries in the northeastern part of the island. **Bläse** ⑰, located about 15 kilometers north of Lärbro, is home to the very informative ***Bläse kalkbruksmuseum**; the former limestone quarry, in operation

Right: An impressive evening contre-jour shot of a rauk on Fårö.

until the 20th century, has been converted into a museum.

The ***Kulturhistoriska museet** in **Bunge** welcomes you to ethnological and archeological expeditions through centuries-old farming culture. In addition to houses, mills and utensils of days past, there is an impressive collection of Gotlandic **rune stones** *(bildstenar)* on display – these are unique memorial stones customarily used between the 5th and 12th centuries. The mighty tower and the embrasures in the cemetery wall reveal that the **church** of Bunge once served as a fortress.

Route 148 ends just three kilometers farther east in the town of **Fårösund** ⑱. Until the bridge to the neighboring island of **Fårö** is completed, you can get there by ferry. If you like lonely beaches and barren sheep pastures, then you will love it here.

The *raukar* on the peninsula of **Langhammer** in the far north present a fabulous natural spectacle – as does ***Digerhuvud** ⑲, Sweden's largest *rauk* area with its six-kilometer-long coastline west of here.

Gotska Sandön is even more remote. After a two-hour ferry voyage from Fårösund, this **national park** welcomes you with dunes, heathland, virgin pine forests and sandy beaches, as well as simple holiday cabins for accommodation.

There are also impressive dunes on Fårö, in the nature reserve of **Ullahau** in the eastern part of the island. The southerly and easterly aligned coastal regions of Fårö and Gotland are considerably flatter and more isolated than those in the west, and boast many sandy beaches. The beach town of **Åminne** ⑳, south of Slite, is especially popular.

Returning to Visby on Route 148, you cannot miss the 55-meter-high church tower of **Tingstäde** ㉑. Not only did the villagers demonstrate their wealth in the 13th century, but also their appreciation for art with the magnificently decorated

The Grand Islands

Romanesque church portals. The square, wooden defense fortification (**Bulverket**) from the Viking Age, long submerged in the village lake, still remains indiscernible to the rapidly passing motorists on Route 148.

In **Bro**, 12 kilometers east of Visby, we are reminded of the grand shipping days of Gotland since the *★church, repeatedly built in Gothic and Romanesque styles between 1200 and 1300, was considered to be an important offertory church by the mariners. The area is teeming with relics of prehistory, most of which date back to the Bronze Age. The grooved stones at the sacrificial spring from pagan times are rather mysterious (southwest of town en route to Hedeby). Around 2,000 such stones have been found on Gotland; no one has succeeded in solving their puzzle.

Central Gotland

Just 17 kilometers after leaving Visby via **Österport** (East Gate) on Route 143, you will arrive at the **Roma kloster** ㉒.

Built on fertile soil around the middle of the 12th century, this is said to have been an unusually rich Cistercian monastery, but served as a source of stone for a long time after the Reformation in the 16th century. Only the majestic nave remains as a roofless ruin.

In the 19th century Visby and its hinterland were provided with a rail connection for the transportation of sugar beets from central Gotland. The old train, which was taken out of service years ago, can be seen at the **Museijärnväg** in **Dalhem**, six kilometers from Roma. The fertile region also displays its wealth by the impressive sacral buildings here. There is, for example, the ★church in **Dalhem**, with valuable glass paintings, the pure Gothic ★church in **Ekeby**, and the uniquely disproportionate ★church of **Källunge** ㉓, which resulted when the elaborate plans for a giant choir were abandoned in the 13th century.

While the region is more densely wooded farther east, the churches of the coastal areas are protected by a *kastal*.

Good examples of this are the church in **Gammelgarn**, with its splendid sculptures at the south portal and the lavishly painted church in ★**Gothem**. But even before the time of Christ, the inhabitants apparently sought protection as well – on the steep limestone plateau of **Grogarnsberget** located on the coast three kilometers east of **Katthammarsvik** ㉔, or in the forest hidden back behind the two-meter-high walls of layered limestone of the **Herrgårdsklint** (commune of Gammelgarn). Also located in the dense woodlands, Sweden's largest fortress grounds, the ★**Torsburgen** ㉕, provided lodging and shelter for many in times of threat, from the Roman Iron Age into the 13th century.

Katthammarsvik, on the east coast peninsula of **Östergarnsholm**, possesses an ideal harbor for shipping the locally quar-

ried limestone (since the 17th century). Today, the *Kalkpatronsgården*, the manor house of a quarry owner, offers accommodations to tourists passing through.

Ljugarn ㉖, 48 kilometers southeast of Visby, has been the most popular seaside resort on the east coast since the 19th century. Its harbor played an important role as early as Gotland's initial seafaring days. A large geographical depression crosses the island between Ljugarn and the west coast. Archeologists built a replica of the Iron Age castle of **Lojsta slott** at the edge of the swampland on a lake. The radiant, colorful glass windows of the village church of **Lojsta**, three kilometers west (Route 142), have been gleaming since the 13th century. The depression continues farther west with the forests, willows and swamps of the **Lojstahajd** region, where the *gotlandsruss*, a species of semi-wild horse, grazes.

Like a fortress, the 12th-century church of **Fröjel** is located on a hill and affords a magnificent view of the central west coast of Gotland and the Karl Is-

Above: Decorated baptismal fonts can be found in many churches in Gotland (Garde). Right: The church of Tofta (13th century) with several typical extensions.

lands located just offshore. The ruins of a *kastal* can be found nearby. During the peak season, boats from the little harbor of **Klintehamn** ㉗ service the island of **Stora Karlsö** daily. Like its sister island **Lilla Karlsö** (accessible by boat from **Djupvik**), it appears to rise off the coast like a platform. Day tourists can take walks through opulent flora to the bird cliffs and Stone Age caves.

Many interesting prehistoric findings are located near the coast, for example, Bronze Age stone settings in the form of ships at ***Gannarve** ㉘ and **Gnisvärd**; or **Vallhagar**, a large community from the Iron Age with an extensive burial site near Fröjel. The settlement, for reasons still unknown, was suddenly abandoned in the 6th century. The present-day harbor of **Västergarn** was a significant competitor for Visby during the Viking Age.

Located 20 kilometers from the island's capital city is **Tofta strand**, a large sandy beach with an adjacent pine forest – a real magnet for summer vacationers. Closer to Visby, the west coast cliffs become more prominent and reach a peak in **Högklint**, with a beautiful view of the city eight kilometers away. Princess Eugénie enjoyed the wooded, hilly landscape and Gotland's mild climate so much that she had a Swiss-style summer house (**Fridhem**) built in the area, which is now used as a hotel. The extensive vacation resort of **Kneippbyn**, with a large amusement park, is particularly suitable for families with children. From here it is only five kilometers to **Söderport** (South Gate) from Visby's city wall.

Southern Gotland

The island of Gotland, flat – with gently flowing ripples at most – is an ideal landscape for bicycling. The roads are maintained in excellent condition and some bicycle routes are marked. You do, however, need to reckon with strong winds, especially in the south. Here, on

The Grand Islands

the peninsula of **Näsudden**, the rotors of a wind-power station are in practically continuous operation.

Hemse ㉙ – where routes 141, 142 and 144 converge – imparts the overall impression of a new town with a modern shopping center. Nevertheless, the well-preserved remains of a timber church from the first half of the 12th century were found here; so valuable that they were even adopted by Stockholm's history museum. The stone church from the Middle Ages, on the other hand, remained in the village, as did the Romanesque stone church of the 12th and 13th centuries located in **Fardhem** four kilometers away. This is the southernmost of the three Gotlandic *tingstäde* (council and court towns) from the beginning of Christianization – and the third one having a church at all, a wooden one, though, that is since long gone.

Route 142 leads to the southern tip of Gotland via **Grötlingbo** ㉚, with its massive church. Relief works of the master stonemason Sigraf (early 13th century)

were taken from its Romanesque predecessor and used in the 14th-century Gothic *church; he also crafted the baptismal font. Only three kilometers away, the medieval court building of the **Kattlunds gård** in the center of town reminds us of the island's significant agricultural and mercantile tradition. Located on the isthmus of the southern peninsula, the church tower of *Öja served as a navigational point until recent years. The community was able to afford a magnificent triumphal crucifix in the second half of the 13th century and built a *kastal* to protect themselves from pirates.

The giant depiction of *The Weighing of the Soul of Emperor Henry II by the Archangel Michael* leaves the most lasting impression of all the murals in the *church of **Vamlingbo**.

The village of **Sundre ③**, not far from the coast, was also protected by a fortification tower close to the church. The ex-

tremely fine sandstone, which has been quarried here for two centuries and processed into whetstones in the *Slipstensbrott*, comes from the rural commune of **Kättelvik** located directly on the west coast. Gotland's sandstone and limestone were important exports as early as the Middle Ages.

Hoburgen, the often storm-buffeted, southwestern tip of Gotland 37 meters above sea level, is personified in its impressive 4.5-meter-high **Hoburgsgubben** *rauk*, the "Old-timer of Hoburgen." The expansive view and the various flora of the limestone heath (*alvar*) continue to fascinate hikers. They also enjoy wandering to the *raukar* in the cozier bays of **Holmhäller** on the east side of the southern peninsula or to the numerous small nature reserves in the area. An abundance of orchids and other flowering plants flourish here, especially during May and June. In addition to the *alvar* areas, the grassy meadows interspersed with light woods have an especially large number of varieties of blossoms.

Above: The nature reserve near Holmhällar is a treasure trove for orchid lovers in the spring.

ÖLAND (☎ 0485)

ℹ️ PO Box 74, 38621 Färjestaden, tel. 39000, directly at the Öland bridge.

🛏️ 🌀🌀 **Strand Hotell**, Vilagatan 4, Borgholm, tel. 88888, fax 12427. **Sunwing Ekerum**, Borgholm, tel. 80000, fax 80010. **Halltorps Gästgiveri**, Borgholm, tel. 85000, fax 85001. 🌀 **Guntorps Herrgård**, Guntorpsgatan, Borgholm, tel. 13000, fax 13319, typical Öland country estate. **Hotell Borgholm**, Trädgårdgatan 15, Borgholm, tel. 77060, fax 42107. **Skansen Hotel**, Tingshusgatan 1, Färjestaden, tel. 30530, fax 34804.

🏕️ **Neptuni Camping**, Byxelkrog, tel. 28495. **Krono Camping Saxnäs**, Färjestaden, tel. 35700, fax 35664. *CABINS:* **Krono Camping Böda Sand**, Byxelkrog, tel. 22200, fax 22376. **Ekerums Camping**, Borgholm, tel. 55190. All campgrounds are near the beach.

❌ Excellent restaurants in **Halltorps Kro** (*Gästgiveri*) for lamb and in **Hotel Borgholm** for seafood specialties. **Sandviks Kvarn**, Löttorp, tel. 26172, eight-story windmill, meals made from historic recipes. **Lammert & Grisen**, Löttörp, roast lamb and suckling pig at a fixed price, tel. 20350.

🏛️ Lighthouses: **Långe Jan** and **Långe Erik**, June-Aug 10 am to sunset daily. **Refuge Eketorp**, May 1-June 17 and Aug 8-31, 9 am-5 pm daily, June 18-Aug 7, 9 am-6 pm daily. **Gråborg**, **Ismanstorp** and **Himmelsberga**, May-Aug 10 am-6 pm daily. **Gårdlösa Church**, 10 am-6 pm daily, except during services. **Borgholm slott**, May-Aug 10 am-6 pm daily. **Solliden slott**, June-Aug 1-5 pm daily.

🚢 The **island of Blå Jungfru**, departures from Byxelkrog, mid-May to mid-August daily 10 am, return 4 pm. Only when weather permits, info: tel. 24005.

📅 July 14: **The Crown Princess' birthday celebration.**

GOTLAND (☎ 0498)

ℹ️ Gotlands Turistförening, main administration: Hamngatan 4, 62125 Visby, tel. 247065.

Information office Visby city center: Donnerska huset, Donners plats, tel. 247065.

Reservation office for accommodations (also vacation homes), ferries and *BICYCLE RENTALS* as well as organized bicycle and camping tours: Turistcenter, Färjeleden 3, 62158 Visby, tel. 279095, e-mail: bokningen@gotlandsresor.se.

📱 *BOATS / FERRIES:* **Nynäshamn-Visby** (1-3 times daily, also catamaran, shipping company Destination Gotland) and **Oskarshamn-Visby**, one day and one night ferry per day, more often from June to the end of

August. Good fares for ferry trips to Gotland in conjunction with ferry bookings from Germany at all providers: TT-Line, Stena, DFO, Silja.

Ferries from Öland: **Grankullavik-Klintehamn** during the peak season twice daily with Litorina Line.

The islands of **Stora** and **Lilla Karlsö** (from Klintehamn, i.e., Dragsvik) and **Gotska Sandön**, reservations: Turistcenter; departures weather permitting.

PLANE: June to the end of August, direct flights from Hamburg to Visby twice weekly (Skyways); connections via Stockholm several times daily.

🛏️ 🌀 **Björklunda Värdshus**, Burgsvik, tel. 497190, fax 497850. **Pensionat Holmhällar**, Vamlingbo, Burgsvik, tel. 498030, fax 498056. **Katthamra Gård**, Katthammarsvik, hostel at the manor house of a limestone magnate, tel. 52009.

YOUTH HOSTELS (open year-round): **STF Vandrarhem Garda**, Kommunhuset, Ljugarn, tel. 491181. **STF Vandrarhem Klintehamn**, **Pensionat Warfsholm**, Klintehamn, tel. 240010.

Hostels open only in summer are those of **Fårö**, tel. 223639; **Ljugarn**, tel. 493184; **Lärbro**, tel. 225786; **Näs**, tel. 489116; **Sproge** (Klintehamn), tel. 241097; and **Stora Karlsö** island, tel. 240500.

🏛️ **Sankta Maria kyrka** of Visby and **other churches**, June-Aug 9 am-6 pm daily, except during services. **Museum of Antiquities** (Gotlands Fornsal), Strandgatan 14, May 15-Aug 15, 11 am-6 pm daily. **Bunge Open-Air Museum**, May 15-Aug 31, 10 am-6 pm daily, otherwise 10 am-4 pm.

📅 First week of July: **Stångaspelen**, a type of regional Olympics with historic competitions. Early August: **Medeltidsveckan** (Medieval Weeks). There is a large cultural program in the summer (info: tourist office).

🛏️ 🌀🌀🌀 **Strand Hotel**, Strandgatan 34, tel. 212600, fax 278111, modern hotel in the old town center. **Wisby Hotell**, tel. 204000, fax 211320, tastefully renovated hotel in the city center. 🌀🌀 **Fridhem**, Västerhejde, tel. 296018, Princess Eugenia's summer residence, no alcohol served. **Sunderbys Herrgård**, Västerhejde, tel. 264850, fax 264867, court hotel in the Gotlandic style, 10 km south of Visby. **Hotell Toftagården**, Tofta beach, tel. 297000, fax 265666, quiet vacation resort, wooded area 18 km south of Visby. 🌀 **Hamn Hotellet**, Färjeleden 3, tel. 201250, fax 219720, efficient hotel at the ferry harbor. **Hotel Gute**, Mellangatan 29, tel. 248080, fax 248089. *YOUTH HOSTEL:* Tel. 269842.

❌ In the **Wisby Hotell** there is a good restaurant. The restaurant in the **Hotel Toftgården** is among the best in Sweden. **Donners Brunn**, Donnersgatan 2, tel. 271090.

The Grand Islands

ER LIVS

ATG

SVENSKA SPEL

MJÖLK
BRÖD
ÄGG

9-20

MINIGOLFBANAN

Öppet FJÄLLBACKA
alla dagar

SJÖ

SERVERING-KIOSK
FLIPPERSPEL
TENNISBANA

HÄR KÖPER DU
TELEFONKORT

Sibylla

JACKPOTS
V.35
LOTTO 10 MILJ
POKER 3

BINGO 700

GB
GLACE

GB
GLACE

THE SWEDISH WEST COAST

HALMSTAD
FALKENBERG / VARBERG
GOTHENBURG (GÖTEBORG)
BOHUSLÄN
TANUM

West Coast

HALLAND AND BOHUSLÄN
One Coast, Two Landscapes

The regions of Halland and Bohuslän are like narrow strips stretching along the western coastline of Sweden from Helsingborg to Svinesund. Each region is 160 kilometers long and up to 50 kilometers wide. Although the two types of landscape are strikingly different, the historic development of the two is very similar.

Sandy beaches and dunes are predominant along the coast in **Halland**, and in its northern section coniferous forests stretch all the way to the beaches. Since the 19th century, they have been adding calcium carbonate marl to the heavy moor soil in the hinterland, successfully increasing its productivity after the region had become poverty-stricken following the practice of clearing the land by fire in the 17th century. Even people sentenced to death during that time reportedly preferred the gallows to taking over a farm in Halland.

Historically speaking, it wasn't until the Treaty of Brömsebro (1645) that the region became a permanent part of Swe-

Preceding pages: Taking time for a chat – vacation in Fjällbacka. Left: In the past, the people in Bohuslän depended upon fishing for their livelihood.

den; it had been a bone of contention between Denmark and Sweden for quite some time. This also explains the large number of fortifications spread out along this coastal stretch.

Although formally belonging to Norway until 1645, **Bohuslän** was governed by Copenhagen. As Sweden, especially after America was discovered, was doing everything in its power to gain access to the North Sea, the two regions were under pressure from Sweden for a long time; the Danes and Norwegians could only partially hold their ground. In addition, in 1621 the city of Gothenburg became a Swedish wedge between Halland and Bohuslän, interrupting trade between the two regions.

The coast of Bohuslän is marked by granite cliffs, smoothly rounded rock knolls and countless islands with hardly any vegetation. Narrow fjords cut deep into the interior. The main traffic route, the E6, runs through both regions.

The Kattegatt Coast

Approaching from **Helsingborg** ❶ you can reach the Kattegatt coast by crossing the **Hallandsåsen** foothills of the southern Swedish high country at **Hjärnarp** ❷. The foothills extend over 40 kilometers in an east-west direction,

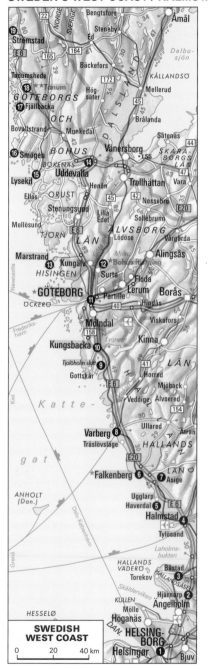

and the highest point is **Högalteknallen** (226 meters). This range of hills separates Skåne from Halland.

If you are interested in prehistoric artefacts, you should definitely pay a visit to the burial mound of **Lugnarohögen**: just stay on the E6, take the exit to Våxtorp and then the 115; the site is on the outskirts of **Hasslöv**. It is the only burial mound from the Bronze Age in Scandinavia which contains a ship made of stone; it is eight meters long. After its discovery they lined the mound with concrete so the grave could be viewed from the inside as well.

The posh beach resort of **Båstad** ❸ (Route 115 heading west) is Sweden's only seaside resort with an international flair. The street of beautiful villas above the town's center is appropriately called "Italian Street." Today, Båstad is a center for tennis in Sweden; from Borg to Wilander to Edberg, every Swedish tennis ace has trained here.

HALMSTAD
A City of Artists

Halmstad ❹ is the present-day capital city of Halland; it has a population of 80,000 and lies at the mouth of the Nissan River at the outflow into Laholm Bay. The brown sign on the E6 displays the emblem of the city: a sailboat. The original sailing vessel, the *Najaden* (1897), is picturesquely moored on the river directly in front of the castle.

Similar to the group of artists in Germany, *Die Brücke*, there was also a loose union of artists in Sweden that introduced Expressionism and Surrealism to this country: the *Halmstad Group*, the most renowned members of which are the Olson brothers. Like numerous other artist associations, this group was also formed in Paris in the 1930s.

Halmstad also owes its rich repertoire of modern artworks to this group of artists, such as the **Picassostatyn** on the

banks of the river, a monumental replica of this artistic genius' small sculpture *Man and Woman*, or Carl Milles' **Europe Fountain** on the market square of **Stora torg**. The **City Hall** is also located here; Stig Blomberg designed the carillon and its movable figures.

Tre Hjärtan (The Three Hearts) from the 15th century is the oldest half-timbered house in town; Halmstad lies on the northern border for half-timbered houses in Scandinavia. Also on Stora torg is the **Kungastenen**; a granite stone memorial from 1952 commemorating the historic meeting between Gustavus II Adolphus and the Danish king Christian IV in 1619 during the negotiations for Sweden's access to the North Sea. The exact history of the construction of **Sankt Nicolai kyrka** at the market is no longer known, however, artists of the Halmstad Group designed its stained-glass windows. South of the market is the 17th-

Above: In the harbor of Glommen near Falkenberg.

century castle, today the seat of the head of the provincial government.

*FALKENBERG AND VARBERG
Sweden's "Bathtub"

You should take the old coastal road between Halmstad and Falkenberg instead of the E6. It passes through **Tylösand**, which you could almost call an elegant seaside resort with its golf course, tennis courts and frequently overcrowded beaches. For those who don't care much for hustle and bustle, there are plenty of beaches along the coastal route farther on where you can enjoy a quiet, peaceful stay at the beach, for example in **Haverdal** ❺, with dunes 36 meters high, or in **Ugglarp**. The water temperature along the Halland coast can reach 20°C in August.

Nowadays, ***Falkenberg** ❻ is also completely geared to tourists. The beaches are long and wide, and the city on the Ätran River is famous for **salmon fishing** – which is permitted from March to September for those in possession of a fishing permit. The **Sankt Laurentii kyrka**, located in the center of an old section of town from the 18th century, has an interesting history. It has a painted barrel vault which was not uncovered until the 1920s after the building had been used as a gym and a shooting range for decades. Sweden's oldest pottery is still producing in this quarter around the **Gåstorget** (Goose Market).

It pays to take an excursion from Falkenberg via Årstad to **Asige ❼**: the four **memorial stones** (unengraved tombstones from the Bronze Age) you see before you reach the town have been dubbed "Hagbard's Gallows" by the locals. The position of the stones actually does resemble a double gallows used in the Middle Ages; the only thing missing is the wooden crossbar. The saga of Hagbard is basically a Scandinavian version of the Romeo and Juliet story.

From Falkenberg it is 30 kilometers to **Varberg ❽**, which was originally called Vardberg (Lookout Mountain). The city, which burned down numerous times in the past, has a present population of 50,000, and its skyline is dominated by the massive ***Fästning** (fortress). The oldest sections are from the 13th century and originate from Jakob von Halland. He and his descendants used the castle into the 16th century. The Danish king Christian IV converted it into a fortress. After 1645, the year peace was declared in Brömsebro, the fortress was suddenly on Swedish soil and thus became superfluous. It was then turned into what abandoned castles in Sweden were usually used for: first it was a prison, then a liquor distillery. The oldest section of the castle was restored in the 1920s and it now houses a **museum**. The showpiece of the collection is the *Bocksten Man*, a corpse from the 14th century found in a bog. The

body, pierced by a wooden stake, was recovered perfectly preserved and fully clothed.

Varberg has a long tradition as a seaside resort. As early as 1823 they built the **Brunnpark** and the **Societetspark** (Community Park), as well as the **Kallbadhuset** and **Societetshuset**. The prettiest beaches are in the **Getterön** nature reserve, close to **Apelviken** and **Träslövslägen**.

You can also take the old coastal road from Varberg to Kungsbacka. Just 10 kilometers before you reach the town, a small path leads to **Tjolöholm slott ❾**, probably the most unusual castle in Sweden. A Scottish merchant from Gothenburg had the castle built of red granite on the Kungsbacka Fjord in the English Tudor style; it stands in the center of a magnificent park. In the meantime, the castle belongs to the city of Gothenburg and is open to the public.

Kungsbacka ❿ has been through many firestorms, but it has retained its small-town charm, which especially comes to light on the first Thursday of the month when the market is held. Leaving this small town you can reach, via **Fjärås**, **Lake Lygnern**, teeming with fish, and its sparse birch forest offers tranquillity and relaxation.

*GOTHENBURG (GÖTEBORG)
Gustavus Adolphus' City

Up until the 17th century, in practical terms Sweden had no outlet to the North Sea. In peaceful times, however, the Danes would allow the Swedes to use the mouth of the **Göta älv** (Göta River), and to control the exporting and importing of the goods from the **Älvsborg** fortress located there. In 1603, Charles IX of Sweden laid the cornerstone for a new city right next to the fortress; he called the city ***Gothenburg ⓫** (Swedish: Göteborg). Just eight years later the Danes destroyed the city and occupied the fortress as well.

Right: Gothenburg, Sweden's gateway to the west since the 17th century.

In addition, they demanded a million Rikstaler to again allow access to the sea. In those days this horrendous sum of money equaled 3,500 tons of copper. Gustavus II Adolphus, who foresaw the tremendous future value of this shipping port, managed to raise the money, and in 1619 the Treaty of Halmstad was signed. This regulated Sweden's access to the North Sea and also provided for the construction of a harbor.

Gustavus Adolphus (see also pp.18-19) wasted no time and immediately started planning the new city, which now was to be just south of the mouth of the Göta älv. Specialists, however, were needed for the construction of a city in the mud of the river's mouth; at that time the specialists were all from Holland, and the king had large numbers of them brought to the country. The Dutch first constructed a right-angled system of canals to drain the area set aside for the city, and they then built Gothenburg into one of the strongest fortresses in Europe. The seats in the city government were granted by royal decree based on population. Four Swedes, three Dutch and three Germans, as well as two Scots, sat on the city council.

This multinational population is still mirrored today in the proverbial worldliness of the citizens of Gothenburg, who have always lived with a population made up of 10 percent (or more) foreigners. The geographical location corresponds to the mentality of the citizens of Gothenburg, who have always oriented themselves toward London rather than to their own capital city. Stockholm, they say, is situated on a dying ocean, and beyond the ocean is Siberia. Another indication of the liberality of the city: Gothenburg is the only city in Sweden with a nightlife worth mentioning.

The Company Period

Gothenburg experienced a rapid upswing when merchants in the 18th century founded their own "East India Company," modeled on the Dutch enterprise. These companies were noth-

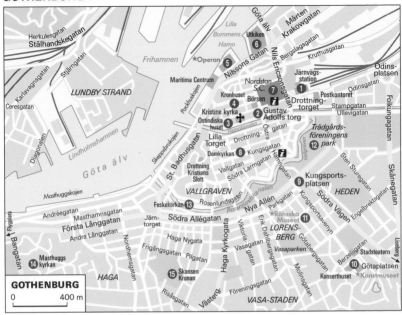

**The Hamn Canal –
The City's Historical Artery**

ing more than the successful attempt to divide the risks of lengthy trade voyages among as many merchants as possible and to distribute the profits based on their individual investments. When products from China, especially fine Chinese porcelain, became fashionable in Europe, the company had to struggle to meet the enormous demand. The affluence of the East India Company also provided the city with immense advantages: the city received substantial donations and tax revenue. Following Napoleon's continental blockade, trade with East Asia was interrupted, and it was not until the beginning of the Industrial Age that the city was finally able to recover.

The shipbuilding industry, which ushered in the new boom, has closed down in the meantime, while automobile and engineering industries have taken its place. Today, businesses in the service sector and high-tech industries guarantee

Right: The business metropolis of Gothenburg has always been a multinational city.

growth and employment. Gothenburg has half a million inhabitants, while another quarter of a million live in satellite towns outside the city limits. There are approximately 40,000 students enrolled here at the university.

The city is not very "car friendly." The only way to drive into the sections of the inner city is from the **Nya Allén**, the old street along the city's walls; streets for automobile traffic do not connect the different sections. The fees for parking are so exorbitant that it definitely pays to buy the tourist ticket, called the *Göteborgskortet* (see *INFO*, p. 100). It gives you free admission to all of the museums and free travel with public transportation. You can purchase it on all of the ferries leaving for Gothenburg from Germany, England and Denmark.

The Hamn Canal –
The City's Historical Artery

The best way to start your tour is at the **train station ❶**; the town's citizens say it

is the most beautiful train station in the country. The **Drottningtorget** (Queen's Market) south of the train station extends to the **Hamn Canal** (Harbor Canal). This is also where the **Vallgraven** (Wall Moat) empties into the canal. The moat runs around the old part of the city and was part of the city's fortifications in the 17th century. All of the other waterways have been filled in.

At Drottningtorget, follow the Harbor Canal westwards until you arrive at Norra Hamngatan. **Hotel Eggers** on the corner of the Queen's Market was recently classified as a historic monument. The Sunday brunch served at the hotel's restaurant (from 10 a.m. to 3 p.m.) is legendary: it is guaranteed to satisfy every culinary desire.

At the intersection of **Norra** and **Östra Hamngatan** is the equestrian statue of Gustavus II Adolphus, looking down over his city. On the north side of **Gustav Adolfs torg ❷** is the **Stadshuset**, and the **Wenngrenska huset** is to its left. Both are from the 18th century and were later modified to conform to each other. To the right, at the end of the row of houses, is the former **stock exchange** (1849) – nowadays, it houses the city's administration offices. Unfortunately, its marvelous 19th-century banquet hall is only rarely open to the public.

The attractive **Rådhuset** on the west side of the square houses, among other institutions, the registry office; on Fridays you can often witness some see extremely interesting wedding celebrations here. A few meters farther along the Harbor Canal is the **Kristine kyrka**, which was originally built in the 17th century as a church for the local Dutch population. For the last hundred years or so it has served the German community and is therefore also referred to as the *Tyska kyrkan*, or German Church.

In the **Ostindiska huset ❸** (House of the East India Company) next to the church, the city museum has installed exhibitions displaying its extensive archeological, ethnological and historical collections.

The Harbor Quarter

Next to the East India Company, a narrow passageway leads to the **Kronhuset** ❹. The oldest secular building in the city has hardly changed in appearance since the 17th century, unlike many other buildings. Once a royal armory, today it contains boutiques and artisans' workshops. The courtyard inside has a nice café.

If you walk down the Västra Hamngatan from here towards Göta älv, you arrive at the former **Packhuskajen**, which is now home to the **Maritime Center**. Several old ships, no longer in service, are on display here. The excursion boat trips to the skerries also leave from here. On the northern end of the quay is the hyper-modern opera house, the ***Operan** ❺, which opened in 1994. On the other side of **Lilla Bommens Hamn**, a small dock next to the opera, Gothenburg's only

Above: The Kronhuset, a former arsenal, today a handicraft center. Right: Utkiken's terrace has the best view of the city.

highrise building reaches up to the sky: **Utkiken** ❻. There is a magnificent panoramic view of the city from its terrace.

The Business District

Back to Lilla Bommens Hamn, where a pedestrian bridge crosses over to Östra Hamngatan: the covered **Nordstan Shopping Center** ❼ encompasses an entire city quarter. From alcoholic beverages to newspapers, everything imaginable is for sale here. Numerous cafés, restaurants and fast-food stands provide ample opportunity for taking a break.

Östra Hamngatan crosses the Hamn Canal and the Vallgraven, heading south. The quarter between the two moats is the old residential area of Gothenburg. Nowadays you will find here countless boutiques, bars, ice-cream parlors, cinemas, and restaurants serving just about every type of cuisine. In this quarter, along Kyrkogatan in the middle of a park, is the **Domkyrkan** ❽, a rather modest 19th-century building.

The Promenade: Avenyn

Östra Hamngatan ends at **Kungsportsplatsen** ❾, where the royal gate in the city walls once stood. Today the **equestrian statue of Charles IX** stands where the so-called "King's Gate," part of the city's fortification wall, used to be; in the vernacular the statue is called "The Copper Mare." From here the **Kungsportsavenyn**, called *Avenyn* for short, runs directly to **Götaplatsen**. Avenyn is rightfully called the Champs Elysée of Gothenburg. In the high-class buildings are banks, insurance and airline companies, boutiques and sidewalk cafés, where on warm days – in Scandinavia that means about 16°C – it is hard to find a spot to sit down. Avenyn is a meeting place for beautiful people who want to see and be seen.

Surrounding the **Poseidon Fountain** by Carl Milles, which is in the center of the **Götaplatsen** ❿, are, clockwise, the **Stadsteatern**, the ***Konstmuseet**, the **Konsthallen** and the **Konserthuset**. The art museum has Sweden's second-largest collection of paintings; native painters such as Gustav Cederström and Anders Zorn are represented here, as are modern European painters, from Georges Braque to Pablo Picasso.

A must for amateur photographers is the **Hasselblad Fotomuseet** in the same building. The ***Röhsska Museet** ⓫ is a treat for people interested in design and modern arts and crafts.

Amusement Park, Shrimps and Roses

Southeast of Götaplatsen is the ***Liseberg** amusement park, more or less a permanent fair. Theater and dance performances as well as pop concerts take place here in the summer. The giant multipurpose structure **Scandinavium** nearby seats 12,000; right next to it is the **Ullevi Stadium**, where the World Track and Field Championships were held in 1995.

West Coast

Those more interested in flora will find the largest tropical greenhouse in Europe, and a rosarium with over 3,000 varieties of roses in the eastern wall rampart in **Trädgårdsföreningens Park** ⓬ (Garden Club Park).

If you are interested in cuisine, you shouldn't miss the fish market along the moat – called **Feskekörkan** ⓭ (Fish Church), it's located on the moat close to the Rosenlunds Canal. Everything the ocean has to offer is either being sold or auctioned off here from the early morning hours until 5 p.m. Fresh shellfish in small portions is sold, ready to eat, at the multitude of snack bars.

A wonderful lookout point is on the hill above the **Masthuggskajen**, where the ferries dock on the Göta älv (west of the city center). Here is the **Masthuggs kyrkan** ⓮. For a long time this red granite church with its 42-meter tower was Gothenburg's church for seamen. The structure of the wooden barrel vault reminds you of a ship's hull turned upside down. From the platform in front of the

church you have a vast view of the harbor and parts of the city.

The climb to the **Skansen Kronan** ⑮ (a fortress tower with a military museum) also offers panoramic views.

★★BOHUSLÄN
Land of Fortresses

You should leave the E6 20 kilometers north of Gothenburg. Route 45 leads directly to the **★Bohus fästning** ⑫, which gave the entire Bohuslän region its name. From 1482, when it was built as a Norwegian border fortress, up until 1678, the date of the last attack, Bohus was subjected to 14 sieges. None of them were successful. A contemporary chronicle reported that during the last siege 20,000 cannonballs and 384 stones were fired at Bohus. In addition, 161 red-hot cannon-

Above: The picturesque boathouses in Fjällbacka are now lodgings for tourists. Right: "The Lovers," a famous rock carving in Tanum from the Bronze Age.

balls were fired to set the fortress on fire, and 216 sacks of excrement thrown in, in an attempt to induce "inner fever" in the defenders. After this last attack the fortress remained Swedish, but it lost its importance and was used as a quarry for a long time. But Bohus is still a good example of a 15th-century fortress.

On the other side of the Göta älv, in nearby **Kungsälv**, a visit to the old 17th-century wooden church is recommended. The church's barrel vault was painted immediately after construction ended, "under contract" for 300 taler.

If you have time you can take an excursion to **Marstrand** ⑬ (Route 168) and then cross the island of Orust to reach Uddevalla. Marstrand also has a fortress; it was built after the region became part of Sweden, but it was never needed. The Norwegian king Håkon Håkonson founded the city in 1250. In the 16th century, Marstrand was an El Dorado for herring fishermen on what was then the Norwegian coast. Today the harbor is a meeting place for sailors on the coast of

Bohuslän. The city consists of beautifully decorated wooden houses in the Oscarian style of the turn of the century, but it is very crowded during the high season, especially on weekends. Route 160 runs south-north through an attractive landscape across the island of **Orust** and continues on to the **Bokenäs** peninsula. The **Bokenäs Gamla kyrka**, on Route 161 heading west, is worth the trip. The oldest church in the region was built in the 12th century. Its rustic 18th-century paintings are in excellent condition; the church furnishings are also from this period.

A visit to the industrial city of **Uddevalla** ⓴ (Route 161 eastwards) is only recommended on St. John's Day (Midsummer Day), when people dance on the harbor docks, the only place of amusement in the city. In general, it makes more sense to stay on Route 160 and do a "four-island tour," visiting the picturesque fishing villages of **Lysekil** ⓰, **Smögen** ⓱ and **Fjällbacka** ⓲ – these villages have retained their nostalgic charm in spite of the tourist industry, and many people also come here for their annual vacation.

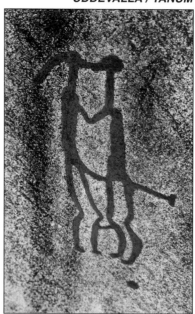

West Coast

**TANUM
Prehistoric Cult Sites

The rock carvings at ****Tanum** ⓳, 40 kilometers north of Uddevalla and four kilometers south of Tanumshede, were designated as UNESCO World Heritage Sites in 1994. Many of the carvings (*Hällristningar*) here, scattered over a very large area, are from the Bronze Age between 1500 and 500 B.C. They were chiseled or carved into the surface of the flat rocks, more than likely with stone tools, and then they were painted with red-brown mineral paint, as traces of the pigment have revealed. The present-day painted carvings therefore approximate the original condition.

Most of the carvings to be seen here are of boats, some with and some without railings. Some of the boats have passengers, some of them are empty. Sometimes the passengers are only stick figures. Figures carrying axes and clubs suggest battle scenes, but they could also be interpreted as processions. Dotted lines appear to signify borders. There are also drawings of animals – mostly reindeer – and they are depicted either as a hunting kill or harnessed to a sled or a boat. Especially impressive is the portrayal of two "lovers": they are receiving a priest's blessing and making love standing up; this is the only figure clearly identifiable as being female.

The small museum located at the site's parking lot suggests possible interpretations to the many riddles these carvings still present.

Past **Strömstad** ⓴, a vacation resort with decorated wooden houses and a large sailing port, you arrive at the Swedish-Norwegian border at **Svinesund**. A bridge 420 meters long and 65 meters high, built in 1946, connects these two northern neighbors, who in the past were enemies for so long.

BÅSTAD (☎ 0431)

i Torget, 26921 Båstad, tel. 75045.

🛏 😊😊 **Buena Vista Hotel**, Tarravägen 5, tel. 78000, fax 79100, old villa, recently renovated. 😊 **Hallandås Rasta**, Östra Karup (E6), tel. 74270, fax 74654.

YOUTH HOSTELS: **Vandrarhem Båstad**, Korrödsvägen 17, tel. 75911, directly at the tennis center.

🏕 **Krono Camping** Båstad/Torekov, tel. 64525.

❌ **Hotel Buena Vista** has a nice restaurant. **Svensons Krog & Café** in Torekov, tel. 64590.

🏛 **Burial Mounds of Lugnarohögen**, May 15-Aug 31 Tue-Sun 2-4 pm.

🎨 Meta Måås-Fjetterström, Agardsgatan 9, tel. 70183, beautiful country-style **textiles** and **carpets**.

HALMSTAD (☎ 035)

i Lilla Torget, tel. 109345.

🛏 😊😊😊 **Scandic Hotel Hallandia**, Rådhusgatan 4, tel. 218800, fax 148956. 😊😊 **Hotel Continental**, Kungsgatan 5, tel. 218070, fax 128604. **Provobis Grand Hotel**, Stationsgatan 44, tel. 219140, fax 149620. 😊 **P&J Lindbergs Krog**, Golfbanevägen, 30273 Halmstad, tel. 32550, fax 32650.

❌ **Tre Hjärtan**, Stortorget, tel. 112485, restaurant in the oldest half-timbered building in town. **Café-Restaurant Nygatan**, Nygatan 8, tel. 121088, pasta and vegetarian dishes. Excellent restaurant **Stefan Holmström**, Strandgatan 6, tel. 111711.

FALKENBERG (☎ 0346)

i Stortorget, tel. 17410.

🛏 😊😊 **Grand Hotel i Falkenberg**, Hotellgatan 1, tel. 14450, fax 82925. 😊 **Hotell Strandbaden**, Havsbadallén, tel. 58000, fax 16111, nice old hotel directly on the beach, in the summer a beach pub.

❌ **Bon Appetit**, Storgatan 37, tel. 84290. **William's Pub**, Storgatan 34, tel. 14813.

🎨 **Töngrens Krukmakeri**, Krukmakergatan 4, tel. 10354, Mon-Fri 10 am-12 pm and 1-4 pm, pottery since 1789.

🎣 *FISHING*: Ätran, a good place for salmon and sea trout fishing. Fishing bridge open March-May 6 am-10 pm, June 1-Aug 15, 5 am-11 pm, Aug 16-Sept 30, 6 am-9 pm daily, fishing permits available at tourist office.

VARBERG (☎ 0340)

i Brunnsparken, tel. 88770.

🛏 😊😊 **Comfort Hotell Fregatten**, Hamnplan, tel. 77000, fax 611121. **Varbergs Kurort och Kunst-**hotell, 43658 Apelviken, tel. 29801, old resort hotel directly on the beach. 😊 **Strandgården**, Getterön, tel. 15855, fax 16855.

YOUTH HOSTELS: **Fästningen Vandrarhem**, tel. 88788, accommodation in the former prison.

❌ **Borggården**, in the old fortress, tel. 76990, beautiful view. **Societén**, in the old Community Center, tel. 76500. **Otto's Skafferi**, Kungsgatan 12, tel. 78900, restaurant, open during the day.

🏛 **Museum in the fortress**, June 13-Aug 15, 10 am-7 pm daily, guided tours on the hour from 10 am to 5 pm.

👫 **Tjolöholm Castle**, June 15-June 15, 11 am-4 pm daily, April 3-June 13 and Aug 16-Sept 30, Sat-Sun and holidays 11 am-4 pm.

GOTHENBURG (☎ 031)

i Kungsportsplatsen 2, 4110 Gothenburg, tel. 100740, e-mail: info@gbg-co.se.

The **Göteborgkort** is available in the tourist office, good for free parking, public transportation, sightseeing boats and free entrance (but not everywhere). This special card is also part of the **Gothenburg package**, which is available in various price categories for a maximum of three nights.

🛏 😊😊😊 **Sheraton Gothenburg Hotel & Towers**, Södra Hamngatan 59-65, tel. 806000, fax 159888, Atrium six stories high with a waterfall, two restaurants, casino, disco and bar. **Radisson SAS Park Avenue Hotel**, Kungsportsavenyn 36-38, tel. 176520, fax 169568, in a district of fine cafés, restaurants and bars. **Scandic Crown Hotel**, Polhemsplatsen 3, tel. 800900, fax 15488, near the train station, restaurant and bar. 😊😊 **Hotell Eggers**, Drottningtorget, tel. 806070, fax 154243, tasteful hotel, great restaurant, Sunday brunch special. **Hotel Lorensberg**, Berzeliigatan 15, tel. 810600, fax 205073, beautiful, centrally located hotel, murals. **Hotel Onyxen**, Sten Sturegatan 23, tel. 810845, fax 810845. **Hotel 11**, Maskingatan 11, tel. 7791111, fax 7791110, at the harbor, bar with view of the harbor. 😊 **Hotel Robinson i Palacehuset**, Södra Hamngatan 2, tel. 802521, fax 553982. **Hotel Vasa**, Vasagatan 6, tel. 173630, fax 7119597. **Sankt Jörgens Hotell & Pensionat**, Gamla Lillhagsvägen 127 B, tel. 553981, fax 553982, old villa, somewhat rural, but still close to the city.

YOUTH HOSTELS: **MS Seaside**, Packhuskajen 8, tel. 105970, open April 3-Sept 27, fabulous, old ship, a favorite. **Masthuggsterrassens Vandrarhem**, Masthuggstorget, tel. 424820, open year-round.

🏕 **Delsjö Camping**, Liseberg, Brudaremossen, tel. 252909. **Kärralund**, Liseberg, Olbergsgatan, tel. 840200.

⊠ *FISH:* **GG 12**, Kungsportsavenyn 35, tel. 105826. **Räkan**, Lorensbergsgatan 16, tel. 169839. **Fiskekrogen**, Lilla Torget 1, tel. 101005. *SWEDISH:* **Kometen**, Vasagatan 58, tel. 137988. **Ferb**, Första Långgatan 8, tel. 141673. **Smaka**, Vasaplatsen 3, tel. 132247. *ITALIAN:* **Fontana di Trevi**, Kungsgatan 6, tel. 137372. **Grappa**, Viktoriagatan 12 C, tel. 7017979. **La Gondola**, Kungsportsavenyn 4, tel. 7116828. *FRENCH:* **Cyrano**, Prinsgatan 7, tel. 143110. **Léscalier**, Övre Majorsgatan 4, tel. 144800. *DUTCH:* **Amsterdammertje**, Odinsgatan 21, tel. 155709. *CHINESE:* **Ching Palace**, Södra Hamngatan 2, tel. 158086. **Ming**, Kristinelundsgatan 9, tel. 180479. *GREEK:* **Dionysos**, Sveagatan 24, tel. 136112, **Mykonos**, Linnégatan 58, tel. 145770. *JAPANESE:* **Mikado**, Vasagatan 43 B, tel. 814805. **Sushi**, Erik Dalbergsgatan 4, tel. 7116699. *INDONESIAN:* **Bali**, Vasaplatsen 1, tel. 7113833. *AMERICAN:* **McDonald's**, Avenyn 5, tel. 130025.

▼ *THE "IN" MEETING POINTS:* **Nivå**, Kungsportsavenyn 9, tel. 7018090. **Déjà vu**, Götaplatsen, tel. 182212, bar and pub. **Havanna Bar**, Kungsportsavenyn 15, tel. 7110070. *CAFÈS & BARS:* **Café Capuccino**, Östra Larmgatan, tel. 136695. **Café Tintin**, Engelbrektsgatan, tel. 166812. **Café Engelen**, Engelbrektsgatan 26, tel. 7781200, night café. **Junggrens Café**, Kungsportsavenyn 37, tel. 161751, the café with the storybook smörgåsbord. **Harley's Pub**, Kungsportsavenyn 12, tel. 107161. **Lemon Bar**, Teatergatan 18, tel. 7119911. **Trädgår'n**, Nya Allén 17, tel. 7111511, bar, stage, restaurant. **Bubbles Nightclub**, Kungsportsavenyn 8, tel. 105820. **Jazzhuset**, Erik Dahlbergsgatan 3, tel. 133544. **C@fé Hörnet**, Internet café: www.cafe-hornet.com.

▓ **Sheraton Hotel & Towers**, Park Lane, Kungsportsavenyn 7, tel. 206058. **Trädgårdsföreningen**, Vasagatan 4, tel. 183093. **Summer discotheque** in the Liseberg amusement park, May 13-Aug 23, only on weekends, weather permitting, tel. 400100.

▣ **Operan**, Christa Nilsons Gata, tickets: tel. 131300, **Gothenburg's Konserthus**, Götaplatsen, tickets: tel. 615310. **Ullevi**, Skånegatan, tickets: tel. 611020, rock concerts. **Stadsteatern**, Götaplatsen, tel. 819960. **Stora Teatern**, Kungsparken 1, tel. 613650.

▤ **Nordstan**, Nordstadstorget, 135 stores under one roof. **Nordiska Kompaniet (NK)**, Östra Hemngatan 42, 80 expensive stores under one roof. **Antikhallarna**, Västra Hamngatan 6, antiques, curiosities. **Kronshusbodarna**, Postgatan 6-8, daily 11 am-4 pm, gold, silver, glass, horologist.

▥ **Kristine Kyrka**, **Masthuggskyrkan**, can be visited outside of the service hours. **Museums** at **Ostindiska huset**, Norra Hamngatan 12, Mon-Fri 12-6 pm, Sat-Sun 11 am-4 pm. **Maritima Centrum** March-April and Sept-Nov 10 am-4 pm daily, May 1-June 30, 10 am-6 pm daily. **Utkiken**, panorama terrace, May-Aug 11 am-7 pm daily, Sept 1-27, 11 am-4 pm daily, otherwise Sat-Sun 11 am-4 pm. **Konstmuseet**, **Konsthallen**, Götaplatsen, Mon-Fri 11 am-4 pm, Sat-Sun 11 am-5 pm. **Trädgårdsföreningenspark**, with palm and rose gardens, April-May and Sept 10 am-4 pm daily, Aug 10 am-5 pm daily. **Fish Hall** (*Feskekörkan*) Mon-Sat 6 am-5 pm.

▦ **Bohus Fortress**, June-Aug 10 am-4 pm.

▧ February: **Gothenburg Film Festival**.

▨ *BOATS:* **Paddan Boote**, on the canals of Gothenburg, April 25-Oct 4 daily from Kungsbron, tel. 609670. **Marstrand**, June-Aug daily from Lilla Brommen, 9:30 am, return 3 pm from Marstrand, tel. 800750. **Disco boat Brännö Brygga**, three-hour journey with food, drink, dancing, runs between June 11 and Aug 13 from Lilla Brommen, tel. 609660.

BUS: From the Stena dock in Gothenburg buses go to **Stockholm** and **Oslo**, the ferries coming from Kiel leave the dock at 9:40 am. You reach your destination after four to seven hours of travel time. Tickets are available on board.

MARSTRAND (☎ 0303)

▣ Båtellet, 44030 Marstrand, tel. 60087.

▤ ⑤⑤ **Villa Maritime**, Hamngatan, tel. 61025, fax 61620, with restaurant. ⑤ **Båtellet**, Hamngatan, tel. 60010, simple rooms with multi-bedded rooms.

▧ 1 km north of the harbor, tel. 60584, reservations recommended in summer.

▥ **Marstrand Fortress**, June-Aug 10 am-4 pm in guided groups.

TANUM (☎ 0525)

▤ ⑤⑤ **Hotel Tanum Strand**, tel. 19100, fax 19147, directly on the sea.

⊠ **Tanums Gestgifveri**, tel. 29010, directly on the E6, Sweden's oldest inn has been in operation since the 17th century.

UDDEVALLA (☎ 0522)

▣ Kampenhof, 45181 Uddevalla, tel. 11787.

▤ ⑤ **Hotel Ritz**, Lagerbergsgatan 10, tel. 14225, fax 14304.

▥ **Bokenäs Kyrkan**, June-Aug daily 10 am-4 pm.

▧ **Tanum**, **Rock Carvings**, open from sunrise to sunset. **Museum**, April 15-June 30 and Aug 15-Sept 15, daily 10 am-5 pm, July 1-Aug 14, 10 am-6 pm daily.

West Coast

101

THE REGION OF THE GREAT LAKES

VÄNERN

TROLLHÄTTAN

DALSLAND

KARLSTAD

VÄRMLAND

SKARA

ÖREBRO

★VÄNERN (LAKE VÄNERN)
Sweden's Inland Sea

According to the saga, Lake Vänern was formed by the Goddess Gefijon. She was promised as much land as she could plow up in one night, so she turned her sons into steers and plowed the area of the present Lake Vänern. She removed the clods and piled them off the coast. These became the Danish island of Seeland; and, as the legend has it, she then filled the open basin with water to create Lake Vänern.

★**Vänern** is Sweden's largest lake, and with an area of 5,600 square kilometers, nearly three times the size of Lake Vättern located 40 kilometers farther east. Reaching depths up to 92 meters, the lake was the inland part of a long fjord stretching from Gothenburg to far beyond Karlstad after the last Ice Age. Due to the land mass rising after the Ice Age, the connection to the sea dried up leaving the lake with thousands of skerry islands.

Lake Vänern is surrounded by four regions: Värmland lies to the north, Närke, to the northeast, nearly extends to the sea,

Preceding pages: Every second Swede owns a boat (sailboats on Lake Vänern). Left: Saint Lucia is said to drive darkness away – the saint's feast is celebrated on December 13.

Dalsland lies between the lake and the Norwegian border, and Västergötland encompasses the area to the south and east. Five major roads circumvent the lake forming a ring.

TROLLHÄTTAN

Route 45 follows the valley of Göta älv from **Gothenburg ❶** to Trollhättan. The river has cut into the alluvial land, but the river valley itself, a part of the **Trollhätte Canal** at this point, has to accommodate two country roads in addition to the railway and the **★★Göta Canal**. There are also many industrial firms which have been established in the lower area of the valley. Sweden's only harbor opening westward to the North Sea was located near **Lödöse ❷** until into the 12th century; the **Lödöse Museum** illustrates the history of the once important maritime trading city, which lost its function when the harbor was moved closer to the sea and its citizens were relocated to Gothenburg. A power station dams up the Göta älv in **Lilla Edet ❸**; a specially designed ladder allows the salmon to bypass the barrage and reach their spawning grounds. In addition, the first of many paper mills – transforming the forests of western and northern Sweden into newsprint – billows forth its smoke here.

Map p. 106, Info pp. 118-119

The Great Lakes

THE GREAT LAKES

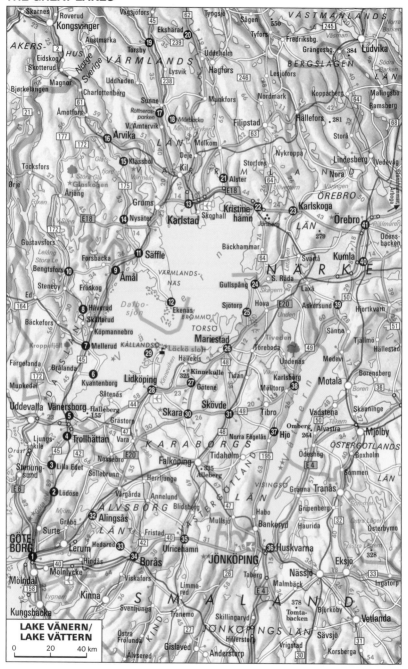

LAKE VÄNERN/
LAKE VÄTTERN

0   20   40 km

Trollhättan ❹ is located where the Göta älv has forced its way through a gneiss ridge – creating a 33-meter-high waterfall. This obstacle to shipping between Lake Vänern and the North Sea challenged master builders and engineers early on, but not until 1916 did the system of locks become fully functional. The capacity allows passage for ships up to 13,500 gross registered tons. The power of the waterfall has long since been tamed: it drives the turbines of an electric power station.

The **King Oscar Bridge** affords the best view of the Göta älv surging down the cliff. Because of the electricity production, it is unfortunately dry most of the time; only on three days in the summer *Fallens dagar* (Waterfall Days) are the weirs opened, and the river is allowed to flow over the cliff for a short time in a tremendous roar. Following the *Slussarna* signs via the old canal, you'll arrive at the system of six sluice chambers which you can tour. There is also the interesting **Canal Museum** nearby.

Trollhättan is an industrial city with a population of 50,000. Famous far beyond the country's borders, the city's largest employer, the SAAB automobile works, is located here.

After traveling a few kilometers upriver, we reach **Vänersborg** ❺ on Lake Vänern, the capital of Älvsborgs län, the southern province of Västergötland. In summer, elk-watching excursions are offered in the lake and forest areas surrounding the 154-meter-high Hunneberg.

*DALSLAND
Sweden in Miniature

The *Dalsland (valley country) region begins north of Vänersborg. Its valleys, gouged out by glaciers during the last Ice Age, run roughly from north to south. Immediately following the Ice Age many valleys were still fjords. Not until the land

mass began to rise did they dry up; however, many lakes remained in the valleys, often connected by the course of a river. Dalsland was Norwegian until being granted to Sweden in the 12th century, and it was rarely involved in the conflicts among its neighbors in the following period.

Dalsland is marked by two noticeably different landscapes: there are the plains of Lake Vänern, a fertile agricultural area; and the pine forests covering the majority of the region. The forests are the wealth of the province and made a flourishing iron industry possible in the 19th century. When England succeeded in smelting iron with the help of hard coal at the end of the 19th century, Dalsland's iron works could no longer compete and completely disappeared within 25 years. At that time, the population had increased to a density of 40 inhabitants per square kilometer, and the farmlands alone could not possibly provide for everyone. A mass exodus resulted, mainly to America. Not until the end of World War II and after the construction of paper mills did the population stabilize again at 10 people per square kilometer.

With bathing beaches at Lake Vänern, extensive forests, rivers, lakes and moors, Dalsland offers everything that makes for scenic charm. For this reason, it is presented as a miniature version of Sweden as a whole. The numerous rivers, lakes and canals connecting Lake Vänern and the Norwegian border make Dalsland, together with Värmland, the most attractive canoeing area in the country.

Directly on Lake Vänern there is a turnoff near **Brålanda** on Route 45 leading to **Kvantenborg** ❻. Here are the remains of the 14th-century Danish **Dalaborg**, where Margaret of Denmark was elected the Scandinavian Union's first queen (1397). The road follows the lakeshore farther north, skirts **Vita Sannar**, Dalsland's most beautiful beach, and converges with the railway hub of

The Great Lakes

Mellerud ❼ again on Route 45. **Kroppefjäll** lies to the west, a wilderness area 30 kilometers long and 10 kilometers wide. There are charming marked hiking trails through this protected area of flora and fauna. The *Karolinerleden*, by the way, follows the trail the soldiers used when accompanying Charles XII on his last campaign.

Located north of Mellerud and just a few kilometers west of Route 45 is the inviting wooden church of **Skållerud** from the 16th and 17th centuries. Painted in warm colors, its Baroque furnishings are particularly impressive.

In **Håverud** ❽, six kilometers north, we come to the *Dalsland Canal, built between the Norwegian border and Köpmannebro on Lake Vänern for the transportation of timber. Håverud had to be connected to the canal via the deep Upperudälv gorge. A riveted steel trough 32 meters in length solved the problem in 1868. Later a railway bridge as well as a road bridge spanned the gorge. The Dalsland Canal has long outlived its usefulness for transporting timber; it now merely serves as a tourist attraction. The history of its construction is documented in a small **museum** located directly at the canal bridge.

Åmål ❾ on Lake Vänern (Route 45) is Dalsland's only city. Founded in 1640, it was granted a municipal charter three years later. This enabled Åmål to collect more taxes from the farmers, who had to sell their goods here. The manor house of **Forsbacka** (seven kilometers northwest of Åmål) and the red wooden church of **Fröskog** might lure you to the hinterland. The iron crosses in the cemetery there are considered to be the best examples of "iron culture" from the 19th century.

Bengtsfors ❿ not only has an attractive open-air museum, but it is also a popular starting point for canoeists, who

Right: Sailing – a popular activity in Sweden (here on Lake Vänern).

equip themselves accordingly in the local specialty shops. Excursion boats run between Bengtsfors and Köpmannebro on the historical canal route. The nostalgic trolley running on the disused railroad tracks between Bengtsfors and Årjäng in Värmland is ideal for enthusiasts of unusual modes of transportation.

KARLSTAD
North of Lake Vänern

When arriving at **Säffle** ⓫ you will also have arrived at the southernmost tip of *Värmland. It is also the center of the **Värmlandsnäs** peninsula, which projects some 40 kilometers into Lake Vänern. You can rent motorboats in **Ekenäs** ⓬ at the southern tip of the peninsula and then explore the offshore skerry world. **Lurö**, the largest of the islands, is a nature reserve.

The *Säffle Canal, between Säffle and Arvika at Glafsfjorden, has been in existence since 1837. Nowadays, this charming waterway is primarily of touristic significance.

Charles IX not only granted the capital of Värmland, **Karlstad** ⓭, municipal charter rights in the 16th century, but also gave the former *tingstäde* its name. Located at the mouth of the 500-kilometer-long Klarälven River flowing into Lake Vänern, the city was a very important trading post between Värmland and Västergötland as far back as the early Middle Ages. Karlstad is a fire-ravaged city; the last one having occurred in 1865. The mayor's house is said to have burned down at that time because instead of helping, he only cried and prayed, but the bishop, on the other hand, helped to extinguish the fire, and his house remained standing – at least, that is what the inhabitants like to say. It is more probable that the park surrounding the bishop's palace prevented the fire from spreading to the building. Apart from the palace, only six other houses escaped the blaze; the **Östra**

The Great Lakes

Bron, the old stone bridge, with 12 arches, also survived the fire.

The statue at Stora Torget commemorates negotiations which took place to dissolve the union with Norway in 1905. There is a modern crucifix in the **Domkyrkan** (also heavily damaged in the fire) made of silver-plated stainless steel and Orrefor crystal worth seeing. The **Gamla Gymnasiet** opposite has been converted to a school museum.

VÄRMLAND
Pure Nature

You can cover the center of Värmland – the area between Säffle and Arvika in the west, and Karlstad and Torsby in the east – on a wonderfully scenic stretch in relatively little time. Following the side road toward **Nysäter** ⓮, after about 10 kilometers you arrive at **Echstedtska gården**, an 18th-century estate complete with Rococo furnishings, as well as two pavilions flanking the main building. Farther north, Route 175 swings to the east

side of **Glafsfjorden**. The circular tour called *Hantverksrundan* begins in **Klässbol** ⓯; it passes one artisan shop after another (offering souvenirs as well as coffee and cake), including the former artist colony of the painter Christian Erikson in **Rackstad** on **Lake Racken**.

Arvika ⓰, a beautiful, nearly circular cove located near Glafsfjord, was one of the centers for Finnish immigrants during the famine of the 18th century.

Nature lovers adore the area between Arvika und Årjäng: lake **Stora Gla** is located here in the nature reserve of ***Glaskogen**, which has many marked hiking trails.

In the Footsteps of Selma Lagerlöf

The chain of the three elongated **Fryken Lakes** is longer than Glafsfjorden 30 kilometers away. You can enjoy a breathtaking view of the forest in varying shades of green, as well as the Fryken Lakes system, from **Fryksdalshöjden**, four kilometers west of **Västra**

Ämtervik on **Mellan Fryken**. The course of a river connects the Upper, Middle and Lower Fryken. In her novel, *Gösta Berling's Saga,* Selma Lagerlöf uses the individual lakes called "the long lake of Löven," as an allegory to youth, maturity and old age.

Driving north on Route 45, you arrive at the manor of ★**Rottnerosparken ⑦** directly on Mellan Fryken. It, too, plays an important role as the "Ekeby" in *Gösta Berling's Saga.* There is an animal enclosure and a restaurant here, as well as a vegetable and rose garden. The large number of sculptures decorating the park are mainly replicas of famous works, including those of Vigeland and Milles.

The rural town of **Sunne** developed on the flat promontory between Mellan and **Övra Fryken**; it is a popular vacation resort offering numerous activities from fishing to rafting.

Driving south on route 238, you'll arrive at ★**Mårbacka ⑱**, the farmhouse estate where Selma Lagerlöf was born in 1858. It had to be sold after the death of her father in 1882. Selma Lagerlöf earned her living as a teacher, but never remained in a lasting position; she instead traveled extensively to Italy and Palestine between her periods of employment. After the successes of her first literary works, particularly the "geography textbook" *The Wonderful Adventures of Nils,* she was able to buy back the family house. She was awarded the Nobel Prize for Literature in 1909, and was the first woman ever admitted to the Swedish Academy of Language and Science. Her Mårbacka estate has remained unchanged since she had it renovated in the 1920s, and it is now open to the public. Selma Lagerlöf was laid to rest in the small cemetery of **Östra Ämtervik**.

From Sunne, Route 238 winds along the eastern shore of Övra Fryken to

Right: Nowadays, timber is only transported along the Klarälven.

Torsby ⑲. Turning east there, near **Ekshärad ⑳**, you arrive at the valley of the ★**Klarälven**, where Route 62 will take you to Karlstad. This stretch is one of Värmland's most beautiful; you should allow at least a day for it.

The Klarälven is the longest river in Scandinavia and the only one in Sweden where rafting trips are offered. Those interested in such a merry adventure can rent a raft or even build their own and drift towards Karlstad. Route 62 leads from Karlstad to the Norwegian border and on to Trondheim; this is the old pilgrim route to the grave of Saint Olav.

In the Northeast of Lake Vänern

The poet Gustav Fröding (1860–1911) chose **Alster ㉑**, 10 kilometers east of Karlstad on the E18, as his place of residence. The author, known throughout Sweden, was an inwardly torn character who counterbalanced his gloomy verse with humorous poems.

The city of **Kristinehamn ㉒**, named after the young queen of the 17th century, enjoyed its heyday in the 19th century, when iron ore from **Bergslagen** was transshipped from here to Dalsland. In today's harbor, timber from the surrounding area is loaded onto ships. **Tête de femme**, a 15-meter-high sculpture by Picasso, stands at the end of the **Vålösund**, an area of villas with its own yacht harbor. A local artist, Bengt Olson, brought the model of the sculpture here from Paris, and the Norwegian Carl Nesjar later cast it in concrete. Picasso himself, who had never been to Sweden, presented it to the city.

Founded by Charles IX, the old mining town of **Karlskoga ㉓** on the E18, is 24 kilometers east of Kristinehamn. It became world famous when Alfred Nobel bought the Bofors steelworks here and produced dynamite – his invention. The Nobel Foundation annually distributes its accrued interest in the form of "Nobel

Prizes." Nobel's summer residence, **herr-gård Björkborn**, is now a museum.

Heading south on Route 64 from Kristinehamn, it's worth taking a westward detour to the rune stone of **Järsberg**, near Gårdsberg. It dates from the 9th century and is the oldest one in Värmland.

You should plan on taking a break in **Gullspång ㉔** on **Lake Skagern**, as the church of **Södra Råda** here is a true art-historical jewel: built in the log-cabin style in 1260, it has remained unchanged ever since. The choir was painted in the High Gothic style in 1323 by unknown artists; the nave by the master craftsman Amund in 1494. As a matter of interest, it was recently discovered that for his depiction of the Virgin Mary he copied a French work from the 13th century.

Between Lakes Vänern and Vättern

The boundary between Värmland and **Västergötland** runs north from Gullspång, near **Sjötorp ㉕**; the Göta Canal leaves Lake Vänern heading east. Västergötland is the region between lakes Vänern and Vättern extending nearly 100 kilometers to the south. Unlike in many other landscapes in Sweden, Cambrian and Silurian sedimentary deposits – sandstone, limestone and slate – remain because a magmatic flow of greenstone blanketed these soft layers and acted as a protective covering. Hard greenstone plates form distinctive plateaus in the north, while fertile plains of clay soil are more typical of the south.

Västergötland is Sweden's heartland: it has never been under foreign rule and therefore was never forced to undergo destruction and pillaging. This region first made history with the construction of the Skara cathedral in the 12th century, however, numerous megalith graves and stone burial mounds, stone settings and cave drawings verify prehistoric settlements on this land which is still used for farming today.

Routes 40 (Gothenburg-Jönköping), 195 (Lake Vättern; west shoreline), and

E20, with its side roads 64 (north) and 44 (south) heading east of Lake Vänern, provide a comprehensive introduction to Västergötland.

Mariestad ㉖ is an industrial town located on the E20 where the Tida flows into Lake Vänern. It is worth a visit to the 16th-century **Domkyrkan**, protectively located on an island in the Tida River, and to **herrgård Marieholm**, today the administrative seat of the province and a museum.

The E20 takes us southward toward **Götene** ㉗. From there, continue westward on Route 44 towards Lake Vänern. The prominent plateau of *Kinnekulle affords beautiful views from a tower at 325 meters above sea level, and the *Kinnekulleleden* hiking trail winds around the mountain to places of cultural interest from prehistoric to modern times.

Above: Posing glamorously at the hunting lodge of Lidköping. Right: You can glide across the lake like a swan in these pedal boats (at Läckö Castle, Lake Vänern).

The **Kinnekullegården** is a good place to relax; a **Naturum** is also located here. **Husaby**, south of Kinnekulle and a few kilometers north of Route 44, is an excellent place to begin a tour. A royal court reigned here in the 11th century, which was enlarged to a diocesan town in the 12th century. The former stave church no longer exists, only a stone tower remains; this is presumably Sweden's oldest church tower.

Located on the southern shore of **Kinneviken Bay**, where the Lidan River flows into Lake Vänern, the city of **Lidköping** ㉘ developed in the 15th century. Lord High Chancellor Magnus Gabriel de la Gardie was granted the right to enlarge the city in the 17th century. He laid out a new district on the west bank of the river to develop a uniform, symmetrical townscape characteristic of the Baroque period. He later bestowed his wooden hunting lodge to the city to house the town hall.

North of Lidköping, the peninsula of Kålland reaches out into Lake Vänern.

The Great Lakes

Here, off the coast on the island of **Kållandsö** ㉙, the bishop of Skara had a castle built in the 13th century, which was later remodeled to become ***Läckö slott**. After the Reformation, the castle fell to the Vasa kings, who granted it as a fief – lastly to the De la Gardie family. Magnus de la Gardie intended to have it remodeled in the Baroque style, but due to lack of funds, this was never fully realized; nevertheless, initial changes are noticeable in some of the 280 rooms.

*SKARA

*Skara ㉚, a rural town with a population of 17,000, is located on the E20 on a plateau between lakes Vänern and Vättern. The location was already a cult and *ting* (assembly) site in the Stone Age, and it became a diocesan town in 1150. At the same time, a seminary was established which later became a secondary school (founded in 1641). It is still one of the more elite schools in Sweden. The **Stortorget**, with a "chronicle fountain"

showing episodes of the city's history, marks the center of Skara. The ***Domkyrkan**, Sweden's second-oldest cathedral, rises high behind it. Consecrated in the 12th century as a Romanesque basilica with a crypt, it was rebuilt many times in the following centuries. During the 19th-century restoration, the Gothic elements were returned to the limelight and the towers were added. Tombs of the city's first bishops were found in the Romanesque crypt below the choir. Nothing remains of the medieval furnishings of the cathedral; the interior is now dominated by Italian Baroque. The black-and-white marble sarcophagus of the cavalry colonel Erik Soop and his wife is worth seeing. Soop was honored with this monument for saving the life of King Gustavus II Adolphus in 1629 during the Thirty Years' War.

A side-trip to **Skövde** ㉛ takes us to ***Varnhem Monastery**. It was founded by the French Cistercian order as an annex of the Alvastra Monastery in the 12th century and abandoned after a fire in

1394. After having been in the hands of the crown since the Reformation, it was granted to Magnus de la Gardie as a fief. The church is the final resting place of early Scandinavian kings and nobility (e.g., Birger Jarl). Magnus then had his family crypt established here and the church remodeled in the style of the 17th-century, when it was given the buttresses which now characterize the building.

With 50,000 inhabitants, Skövde, the largest city in the province, has gone up in flames so many times that nothing of the original structures remains. The prehistoric monument of **Askeberga** is worth visiting. It was found 24 kilometers north of Route 200 and is one of the largest known stone settings; it consists of 24 mighty stone blocks laid out within a perimeter of 54 meters.

To the Western Shore of Lake Vättern

Returning to Skara from this excursion to the hinterland on the E20, the rapid Stockholm-Gothenburg connection, we arrive at **Alingsås** ㉜, the center of Sweden's textile industry, after about 80 kilometers. The **Alströmerska magasinet**, a social history museum, allows us to visualize how it was to have more than a thousand workers employed in a single factory in the 18th century.

Route 180 toward Borås takes us past **Hedared** ㉝. This is the location of the last preserved *stave church in Sweden. Almost all of the oldest Scandinavian churches can only be found in Norway today. The church of Hedared is tiny (35 square meters), very plain and most likely from the 12th century. The altarpiece of those days was only a painting directly on the wooden wall.

While the secondary road, Route 180, continues on to **Borås** ㉞ from Hedared,

Right: The last primeval forest of central Sweden – Tiveden National Park.

Route 40 coming from Gothenburg enters the city as a four-lane highway. The **Textilmuseet** testifies to the fact that Borås was also a center of the textile industry. It flourished when Gustavus II Adolphus universally granted the privilege of itinerant trade to the poor; the men known as *knallarna* (literally "trotabouts") would sell the goods the women of Borås made at home.

The former Boge Sound was renamed **Ulricehamn** ㉟ after Charles XII's sister – Ulrica Elenora. There is a nice ensemble of wooden houses on the cobble-stoned Stortorget.

Located 27 kilometers farther south at the opposite end of the long, narrow **Lake Åsunden** is the medieval **Torpastenhus** castle. Its preserved condition is noteworthy; the Renaissance-styled knights' hall and the Baroque palace chapel deserve a visit.

Jönköping ㊱ at the southern tip of ****Lake Vättern belongs to Småland (see also p. 59), whereas the western shore belongs to Västergötland. The charming countryside is easily reached via Route 195. Three old wooden churches, in **Brandstorp**, **Södra** and **Norra Fågelås**, on the way to **Hjo** ㊲, are worth a stop. Hjo is a delightful resort town with wooden villas from the 19th century and a popular beach. An old steamship runs between here and the island of Visingsö (see also p. 60).

Karlsborg ㊳, located where the Göta Canal enters Lake Vättern, is a small fortress town with shops, cafés and vacation apartments. The town was built after Sweden lost Finland to Russia in 1809, and then restructured its inland defense. However, by the time the site was completed, it had already lost all military significance. There is an extensive view of the sea from the ramparts.

Tiveden, an area rich in woodland, moors and lakes, lies between lakes Vättern and **Unden**. Although this "southernmost wilderness of Sweden"

The Great Lakes

has already been threatened by lumbering, the existence of the **Tiveden** national park (13 square kilometers) in the center has, since 1983, been an attempt to retain its primeval-forest character. Hiking trails, canoeing waters and bicycle paths provide a number of attractive recreational possibilities throughout the entire isolated area.

Närke – Shoemaker Country

To the north and adjacent to this wilderness region is **Närke**, a lowland area just 30 meters above sea level; it includes **Hjälmaren**, Sweden's fourth-largest lake, which is located in the center. The few mountain crests in the north and east are actually terminal moraines; leftover glacial debris.

The settlement of this transit country dates back to as far as the Stone Age; easily navigable waterways to lakes Mälaren and Vättern made early trade relations possible. Iron ore mining in the northern part of Närke was the key to economic development in the Middle Ages. The abundance of timber in the region also played a key role in the possibility of processing iron. And in **Glanshammar**, located on the northern shore of Hjälmaren, silver was even mined until as late as 1530. The realm of *Landsförsamlingskyrkor*, extending to the far north, begins in Närke. These 17th-century churches were not only places of worship, but they also served as venues for assembly. An especially pretty example of this is in **Askersund** ❸❾ on the northern tip of Lake Vättern.

Since the soil of Närke was rather acidic and less suitable for agriculture, the farmers were forced to look elsewhere for a source of additional income. They tanned cattle hides and made sacks which were then needed in mining – making shoes seemed to be a natural progression. A flourishing shoe industry developed in **Kumla** ❹❶ and in the surrounding area. It has since been relinquished due to competition from countries using low-wage manpower.

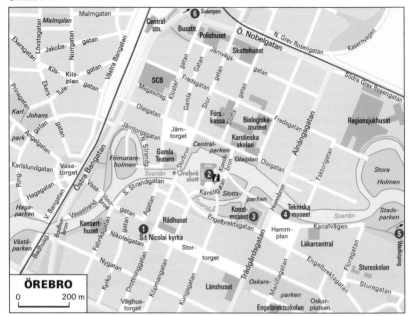

★ÖREBRO

The E18 and E20 intersect in **★Örebro** ❹. The city of 120,000 inhabitants on the borderline between mining and farmland is traversed by the Svartån River, which flows into the Hjälmaren. In the Middle Ages, the only river crossing (the water was much deeper then) was located here. Birger Jarl secured the spot by building a 25-meter-high fortified tower.

Hardly any of the wooden medieval houses remain today; the devastating fire of 1854 destroyed practically everything, and the Old Town was reconstructed with stone houses. The center is located on the elongated Stortorget, where on the west end the **Sankt Nicolai kyrka** ❶ is situated. It was built of brick in the Gothic style of northern Germany in the 13th century and originally belonged to the German merchant community in Örebro. Many gravestones can be seen inside the

Right: View of Örebro with its landmark moated castle.

church; one of them is that of Engelbrekt Engelbrektsson, a legendary national hero who organized a revolt against King Erik of Pomerania in the 15th century. His statue stands in front of the church.

Complete with a moat, **★Örebro slott** ❷ is situated a bit north of the Stortorget. The castle dates back to a 13th-century fortress. Its ground plan is from the time of the Vasa kings; its appearance from the late 19th century. Today it houses provincial government offices and the tourist information office. The **knights' hall**, decorated with coats of arms, is open to the public. It was the setting of many important parliamentary discussions. For difficult negotiations, the parliament retreated to the remote Örebro to prevent decisions from leaking out prematurely. Such was the case in 1810, when the election of the Napoleonic marshal Jean Baptiste Bernadotte as heir to the throne took place. The cafés in the beautiful **park grounds** surrounding the castle are tempting rest spots; with live music and dancing on summer evenings.

The Engelbrektsgatan extends eastward from the castle along the Svartån. After a short walk, you come to the **Konstmuseet** ❸, which houses a collection of ecclesiastical art gathered from the Närke region. At the river nearby, the **Tekniska museet** ❹ covers topics of industrial development and shipping.

Following the Kanalvägen farther, we reach the city park and the **Wadköping** ❺, the cultural center. The name stems from a novel by Hjalmar Bergman describing the city of his childhood. Former merchants' houses of the 18th and 19th centuries from around the city have been re-erected here, forming an open-air museum. Arts and craft shops have been established here as well. It is said that Charles IX once slept in the oldest house, the 16th-century *Kungsstuga* (King's Quarters). The **Svampen** ❻ (Mushroom) water tower,1.5 kilometers north of the castle, is a modern attraction. It is 58 meters high and has a restaurant with an observation deck offering expansive views of the surrounding countryside.

The attempt to provide the satellite towns of Örebro with a metropolitan infrastructure while allowing them to maintain a rural environment by arranging them as villages around the city center has gained worldwide attention.

Arboga

In the Middle Ages, **Arboga** (located north of E20 and 54 kilometers from Örebro) was a trading center for ore from mountainous areas, but it lost this function after the opening of the Hjälmaren Canal. The first Swedish parliament was founded in Arboga in 1435; it was at this meeting that Engelbrekt Engelbrektsson was named Governor of the Realm. The idyllic little town deserves a visit, mainly because of its well-preserved houses on Storgatan and Västerlånggatan. The **Trefaldighetskyrkan** is also worth seeing; it is decorated with frescoes depicting scenes from the life of St. Francis of Assisi. In the Middle Ages it belonged to the Franciscan monastery.

TROLLHÄTTAN (☎ 0520)

ℹ️ Gärdhemsvägen 9, 46184 Trollhättan, tel. 87654.

🛏️ 😊😊 **Kung Oscar**, Drottninggatan 17, tel. 7480280, fax 13116. 😊 **Hotel Trollhättan**, Polhemsgatan 6, tel. 12570, fax 15471. **STF Vandrarhem Gula Villan**, Tingvallavägen 12, tel. 12960, fax 15600, hotel and *YOUTH HOSTEL.*

🔺 **Stenrösens Camping**, tel. 70710, 10 km south on Route 45, nice location.

❌ **Ronnums Herrgård**, Vargön, 2 km outside of Vännersborg, tel. 0521-223270, Sweden's top chef, Ingvar Sandberg, frequently cooks here, often features elk specialties.

🏛️ **Waterfall Days**, May 1-June 14, Sat-Sun from 2:15 pm, June 15-Aug 31, Wed and Sun from 2:15 pm. **Canal Museum**, June 11-Aug 21, 11 am-7 pm daily, otherwise only Sat-Sun and holidays 12-5 pm.

MELLERUD (☎ 0530)

ℹ️ Gamla Tingshuset, 46431 Mellerud, tel. 18308.

🔺 **Vita Sannars Camping**, Sunnarnå, tel. 12260, directly on the most beautiful beach of Dalsland.

🚶 **Church** of **Skållerud**, June-Aug 10 am-4 pm.

📷 Daily journeys to the **Dalsland Canal**, Dalsland Akvedukt-sightseeing, Köpmannebro, tel. 31097.

🚢 *BOAT:* Six-hour **canal cruise** from Köpmannebro to Bengtsfors, following day return (or directly afterward by bus), Rederi Dalslandia, Köpmannebro, tel. 31001.

HÅVERUD (☎ 0530)

ℹ️ Dalsland Center, PO Box 6030, 46490 Mellerud, tel. 30580, located directly on the canal.

🛏️😊 **Håveruds Herrgård**, tel. 30490, fax 30060, with restaurant. **SFT Vandrarhem Håverud**, Museivägen, tel. 30275.

🏛️ **Canal Museum**, June-Aug, Mon-Fri 10 am-6 pm, Sat-Sun/holidays 11 am-4 pm.

ÅMÅL (☎ 0532)
BENGTSFORS (☎ 0531)

ℹ️ Dalsland Turistråd, Box 181, 66231 Åmål, tel. 16060. Bengtsfors Turistbyrå, Tingshustorget, 66630 Bengtsfors, tel. 16105.

🛏️ 😊 **Dalhall Hotell & Restaurang**, Riksväg 45, Åmål, tel. 166990, fax 12967, hotel in the Viking style. **Stadshotellet i Åmål**, Kungsgatan 9, Åmål, tel. 12020, fax 16775. **Furnäs Stugby**, Furnäsvägen 2, Bengtsfors, tel. 12090, fax 12520. **Kanalvillan**, Dals Långed, Bengtsfors, tel. 41116, also *CANOE RENTAL.*

🔺 **Örnäsbadet Camping**, tel. 0532-17097, directly on Lake Värnern, 26 *CABINS.*

❌ **Baldernäs Herrgård**, Dals Långed, tel. 0531-41211, May-Aug only, fish and game restaurant.

🔷 **Bengtsfors** open-air museum, June-Aug 10 am-4 pm. **Church** of **Fröskog**, open daily, except during services.

📷 *FISHING:* Trawling in Lake Vänern, April-Oct, Turiststiftelsen Plantaget, Åmål, tel. 17260. *TROLLY RIDES:* Bengtsfors-Årjäng, Dal-Västra Värmlands Järnväg, Bengtsfors, tel. 10285. *CANOEING:* Silverlake Canoeing, Brogatan Slussen, Bengtsfors, tel. 12173, canoe and outdoor equipment rental, May-Oct. Red Bay Canoeing Center, Grindhöjdsvägen 6 F, Åmål, tel. 16229, May-Sept.

SÄFFLE (☎ 0533)

ℹ️ Billerudsgatan 5-7, 66100 Säffle, tel. 10600.

🚢 *BOAT RENTAL:* Sola Båten, Ekenäs, tel. 0522-12096.

KARLSTAD (☎ 054)

ℹ️ Västra Torggatan 26, 65184 Karlstad, tel. 215220.

🛏️ 😊😊 **Hotell Ritz**, Västra Torggatan 20, tel. 215140, fax 219443. **Stadshotellet Karlstad**, Kungsgatan 22, tel. 215220, fax 188211. 😊 **Comfort Home Hotel Bilan**, Karlsbergsgatan 3, tel. 100300, fax 219214.

❌ **Restaurang Tiffany's**, Västra Torggatan 19, tel. 153383. **Munken**, Västra Torggatan 17, tel. 210216.

🚶 **Echstedtska Gården**, June-Aug 11 am-6 pm daily.

SUNNE (☎ 0565)
TORSBY (☎ 0560)

ℹ️ Sunne Turistbyrå, Mejerigatan 2, 68623 Sunne, tel. 13530. Torsby Turistbyrå, Norra Torggatan 1, 68521 Torsby, tel. 10550.

🛏️ 😊 **Hotel Fryken Strand**, By 80, Sunne, tel. 13300, fax 711691. **Broby Gästgivaregård**, Långgatan 25, Sunne, tel. 13370, fax. 12553. **Hotel Björnidet**, Kyrkogatan 2, Torsby, tel. 13820. **Selma Lagerlöf Hotel**, Långgatan, Sunne, tel. 16600, fax 16620.

🏛️ **Klässbol Hantverksrundan**, stores and workshops Mon-Fri 8 am-6 pm, Sat 10 am-3 pm. **Rackstad Museum**, June-Aug, Tue-Sun 10 am-4 pm. Rottnerosparken May 8-Sept 7, 10 am-7 pm daily. **Mårbacka** manor house, May 10-Sept 7, daily from 10 am (tours), otherwise only Sat from 2 pm. **Alster** manor house, June-Aug 11 am-6 pm daily.

📷 **Selma Lagerlöf Culture Week**, early August, information from tourist offices. *OUTDOOR VACATION:*

Nordmarkens Kanotcenter, Årjäng, tel. 0573-38060 or 38068. *ELK SAFARI:* In Glaskogen, July 8-Aug 14, Tue and Thu from Arvika, tel. 0570-81790. *RAFTING TRIPS:* Sverigeflotten, Transtrand 20, Likens, tel. 0564-40227. Vildmark i Värmland, Torsby, tel. 14040, rafts are self-assembled.

KRISTINEHAMN (☎ 0550)

🛈 Västerlånggatan 22, 68131 Kristinehamn, tel. 88187.

🛏 ☺☺ **Hennickehammars Herrgård**, 2 km outside Filipstad, tel. 0590-12565, sports hotel. ☺ **Hotel Frödich**, Kungsgatan 44, tel. 15180, fax 10130.

⛵ **Boat trips** to the bathing cliffs of **Sibberon**, June 7-Aug 29, eight times daily, tel. 8185.

KARLSKOGA (☎ 0586)

🛈 Katrinedalsgatan 2, 69183 Karlskoga, tel. 61474.

🛏 ☺☺ **Hotell Skotten**, Järnvägsgatan 12, tel. 50160, fax 89827. **Svartå Herrgård**, Svartå, tel. 0585-50003, fax 50303, manor house from the 18th century with park and lake. **Grythyttans Gästgivaregård**, Grythyttan, tel. 0591-14124, villa with morbid charm and a restaurant classified with one Michelin star.

🚶 Manor house of **Björkborn**, June-Aug 1-5 pm daily and by appointment, tel. 83494. **Church** of **Södra Råde**, June-Aug 10 am-4 pm daily.

MARIESTAD (☎ 0501)

🛈 Hamnplan, 54230 Mariestad, tel. 10001.

🛏 ☺ **Rattugglan**, Muggebo, tel. 70035, fax 14897.

LIDKÖPING (☎ 0510)

🛈 Nya Stadens Torg, 53102 Lidköping, tel. 83500.

🛏 ☺☺ **Stadt Lidköping**, Gamla Stadens Torg 1, tel. 51410, fax 21532. ☺ **Hotell Läckö**, Gamla Stadens Torg 5, tel. 23000, fax 62191. **SFT Vandrarhem Kinnekulle**, Gössäter Hällekis, tel. 40022, fax 40509.

🏛 **Husaby kyrkan,** May 25-Aug 15, 11 am-6 pm daily, otherwise 11 am-4 pm. **Läckö Castle**, May 15-Aug 31, 10 am-6 pm daily.

ALINGSÅS (☎ 0322)

🛈 Stora Torget, 75200 Alingsås, tel. 75730.

🛏 ☺☺ **Grand Hotel Alingsås**, Bankgatan 1, tel. 14000, fax 17100.

❌ The **Grand Hotel** restaurant specializes in potato dishes.

🏛 **Alströmerska Magasinet** (social history museum), Lilla Torget, May 1-Aug 15, 11 am-5 pm daily, otherwise Tue-Fri 12-4 pm.

🚶 **Hedared** stave church, May 10-Sept 10, 10 am-6 pm daily.

SKARA (☎ 0511)

🛈 Skolgatan 1, 53288 Skara, tel. 32580.

🛏 ☺☺ **Skara Stadshotellet**, Järnvägsgatan 5, tel. 31000, fax 13360. ☺ **Hotell och Restaurang Stadskällaren i Skara**, Skaraborgsgatan 15, tel. 13410, fax 12148, with original restaurant.

🏛 **Domkyrkan**, 9 am-6 pm daily, except during services.

🚶 **Varnhem Monastery**, church open May 15-Aug 31, 11 am-5 pm daily.

KARLSBORG (☎ 0505)

🛈 Norra Kanalgatan 2, 546 33 Karlsborg, tel. 17350.

🛏 ☺ **Kanalhotellet**, Storgatan 94, tel. 12130, fax 12761.

🏛 **Torpa Castle**, May 1-Aug 15, 11 am-5 pm daily, tours on the full hour. **Churches** of **Brandstorp**, **Södra** and **Norra Fågelås**, 9 am-6 pm daily, except during services.

🚶 National park of **Tiveden**, info: tel. 019-193000.

ÖREBRO (☎ 019)

🛈 Örebro slott, 70135 Örebro, tel. 212121, e-mail: destination@orebro.se.

🛏 ☺☺☺ **Scandic Hotel Grand Örebro**, Fabriksgatan 21-23, tel. 150200, fax 185814. ☺☺ **Stora Hotellet**, Drottninggatan 1, tel. 124360, fax 6117890. ☺ **City Hotel Örebro**, Kungsgatan 24, tel. 6014200, fax 6024209.

🅰 **Gustavsvik Camping**, tel. 196950, fax 196961, 2 km south of the center, with lake for swimming, fun pool and *CABINS*.

❌ **Slottskrogen**, in Gustavus Vasa's old parliament hall, Örebro slott, tel. 134269, with terrace. **Restaurant Boat Örebro III**, Hamnplan, tel. 261818.

🏛 **Örebro slott**, June-Aug tours 10:30 am, 11:30 am, 3 pm and 6 pm daily. **Länsmuseum, Techniska Museet,** June-Aug 11 am-5 pm daily. Open-air museum of **Wadköping**, same opening hours. **Svampen** water tower with restaurant, April 30-June 5 and Aug 14-Sept 3, 10 am-6 pm daily, June 6-Aug 23, 10 am-8 pm daily.

⛵ **Palace Festival**, last week of July. **Longboat Festival**, second week of August.

AROUND LAKE MÄLAREN

NYKÖPING
GRIPSHOLM
SALA
VÄSTERÅS
UPPSALA
SIGTUNA

**LAKE MÄLAREN
The Heart of the Svear Empire

Three regions are grouped around **Lake Mälaren**: Södermanland to the south, Västmanland to the northwest and Uppland to the northeast. In the 5th century, they made up the nucleus of the *Svear rike* (Svear Empire), whose borders were never finalized. But the central area offered a rough configuration nevertheless: *Uppland* represented the center; south of Uppland lived the "southmen" and to the west, the "westmen."

Lake Mälaren provides all three regions with a common heart. In the Middle Ages, the lake was still connected to the Baltic Sea, but today dams and locks have separated the two bodies of water and, as a result, Lake Mälaren has become Sweden's third-largest lake. The lake stretches from near the Baltic Sea to as far away as Köping (100 kilometers inland), and is marked by numerous bays, tributaries and islands. Many of Sweden's historic cities can be found in this area – Birka, Old Uppsala, Uppsala and Stockholm. Västerås, Strängnäs and Sigtuna

Preceding pages: Trosa, an idyllic seaside resort south of Stockholm. Left: A novel by Kurt Tucholsky brought Gripsholm Castle worldwide fame.

are three additional centers going back to the Middle Ages that lie on the shores of the lake. Today, Lake Mälaren is connected to the Baltic Sea by the Södertälje Canal and is even navigable for seagoing vessels with up to 5.5 meters of draft. This led to the construction of large industrial complexes in Södertälje, Eskilstuna and Västerås.

The Land of the Southmen

Södermanland is marked by gently rolling hills and numerous lakes, forests and rivers; the only highlands appear in the south with **Kolmården** and in the west with **Mälarmården**. Off the Baltic Sea coast lies a scattered archipelago of over 5,000 islands. The region was already settled during the Stone Age, and the early inhabitants left a rich inheritance of cultural and historical treasures. Over 100,000 burial mounds, stone settings, rune stones and castle fortresses have been estimated. The close proximity to Stockholm and the lure of the landscape motivated wealthy noblemen of the 17th century to have a large number of mansions built here. The combination of delightful countryside and an abundance of cultural and historical monuments makes Södermanland one of the most popular vacation spots in Sweden.

Around Lake Mälaren

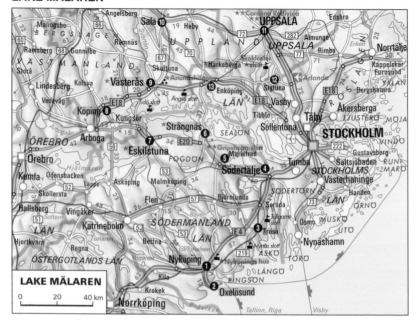

0   20   40 km

The region is served by an admirable traffic system: the E4 crosses through from north to south and the E20 from east to west. Railway lines connect all the major cities and bus routes provide service to even the smallest towns.

NYKÖPING
The City With the Key

An giant key on the roof of a building at a rest stop on the E4 about 10 kilometers before **Nyköping** ❶ recalls a fateful banquet that took place at the castle of *Nyköpings hus in 1317. King Birger Magnusson invited his brothers, who had been disputing his right to the throne, to a reconciliation dinner at the castle. However, instead of feasting them, he had them thrown into the dungeon and dropped the only key into the Nyköpingsån River and, in so doing, condemned his brothers to death by starvation.

Right: If only to see its original furnishings, Nynäs Castle is well worth a visit.

Out of a 12th-century watchtower developed a fortress that later became a Renaissance castle under Charles IX. After a devastating fire in 1665, the castle was only partially reconstructed. The castle gate, known as the **Vasaporten**, and the **Kungstornet** (King's Tower), where the infamous dungeon was once located, still remain. Here models of the original castle are on display. In July, the castle ruins are used as an open-air stage, where a presentation of the *Nyköpings Gästabud*, "The Nyköping Banquet," is performed.

The seaport of Nyköping was granted a charter in 1260; Magnus Ladulås, who was proclaimed king here, heartily patronized the city. After the conflagration of the Old Town in the 17th century, only the two churches of **Sankt Nicolai** and **Allhelgona** (All Saints) survived. St. Nicolai is located on the Stortorget across from the 18th-century **Rådhuset** (City Hall); the Church of All Saints is on the other side of the river opposite the castle.

From **Oxelösund** ❷, Nyköping's modern harbor, ferries provide service to

Tallin and Riga. You should continue on the E4 to Södertälje, then on Route 219 following the archipelago coast.

Royal Castles

Nynäs slott (35 kilometers from Nyköping, east of Route 219) was built in the 17th century and was privately owned until the 1980s. Today, visitors are welcome inside; this is good opportunity to marvel at a castle with original furnishings and to become acquainted with the lifestyle of a nobleman and his servants. The former orangery today houses the castle restaurant.

The town of **Trosa** ❸, on the northernmost tip of Route 219, consists of small, cramped cottages with pretty gardens. In the fish smokehouse there you can buy provisions for a picnic on the beach.

Until the beginning of the 20th century, Swedish kings spent their summer vacations at **Tullgarn slott** (12 kilometers to the north), until they moved quarters to Solliden on the island of Öland.

Södertälje ❹, on the E4, profited from the opening of the **Södertälje Canal** in 1819 and became an industrial city. The engine plant for SAAB has become the largest employer here. At **Mount Torekäll**, in the open-air museum, the visitor is treated to museums dedicated to photography, automobiles and fire-fighting. In Södertälje, the E20 branches off from the E4 and leads westward along the southern shores of Lake Mälaren crossing through Södermanland.

As a prelude to a whole series of interesting tourist sites, you can visit the old stone church from the 12th century at **Turinge** (driving from Södertälje, on the right-hand side of the E20). In the 17th century, a burial chapel for the field marshal Erik Dahlberg was added. He was a sensitive artist who created a multitude of drawings. In the chapel, numerous reproductions of his work are on display. The country estate of **Taxinge Näsby** (also to the right of the E20) boasts a large park, where the English, French and Italian sections compete for attention.

Around Lake Mälaren

**GRIPSHOLM
Tucholsky's Dream Castle

In **Läggesta**, the road to **Mariefred** ❺ branches off from the E20 in a northeasterly direction and leads to ****Gripsholm slott**. As an alternative to driving, you can also board a historical narrow-gauged train to Mariefred.

Kurt Tucholsky's novel *Gripsholm Castle: A Summer Story* brought worldwide fame to the castle. When the German author published his novel after a two-year stay in Mariefred, he had no idea that it would become his most successful work. In 1933, the critical journalist was banned by the Nazis from further publication; Tucholsky went into exile, eventually ending up in the Swedish town of Hindas near Gothenburg. Ruined both physically and mentally, the author took

Above: Reliving the past on a trip to Mariefred aboard the museum's narrow-gauge train.
Right: Gripsholm Castle attracts a great many visitors.

his own life there. "Fröken" Gertrude Meyer had his body interred in the cemetery in Mariefred, north of the church. "Everything transitory is only a parable" is inscribed on his tombstone which rests beneath an old oak tree.

Gripsholm Castle dates back to the 14th century. The Lord High Chancellor Bo Jonsson had the castle built in Stockholm's back country to provide refuge in an emergency. He named the castle after the eagle on his coat of arms (*grip*, or bird of prey) and the island (*holm*), the future site of the castle. The epithet was a double entendre, since for the construction costs the royal treasury fell prey to Bo Jonsson and suffered greatly. After a fire, the castle was donated to the newly founded Carthusian monastery of Pax Mariä (*Mariefred*, or Mary's Peace) in 1493. After the Reformation, Gustavus Vasa confiscated the property. The castle was then given it's characteristic appearance: four majestic towers (with living quarters enclosed in between) rest on a wall up to four meters thick. Gustavus Vasa died be-

fore completion. His sons Erik and John took turns playing jailer and prisoner at the castle, though not for fun. The two cannons flanking the **main gate** are trophies of war John III brought from Russia and bear the names "Sow" and "Boar."

Charles IX had the main castle remodeled in the Renaissance style and had the outer section incorporated into the castle itself. Around 1690, the **Queen's Wing** was added to the northern section; from then on, the castle served as residence for a number of widowed queens. Quarters for the servants were established in the outer section, and the so-called **Gentleman's Wing** was the guest house.

In 1773, Gustavus III took possession of the castle and, as a lover of the fine arts, had a **theater** built in one of the towers. The real reason for the addition, joked Tucholsky, was as a deterrent to boredom during times of siege. The theater is in good condition and could be used even today. Plans for elaborate Baroque interior decoration – partially conceived by the king himself – have also remained.

Charles XIV, the first Bernadotte to rule in Sweden (1818-1844), established a collection of portraits that led to the castle being given the nickname "Sweden's Pantheon." Since that time, the collection has expanded greatly and presently includes more than 3,500 portraits of prominent Swedish notables and is spread throughout all the rooms open to visitors. For those who have not intensively studied Swedish history, most of the names will be meaningless: "Gustavus the Constipated" and "Adolphus the Unshaven" quipped Tucholsky irreverently. The castle is now part of the Swedish National Museum.

To get the best impression of the unique setting of the castle, we recommend taking a walk around the entire enclosure on the outside, or else admire the view from Mariefred. The most stylish approach, however, is aboard the ferry from Stockholm. On beautiful days, the towers appear to truly shoot into the blue skies, as you can read in the novel *Gripsholm Castle*.

Southwest of Lake Mälaren

In ***Strängnäs ❻**, 11 kilometers to the west, spans the only auto route over Lake Mälaren. The earlier *ting* was the scene of the assembly that voted Gustavus Vasa to be King of Sweden in 1523. The buildings of the city are grouped picturesquely around a hill, where the ***Domkyrkan** towers above it all. Sanctified in 1291, this house of God was originally a brick church with two aisles ending abruptly at the choir. In the centuries to follow it was often remodeled. After the Reformation, the side chapels were converted to royal **burial chapels**. Sten Sture, who led the revolt against the Danes and prepared the way for Gustavus Vasa to gain the throne, is buried here. Gustavus Vasa's youngest son, Charles IX, ordered a tomb to be erected for himself 15 years before his

Above: A 13th-century statue of the Virgin Mary (Strängnäs Cathedral). Right: Strängnäs – the cathedral by night reflected in Lake Mälaren.

death. The church's reputation as the most beautiful in Sweden stems from the impressive medieval frescoes decorating the nave and choir. The **High Altar**, a 15th-century work from Brussels, is Sweden's largest triptych; when the wings are opened, the seven stations of the Passion of Christ are unfolded; when closed, the story of Christmas is presented.

East of Strängnäser Cathedral, you will find the residence of Bishop Kort Rogge, the 15th-century **Roggeborg** that Gustavus Vasa had converted into a secondary school. Today the building is used as a book depository for the Royal Library.

The church in **Jäder**, en route to Eskilstuna, contains the crypt of the formerly influential Oxenstierna family.

West of Jäder, a byroad leads to **Sundbyholm Castle**, once the main building of a monastery of the Knights of St. John. Not far from here, you will find the **Sigurdsristning**, Sigurd's Pillar from the Viking Age (11th century). The runes inscribed on the stone memorialize a deceased nobleman; a drawing details Sigurd's battle with a dragon, a recurring theme that can also be found in the *Nibelungenlied*.

*Eskilstuna ❼ was created when the twin cities of Tuna and Fors – located on opposite banks of the Tunaån River – merged. The city took its name from Saint Eskil, who was buried here after suffering a martyr's death. In the 17th century, Charles X lured the renowned Latvian metal craftsman Reinhold Rademacher to the city by offering him special privileges, so that Rademacher could lend assistance and give the small metal-working businesses a boost. The **Rademachersmedjorna** (Rademacher Smithies) began producing quality knives, locks and other metal products. Of these, 20 smithies have survived; some are now homes, while others are still in operation and welcome visitors.

The sarcophagi from the Viking Age, with their unusual high-gabled covers,

Around Lake Mälaren

were named after the city where they were first discovered, Eskilstuna. Since then, over 60 of these Eskilstuna-coffins have been located. The suburb of **Torshälla** has also been absorbed by city; the name stems from an ancient sacrificial site dedicated to the god Thor. In the Middle Ages, Torshälla was a trading center for goods being transported between Stockholm and Örebro. Later the function was taken over by Eskilstuna. To the south or east of Eskilstuna, you can meet up with the **Sörmlandsleden**, an 825-kilometer-long round-trip trekking trail.

The Land of the Westmen

Residents of **Köping ❽** to the extreme west of Lake Mälaren are renowned throughout Sweden for being taciturn. The name of the city gives evidence to the charge: simply *Köping* (marketplace) without a single embellishment, such as *Ny-*, *En-* or *Jön-*. Köping's most famous inhabitant was the pharmacist Carl Wilhelm Scheele, who came here from Stralsund in 1775. Early on, he devoted himself to chemical experimentation and discovered, for example, oxygen, nitrogen and glycerine. He was also the first scientist to isolate chlorine in its pure form. A pharmacy has been dedicated to him in the **open-air museum**.

Västmanland takes in 9,000 square kilometers, and the landscape is divided into two distinct regions: the southern lowlands lay just 40 meters above sea level and include fertile farmland as well as industrial areas; in contrast, the northern hills are blanketed with forests and boast elevations up to 400 meters. The mountain chain is a part of the so-called *Bergslagen*, the mining belt of Sweden, which stretches from Västmanland through Närke and Värmland before reaching Dalarna.

Sweden's Mountains of Ore: Bergslagen

Iron ore mining and processing has a 2,000-year history in Sweden. At the be-

ginning, iron was extracted from bog ore, where iron deposits separate from iron-rich water near the earth's surface. In the Middle Ages, men followed the water to the source and began mining the ore there. Timber from the Swedish forests was used as the energy source to smelt the iron; huge bellows to keep the fire burning at the necessary temperature were driven by water power.

Iron production was the backbone of Swedish politics in the manufacturing of weapons, without which all dreams of conquest could only be illusion. From its beginning, mining in Sweden enjoyed the special protection of the king and was supported with special privileges. The landowners were allowed to form production collectives. Guaranteed prices were paid for the finished products, and practically unrestricted use of the forests and

rivers was granted. The mine worker, however, suffered under extreme repression. There was even a special judicial system governing miners; it is reported that some cases resulted in capital punishment verdicts. In short, the *bruksamhäller* (metalurgical communities) were autonomous; their members were even exempt from military service. In the late Middle Ages, a shortage of manpower led the Swedes to first enlist workers from the Finns living in the eastern Swedish provinces, later turning to German and Belgian mining experts who brought along their own mining teams. Also foreign capital – especially from Lübeck – flowed into the country and enabled the further development of mining and smelting. In the 16th and 17th centuries, the iron industry had grown so quickly, resulting in a scarcity of wood, that Finnish miners, who had turned to farming for extra income, were banned from using the slash and burn method to clear land.

To solve the problem of transportation, the **Strömsholms Canal** was constructed

Above: Iron-ore mining in Bergslagen – once the foundation for Sweden's power in Europe. Right: Gustavus I Vasa – elected as the first Swedish monarch in Västerås (1544).

between 1777 and 1795 to connect **Strömsholm** (20 kilometers east of Köping; interesting castle with stables) and **Smedjebacken** (Route 66, 100 kilometers northwest of Strömsholm). The canal was acclaimed as a technical feat: only 12 kilometers of canal had to be dug, and only 26 locks built – the rest of the 120-kilometer-long waterway incorporated natural waters. Years later, the Strömsholms Canal lost its function as a means of transportation for industry; now only pleasure craft ply its waters. In summer, the *Strömsund* cruises the entire length of the canal in just three days.

The smelting works and mines of Bergslagen have long since been abandoned. A few factories continued production until the middle of the 20th century – for example, the plants at **Hallstahammar** and **Surahammar** manufactured track as well as wheels for railway vehicles until after World War II.

*VÄSTERÅS
The City of the Reformation

*Västerås ❾ is the provincial capital of Västmanland. From early on, the city was the spiritual center of the region: in 1120 it became an Episcopal see; it was also home to a number of cloisters. In one of these, the Dominican monastery, the most momentous meeting of parliament to go down in Swedish history took place in 1527. The passing of the *Västerås Recess* set the Reformation in motion by granting the king the right to confiscate church property – sweet relief for the pitiful condition of the state treasury. Another meeting of parliament established the monarchy in Sweden in 1544.

Västerås remained a small, sleepy rural town with 12,000 inhabitants until the end of the 19th century, but with the onset of industrialization, electric companies and ball-bearing manufacturers settled here; the population really began to explode and has since increased tenfold.

As the land mass rose over the centuries, the estuary of the **Svartån** moved increasingly closer to Lake Mälaren, and after every major fire the city was rebuilt accordingly, moving the harbor away from the original settlement. This explains why the medieval town center now lies on the northern edge of the downtown area. This section of Västerås, called **Kyrkbacka**, offers a small-town flair that invites the visitor for a walking tour.

Aside from the modern hotel high-rise, the central building is the ***Domkyrkan** south of Kyrkbacka. In the 12th century, a small fieldstone church stood here on the site of this 16th-century, four-aisled brick basilica. Nicodemus Tessin the Younger raised the steeple to a height of 102 meters. Entering the cathedral, be sure to notice the Flemish high altar from the 15th century and two conspicuous tombs near the choir. One of these is a monument carved from marble and alabaster in 1635 to honor Marshal Magnus Brahe, a nephew of the great astronomer. The tomb of King Erik XIV made of Carrara

Around Lake Mälaren

marble was erected 200 years after his death through a donation by Gustavus III. Erik's first place of rest must have been considerably more humble, since he was known to have participated in a number of bloody deeds and probably died of poisoning – at the hands of his brother John III, next in line for the throne.

Sweden's oldest secondary school was founded in Västerås by the Protestant bishop Rudbeckius in the 17th century. A monument to this man is located in front of the cathedral.

The new **Rådhuset**, completed in 1959, with a 65-meter-high tower and Scandinavia's largest glockenspiel, can be seen on the modern Stortorget, south of the cathedral. Next door, the former city hall houses the **Konstmuseet**.

As a modern city, Västerås employs an ingenious district heating system that not only supplies apartments and public buildings with heat, but also delivers process heating to industry, which saves the city skyline from being spoiled with the usual factory smokestacks.

Around Västerås

"Cucumber City" was the name given to Västerås in the 19th century, when cucumbers grown in the area were processed here into pickles and gherkins. "Cucumber Country" offers a number of attractive excursions.

The burial grounds of *Anundshögen are located east of Västerås near **Badelunda**. The largest burial mound, 10 meters high and 60 meters in circumference, provides a panorama over the neighboring mounds, stone settings and five large constructions laid out in the form of ships. It is speculated that the site was created near the end of the early Iron Age, about A.D. 500.

Right: Bronze stamp used to decorate helmets during the Vendel Age (found in Uppland).

On the banks of Lake Mälaren, 25 kilometers east of Västerås, you will find **Ängsö slott**, which is regarded as one of the most beautiful Rococo castles in Sweden. The frescoes in the little Gothic chapel were painted before the Black Death of 1348-50.

Just 10 kilometers west of Västerås, a byroad branches off from the southbound E18 and leads to **Tidö slott**. In 1625, Prime Minister Axel Oxenstierna ordered the castle to be meticulously built in the Renaissance style. Many rooms still contain period furniture, other rooms accommodate a collection of toys, including those once owned by the present king.

SALA
Silver City of the Old World

Precious metal is the topic of discussion when it comes to the city of **Sala ❿** in Bergslagen (Route 67, 35 kilometers north of Västerås). Rich deposits of silver were mined here beginning in the Middle Ages. Up until the discovery of America, Sala's mines had the reputation for being the most productive in the Old World. John III described Sala as the "death mines" of his kingdom; he was referring to the numerous convicts and prisoners of war sentenced to serve as laborers here. His younger brother, Charles IX, held a different view of the city which he called "the kingdom's gem."

The mining village of **Gruvbyn** is open to visitors; a small museum here documents the history of its mines. The **Landsförsamlings kyrka** is also worth visiting: a house of worship where provincial politics are also discussed. The church was erected in the 13th and 14th centuries, even before the city's founding. The frescoes from the late Middle Ages are well preserved. For the active tourist, Sala also has a lot to offer: hiking trails, quiet camping spots in the middle of the wilderness, fishing on numerous lakes, and sports such as golf and tennis.

The Land That Rose From the Water: Uppland

Geologically, **Uppland** is a very young region. Around the time of Christ, the entire area consisted of an extensive archipelago that slowly began to rise. The process was so far along at the end of the Iron Age that solid ground connections had formed between the islands, making inhabitation possible. Waterways must have been the main links between the settlements in the "Vendel Age" (A.D. 500-800). Not until the Middle Ages had the land risen enough to allow roads and bridges to be built. Many inscriptions on the over 1,000 rune stones found in here describe such building projects. Today, the countryside is flat – only the former rocky isles appear as hills – up to 75 meters high. The fertile ground between the hills was used as farmland during the Viking Age, a function it still retains.

Much nicer than scientific fact is the saga concerning the origin of Uppland, as also narrated by Selma Lagerlöf in *Nils Holgersson*. According to the tale, Uppland began as the poorest region in Sweden. This caused it great shame, so it left on a journey as a beggar. It received a small donation wherever it went: woods, boulders, rivers and farmland. Upon returning home, it arranged the meager alms so cleverly that even the king wanted to live in this lovely countryside.

It is true that all of the early Swedish kings resided in Uppland. Birka, on an island in Lake Mälaren, was one of the major cities of the Svear Empire, and later of the Vikings. Another capital was established in (Old) Uppsala, where the Christian kings of the Middle Ages resided. Soon they had the Bishop of Sigtuna join them and elevated him to archbishop. However, the archbishop moved to the more favorably situated modern Uppsala; and the kings moved their residence to the newer city of Stockholm.

If you count Stockholm as a part of Uppland, to which it historically belongs, then this province is indeed the richest cultural region in Sweden.

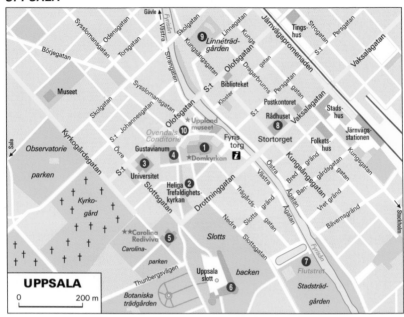

UPPSALA

Because Old Uppsala was inconveniently cut off from the major traffic routes in the country – it had no connection to the existing waterways – the king and the archbishop decided to move their residences in 1273. The archbishop chose a trading center not far away called *Östra Aros* (East Estuary) – as opposed to *Västra Aros* (Västerås), located 70 kilometers to the west, for the new Episcopal see, and just took *Uppsala* from Old Uppsala to name his city. The rising of the land had created a waterfall on the Fyrisån River, which meant that all goods transported inland on the river had to be unloaded and reloaded here, a lucrative opportunity for the development of a city.

Across from the river harbor, on the west bank of the Fyrisån, a hill was selected as the new location for the arch-

Right: From wherever you are, the towers of Uppsala's cathedral direct the way to the center of the city.

bishop's church; it is where a Stone Age settlement, and later in pre-Christian time an important *ting,* had been. The construction of the cathedral drew craftsmen to the city, and the "new" **Uppsala** ⓫ began to flourish. The founding of the university in 1477 provided additional momentum to the city's development. When university professors were granted independent, secular rights in the 16th century, the university became a kind of a city within a city, causing tension and feuding between the institution and the regular citizenry.

In 1702, Uppsala burned to the ground, and the cathedral was also heavily damaged. It took until the mid-18th century for the city to recover from the disaster; construction then recommenced. At this time, the stately stone residences of the professors were built, while most of the humble abodes of the populace were wooden dwellings with sod roofs. Great men of the natural sciences, above all Carl von Linné and Anders Celsius, brought worldwide fame to the univer-

sity. Despite the renown of its university, Uppsala remained a small city, with only 8,000 inhabitants, up to the mid-19th century. Not until the completion of the railway line to Stockholm in 1866 did the city radically change. Industry began to settle here, and the population increased to the current 170,000 – including 20,000 students. Although only the fourth-largest in Sweden, the university is probably the best and most famous in all of Scandinavia; without a doubt, you can even say it is an elite institution. The old university buildings and the cathedral join to mark the heart of the city: this is the logical place to begin a walking tour.

The Coronation Church

The cathedral's transept and choir belong to the "French" construction phase, so called because 13th-century French architects conceived the design, employing sandstone, a rare building material for Sweden. In the 14th century, German architects continued construction using brick. In 1435, the **★Domkyrkan ❶** was consecrated, 50 years after the two front towers were completed. From 1885 to 1893, Hugo Zettervall painstakingly oversaw the restoration of the cathedral, while remembering the original plans and the French precursors, and he had the towers extended to a height of 118 meters. The Neo-Gothic elements are so dominant now that the 800-year history of the cathedral is hardly apparent. The church remains practically unadorned, aside from the doors themselves: the north portal displays St. Olav and the Adoration of the Shepherds; the south portal centers on St. Lawrence, surrounded by prophets and saints. The side doors hail back to the 14th century. The west facade, a redesign of the 19th century, is graced with a statue of Erik IX, a national hero. He is said to have been killed by a Danish prince on the steps of the cathedral. On the south side of the building a number of rune stones have been erected; these were discovered under the floor of the cathedral during restoration.

Inside, the commanding high-vaulted ceiling (27 meters) of the two-aisled basilica evokes a feeling of simplicity. The vault of the center tower is called the "King's Vault" because beneath it, between 1441 and 1719, the Swedish kings took their oath of office before being crowned by the archbishop.

The central chapel of the choir, once dedicated to the Virgin Mary, was converted to the tomb of Gustavus Vasa who rests here with both of his Protestant wives (there were three wives in all). His Renaissance-style tomb, made in Holland of Carrara marble in 1590, is a replica of the ornamental coach which took their remains to Uppsala from Stockholm, where they had formerly been interred. The Vasa Chapel was decorated in the 19th century with seven frescoes depicting the major events in the life of the king.

Above: Flower vendors liven up the Östra Ågatan in Uppsala. Right: Enjoying the sunshine during a break between classes – in front of the university library.

In a neighboring chapel Saint Erik, who, by the way, was never officially canonized, and St. Birgitta's father are buried. The adjoining chapel recalls the murder of Sten Sture and his sons, put to death by Erik XIV. In the third one, the Polish wife of John III, Katharina Jagellonica, found her final resting place.

The former St. Andrew's Chapel in the south part of the choir is where Gustavus II Adolphus' chancellor and friend Axel Oxenstierna found his interment – the greatest posthumous honor the king could bestow. The relief work on the columns of the choir depicting vices and virtues are interesting. Tessin the Younger designed the Baroque pulpit in the nave. A simple stone table serves as the altar; above it hangs a modern silver crucifix and polished rock crystal created by Bertil Berggren in 1976. In the north aisle, near the main entry, the mystic Emanuel Swedenborg is interred; nearby an epitaph honors Carl von Linné.

Just adjacent to the cathedral you will find the **Heliga Trefaldighetskyrkan** ❷

(Church of the Holy Trinity), Uppsala's 14th-century city church.

Across from the church is an 18th-century palace: the residence of Uppsala's Protestant archbishop.

The Stronghold of Education

Founded as a Catholic seminary, the **University** ③ was relieved of the supervision of the Church by the Reformation, and a chancellor was appointed as overseer. Gustavus II Adolphus and his successors granted numerous farmsteads and mills to the institution to assure its independence. Even today, the University of Uppsala is one of the biggest landholders in Sweden.

The **Gustavianum** ④, donated to the university by Gustavus II Adolphus in 1623, is located opposite the main entrance to the cathedral. It is one of the few municipal buildings that survived the great fire of 1702 unscathed. In 1662, Olov Rudbeck supervised the installation of the *Theatrum Anatomicum*, after he had inspected the architecture of such anatomical lecture halls throughout Europe. The bodies were dissected on a simple table in the middle of a circular room, while students followed the procedures from steeply ascending rows with high balustrades. Although some of the students surely became ill during demonstrations, the balustrades prevented falls. The Gustavianum also houses the three archeological museums of the university – displaying Egyptian, Classical and Scandinavian antiquities.

The University Library, ****Carolina Rediviva** ⑤, is located near the Church of the Holy Trinity and contains a copy of every book ever printed in Sweden. The original collection was taken from monastery libraries and presented as an endowment from Gustavus II Adolphus. The current inventory consists of two million volumes and 30,000 hand-written manuscripts. A few of the precious gems of this collection include the so-called ****Silver Bible** (*Codex Argenteus*) from the 6th century, the oldest existing **Edda**

Manuscript, the *Codex Uppsaliensis*, a 13th-century work from Iceland, and the *Carta Marina*, **Olaus Magnus' Map of Scandinavia** (1539). These priceless works are on display in a small museum on the ground floor.

Gustavus Vasa planned the **Uppsala slott 6**, southeast of the library, as a fortress retreat for the city's inhabitants – the large courtyard attests to the castle's original purpose. The structure has undergone a number of renovations and today houses the provincial administration offices; only the **Art Museum** and the **Royal Hall** are open to the public. In this room in 1654, Queen Christina abdicated the throne to embrace Catholicism.

Located directly at the castle's entrance, the Gunilla Bell traditionally rings in springtime on Walpurgis Eve. The ceremony begins in front of the library with a speech by the university's president officially welcoming the coming of spring.

Above: Carl von Linné, the only gardener who is also legal tender.

With full-throated song, the crowd surges from the castle to the **Flustret 7**, a favorite tavern for excursionists located in the city park at the foot of the castle. Here celebrations eventually reach a climax and, for many revelers, often end with a dip in a nearby lake to sober up.

Leaving the city park and heading in the direction of the cathedral and crossing **Västra Ågatan**, you will pass by the so-called *Nationen* houses, where the university fraternities and sororities find their quarters. As opposed to those in other European countries, these organizations serve an exclusively social purpose and are apolitical. If you cross the river via **Drottninggatan**, you will soon reach **Stortorget**, the center of the city and the 19th-century **Rådhuset 8** (City Hall). **Kungsängsgatan** leads from here to the ***Linné Trädgården 9** (Linné Garden, with the Linné Museum), the former botanical gardens of the university. In the 1930s, the park was laid out to demonstrate the classification system of plants as devised by Carl von Linné.

Via **Sankt Olofsgatan** you will reach **Sysslomansgatan**. At its southern end the **Ovendals Conditorie** ❿, another hub of student life with dusty charm and tasty baked goods, is a great place for a coffee break. The narrow Valvgatan branches off at St. Erik's torg. Through the passage of the house on the corner, the **Cathedral Staircase**, a stairway leads directly to the south side of the cathedral, thus completing the round-trip tour.

★Gamla Uppsala

Only five kilometers north of Uppsala lies the former metropolis of the Viking Empire: **★Gamla Uppsala** (Old Uppsala). Already from a distance four large hills catch the eye. From the parking lot, a footpath leading to the community church easily ascends to these elevations. The three hills to the left of the path, it is speculated, are the burial mounds of King Aun, his son Egil and his grandson Adil; the three rulers of the Svear Empire are said to have been interred here in the course of the 6th century. The few burial artifacts found during excavations are in Stockholm's Historical Museum. The fourth hill is suspected to have been a *ting* – one imagines that the Svear kings gathered here with their warriors to decide on important issues; you could call it "the cradle of Swedish Democracy."

A legendary holy grove of the Vikings supposedly once stood on the site of the present church. On this very spot the bishop of Sigtuna had his cathedral erected when he was given the title Archbishop of Sweden in 1164. The construction was more than twice the size of today's church, which was built from the stones of the original. Inside the church there are still the wooden 12th-century Episcopal throne and a pew from the same era; the two pieces are considered the oldest furniture in Sweden. Anders Celsius, the renowned 18th-century physicist, found his final resting place here.

Odinsburg is located near the parking lot; this modern restaurant with Viking-style interior décor stylishly serves a thin mead in a drinking horn.

★SIGTUNA

Just 10 kilometers south of Uppsala, east of the E4, you can visit Carl von Linné's villa: **★Hammarby** is still a Garden of Eden. Linné bought the grange in 1758 and had the main building erected where he sometimes also gave lectures. Today the house is a museum. On the ground floor, furniture and clothing from the 18th century are on display, and an adaptation of Linnés study is also open to inspection. The walls of the upper story are covered with reproductions of the drawings he made of a multitude of plant life. In an additional building left of the main house, a world map displays the numerous voyages Linné took during his research. The building to the right is a café.

The community of **★Sigtuna** ⓬ is halfway between Uppsala and Stockholm. The international airport, **Arlanda**, is within the communal area, while Sigtuna's city center lies 12 kilometers to the west. About 90 percent of the community's 30,000 inhabitants reside here.

Between the 10th and 12th centuries, Sigtuna was the most important city of the Svear Empire: King Olof Eriksson embraced the Christian faith here; the first Swedish coins were minted here; and the very first bishop of Sweden resided here while still under the jurisdiction of the archbishop of Bremen. In the 12th century, the city had five stone churches, which unfortunately, after an attack by Estonian pirates in 1187, were plundered and put to ruin. This first destructive act was followed by many others. Only the Church of Saint Mary remained, the city's main house of worship today. St. Mary's originally belonged to a Dominican monastery which was laid to waste during the Reformation. As a city con-

Around Lake Mälaren

cerned with education (a tradition begun at the monastery in the 14th century), Sigtuna has remained faithful. There are many parochial and state-run educational centers here, including the boarding school where the present king, Carl XVI Gustaf, received his associate's degree.

The General's Castle

Around 20 kilometers from Sigtuna on a peninsula in Lake Ekoln, the northern part of Lake Mälaren, looms the castle of ***Skokloster slott**. The former Cistercian cloister and its possessions were granted to the Von Wrangel family as a fief in the 17th century. Carl Gustav von Wrangel, a general who won fame and fortune during the Thirty Years' War, commissioned the architects Tessin the Elder and De Vallée to construct an ostentatious Baroque castle. The original plans were, however, never completely realized. In the several

Above: On Saturdays, crowds throng Sigtuna's main street.

rooms open to the public today there is still some of the original Baroque furniture, as well as a large collection of art and weapons acquired by Von Wrangel as spoils of war from all over Europe. The well-preserved cloister church served as the family crypt. A rune stone found in the church during one of the renovations is now on display between the castle and church. The cross engraved in the stone is from Christian times; the depictions from the 10th century.

Driving from Skokloster slott near Litslena on the E18, you will reach the next large town of **Enköping** ⑱ (ca. 35 kilometers). Of the city's heyday during the Middle Ages, only the **Vårfrukyrkan** (Church of Our Lady) remained after Enköping was repeatedly destroyed.

*Härkeberga, 10 kilometers northeast of Enköping, prizes its own jewel in the city church: in the 15th century, the Swedish church painter Albertus Pictor created his most impressive masterpiece; he covered the walls and vaults with lifelike representations of Bible stories.

NYKÖPING (☎ 0155)

ℹ️ Stora Torget, 61183 Nyköping, tel. 248200.

🛏️ 😊😊 **Blommenhof Hotell**, Blommenhovsvägen, tel. 202060, fax 268494. **Stadshotellet**, Västra Storgatan 15, tel. 269060, fax 269236. **Scandic Hotel Nyköping**, Gumsbacken, tel. 289000, fax 28305. 😊 **Stiftsgården Sjärholm**, tel. 222700, fax 223002. **Hotell Wiktoria**, Fruängsgatan 21, tel. 217580, fax 214447. **Vandrarhem Nyköpinghus**, tel. 211810, directly at the castle.

🏕️ **Strandstuvikens**, 9 km south of town, tel. 97810, with sand beach, 8 CABINS.

❌ **Värdshuset Stembrogården**, tel. 216738, beautifully located restaurant in manor house style.

🏛️ **Sankt Nicolai, Allhelgona Kyrka**, 6-10 am daily, except during services. **Castle** of Nyköping (tower museum), May 15-Sept 15, 10 am-5 pm daily, otherwise Wed-Sun 11 am-3 pm.

👪 **Nynäs slott**, June 20-Aug 15, 11 am-4 pm daily, with a café in the garden. **Tullgarn slott**, May 15-Sept 14, 12-4 pm daily.

🚣 CANOE ROUTE: On the Nyköpingsån, starting point Andebol on Route 55, info: tel. 0150-57241.

TROSA (☎ 0156)

ℹ️ Torget, 61900 Trosa, tel. 52222.

🛏️ 😊😊 **Bomans i Trosa**, Östra Hamnplan, tel. 13220, fax 13380, fantastic location at the harbor. **Trosa Stadshotell**, Västra Långgatan, tel. 17070, fax 16696.

🏕️ **Havsbadets Camping**, 3 km south on an island, tel. 12494.

❌ **Bomans Hotel**, good regional cuisine. **Café Garvagården**, Västra Långagtan 40, tel. 12220. Smörbröd and small dishes in an enchanting garden.

SÖDERTÄLJE (☎ 08)

ℹ️ Gamla Centralstation, 15189 Södertälje, tel. 55018899.

🛏️ 😊😊 **Park Hotell**, Saltsjötorget, tel. 55034000, fax 55035330. **Scandic Hotel Södertälje**, Verkstadvägen 7, tel. 55034260, fax 55087547. 😊 **Glashyttans Värdshus**, Torpavägen,tel. 55013310, fax 55013310. **Gästhemmet Karlsborg**, tel. 55031470, 55012351. **Vandrarhem Tvetagården**, Tvetavägen 35, tel. 0755-98025, reachable by bus 784 from the train station.

🏕️ **Farstanäs Camping**, 8 km south, on the sea, tel. 0755-50215.

🏛️ **Museen** at **Torekällberg**, June 1-Sept 15, Mon-Fri 10 am-5 pm, Sat-Sun/holidays 11 am-4 pm.

👪 **Church** of **Turinge** June-Aug 12-4 pm daily. Manor house of **Taxinge Näsby**, public park.

MARIEFRED (☎ 0159)

ℹ️ Rådhuset, 64700 Mariefred, tel. 29790.

🛏️ 😊😊 **Gripsholms Värdshus & Hotel**, Kyrkoplan 1, tel. 13020, fax 10974, traditional old building.

🏕️ **Mariefreds Camping**, on Lake Mälaren, tel. 10230.

🏛️ **Gripsholm slott**, May-Aug 10 am-4 pm daily, April and Sept Tue-Fri 10 am-3 pm and Sat-Sun 12-3 pm, Oct-March only Sat-Sun 12-3 pm.

🚢 BOAT: The steamer **Mariefred** runs May 15-Aug 31 daily between Stockholm and Mariefred. Departure from Stockholm (Stadhusbron) 10 am; departure from Mariefred 3 pm, tel. 08-698850 and 0159-10008.

🚂 The **Museum Train** operates from June to August between Läggesta and Mariefred, otherwise by appointment. Information from the tourist office.

STRÄNGNÄS (☎ 0152)

ℹ️ Järnvägsgatan 1, 64580 Strängnäs, tel. 29699.

🛏️ 😊😊 **Ulvhälls Herrgård**, Ulvhälla Allé, tel. 18680, 2 km before Strängnäs. 😊 **Hotell Laurentius**, Östra Strandvägen 12, tel. 10444, fax 10443. **Hotel Rogge AB**, Gyllenhjelmsgatan 20, tel. 13450, fax 18969.

🏕️ **Löt Camping**, on the E20, tel. 25237.

🏛️ **Domkyran**, 8:30 am-6 pm daily, except during services.

👪 **Church** of **Jäder**, 10 am-6 pm daily. **Sundbyholm slott**, today 😊😊😊 romantic hotel with a good restaurant, tel. 016-96500, you can ask to be shown the knights' hall. The **Sigurd Stone** is located in the immediate vicinity.

ESKILSTUNA (☎ 016)

ℹ️ Hamngatan 19, tel. 114500.

🛏️ 😊😊 **Hotell Smeden**, Drottninggatan 9, tel. 137690, fax 127527. **Stadshotellet Eskilstuna**, Hamngatan 9-11, tel. 137225, fax 127588. 😊 **Vilsta Sporthotell & STF Vandrarhem, Vilsta Camping**, tel. 513080, fax 513086.

❌ **Pilkrogs Värdshus**, Djurgården, tel. 132060 home-style fish and game.

🏛️ **Rademachermedjorna**, Rademacherg. 50, June-Aug Mon-Fri 10 am-noon and 1-4 pm, Sat-Sun 10 am-4 pm. **Eskilstuna Sarcophagi** in the **Museum of Local History**, Djurgården Park, May-Sept 11 am-4 pm.

🚌 BUS: To **Torshälla** from Stasjonen (train station).

🎣 FIGHING: In the Eskilstunaän, April-Oct Fri-Wed. Information from the tourist office.

Around Lake Mälaren

HALSTAHAMMAR (☎ 0220)

ℹ 73427 Halstahammar, tel. 24305.

▣ ⑤ Kolbäcks Gästgivaregård, south of Halstahammar, tel. 40360, also a good restaurant with a fabulous Smörgåsbord and a nice view.

⋒ Trågfors Forge Halstahammar, open upon arrangement with the tourist office. **Canal Museum**, June-Aug 11 am-3 pm.

⛴ Boat trips on the Strömsholm Canal, tel. 10011.

SURAHAMMAR (☎ 0220)

ℹ Ekängsvägen 5, 73522 Surahammar, tel. 39083, only June-August.

▣ ⑤⑤ Surahammars Herrgård, tel. 36220, fax 36221.

⋒ Brukmuseum (old railway wheel factory), May 28-Aug 14, daily 2 pm tours also in English.

⋔ Ängelsberg, complete blast furnace village with *CABINS* and vacation apartments. Tours: June 20-Aug 14, 12 and 2 pm daily, June 27-July 31 also 4 pm.

SALA (☎ 0224)

ℹ Norrmanska Gården, 73321 Sala, tel. 13145.

▣ ⑤⑤ BW-Statt Konferenshotell, Bråstagatan 4, tel. 13030, with restaurant. **⑤ Vandrarhem Sala**, Sofielund, Mellandammen, tel. 12730.

Ⓧ Sofilunds familjecamping, Mellandrammen, tel. 12730, June-Sept.

⋒ Grubyn, Museum, June 15-Sept 3, 10 am-5 pm daily, tours: tel. 19541.

VÄSTERÅS (☎ 021)

ℹ Stora Gatan 40, 72187 Västerås, tel. 103710.

▣ ⑤⑤ Hotell Arkad, Östermalmgatan 25, tel. 120480, fax 830050. **Hotel Edison**, Svalgången 1, tel. 303800, fax 303888. **SAS Radisson Plaza Hotel**, Karlsgatan 9, tel. 101010, fax 101091. **⑤ Klipper Hotel**, Kungsgatan 4, tel. 410000, fax 142670. **Hotel Raka Vägen**, Hallsta Gårdsgatan, tel. 300400, fax 300490. **Stadshotell**, Stora Torget, tel. 180240, fax 181012. *VACATION HOMES:* **Björnögården**, Björnö, tel. 26200, fax 26100.

YOUTH HOSTELS: **Vandrarhem Lövudden**, tel. 185230, fax 123036, 5 km south west of Västerås directly on Lake Mälaren, with sauna and tennis court.

Ⓧ Johanisberg Camping, tel. 140279.

☒ Acceptable restaurants in **Hotell Arkad, Stadshottelet** and **SAS Radisson Plaza**. Better restaurants out of town: **Hasslö Värdshus**, Flottiljegatan 73, tel.

0171-800935. **Nykvarns Gästgiveri**, Den Lyklinga Grisen, tel. 0171-442010, 20 km east of Västerås.

☖ Sky Bar, on the 24th floor of the SAS Radisson Plaza Hotel, offers a great view of the city, tel. 101091.

▩ Bronze Factory of Skultuna, 18 km north of Västerås, café and sales room, open May 1-Sept 30, Mon-Fri 10 am-6 pm, Sat-Sun 10 am-4 pm, tel. 75675.

⋒ Domkyrkan, 8 am-6 pm daily, except during services. **Art Museum**, Stora Torget, Mon-Fri 12-5 pm and Sat-Sun 1-4 pm.

⛴ Boat trips to the castles of **Ängsö**, **Tidö** and **Gripsholm**, tel. 189685. **Ängsö slott**, June-Aug 1-5 pm daily. **Tidö slott**, June-Aug Tue-Sun 12-5 pm, May and Sept only Sat-Sun 12-5 pm. **Anundshögen**, always open.

A large **historic market** is held annually on the last Sunday of August.

KÖPING (☎ 0221)

ℹ Barnhemsgatan 2, 73151 Köping, tel. 25655.

▣ ⑤⑤⑤ Kohlswa Herrgård, tel. 50900, fax 51180, 11 km west of Köping, former manor house, beautiful park. **⑤ Scheele Hotel**, Hultgrensgatan 10, tel. 18120, fax 10703.

YOUTH HOSTELS: **Vandrarhem Nygård**, Kristinelundvägen 4, tel. 25655.

Ⓧ Malmöns Camping, 6 km southeast of the city, tel. 24419, with *CABINS* and golf course.

☒ Kohlswa Herregård, tel. 50900, 20 km north of Köping, reservations a must, the restaurant is among Sweden's top 12.

⋒ Scheele Museet, 1-4 pm daily.

UPPSALA (☎ 018)

ℹ Fyristorget 8, 75310 Uppsala, tel. 7274800.

▣ ⑤⑤⑤ Hotell Gillet, Dragarbrunnsgatan 23, tel. 102000, fax 153360. **⑤⑤ Scandic Hotel Uppsala**, Gamla Uppsalagatan 50, tel. 200280, fax 261506. **Hotel Svava**, Bangårdsgatan 24, tel. 130030, fax 132230. **Provobis Hotel Uplandia**, Dragarbrunnsgatan 32, tel. 102160, fax 696132. **Hotell Linné**, Skolgatan 45, tel. 102000, fax 137597. **⑤ Basic Hotel**, Kungsgatan 27, tel. 4805000, fax 4805050. **Grand Hotel Hörnan**, Bangårdsgatan 1, tel. 139380, fax 139380. **Sunnersta Herrgård**, Sunnerstavägen 24, tel. 324220, fax 324220.

Ⓧ Fyrishivs Stugby & Camping, Idrottsgatan 2, tel. 248314, fax 248314, also rents *CABINS*. **Fyris Camping**, Gamla Uppsalagatan, tel. 232323, 30 *CABINS*. **Sunnerstra Camping**, tel. 276084, small family-orientated campground.

Pinos, Svartbäcksgatan 23, tel. 115010. **Wermlandskällare**, Nedre Slottgatan 2, tel. 135756. Fish and shellfish meals are particularly recommendable in both restaurants. **Domtrappkällaren**, St. Eriksgränd 15, tel. 130951, cellar restaurant in a medieval building. You can also eat well in the **Saluhallen** (market hall) at Fyristorg, stands with seating areas. **Restaurant Stallet**, in the Linné Hotel. **Restaurant Odinsborg**, tel. 323522, Mead served in horns and masses of Viking kitsch, also a "heathen" dinner.

CAFÉS: **Ofvendal's Conditorie**, Sysslomannsgatan 1, Uppsala's favorite student café.

Flustred, Munkgatan 13, often live music on weekends.

Arts and Crafts: Uppsala Hantkraft, Övre Slottsgatan 9, tel. 128617. **Ulva Kvarn**, with a café in a former mill 8 km north of Uppsala, tel. 322060, 10 am-5 pm daily.

Domkyrkan, 9 am-6 pm daily, except during services, tours: June 8-Aug 23, Mon-Sat 11 am, 1 and 3 pm (3 pm also in English), Sun 12:30 pm. **Dommuseum, Treasure Chamber**, May 11-Sept 27, Mon-Sat 10 am-5 pm, Sun 12:30-5 pm, tours Mon-Sat 12 and 2 pm. Otherwise Sun only 12:30-3 pm. **Trefaldighetskyrkan**, 9 am-6 pm daily, except during services. **Church Gamla Uppsala**, 9 am-6 pm daily, Sept-March 9 am-4 pm daily. **Gustavium Museum (Theatrum Anatomicum**, archeological museum), Sept 15-May 15, Wed and Fri 11 am-4 pm, tours at 12, 1 and 3 pm, Thu 11 am-9 pm, tours 12, 1, 3, 7 and 8 pm, Sat-Sun 11 am-4 pm, tours 12, 1 and 3 pm, May 16-Sept 14, 11 am-4 pm daily, Thu to 9 pm. **Carolina Rediviva** (university library), **museum**, June 27-Aug 15, Mon-Fri 10 am-6 pm, Sat 10 am-4 pm, May 31-Sept 20, also Sun 11 am-4 pm, otherwise Mon-Fri 9 am-8 pm. **Castle**, June 20-Aug 23, 11am-4 pm daily, tours in English 12 and 4 pm daily, Aug 10-23, 2 pm daily. **Linné Trädgården,** Svartbäcksgatan 27, May-Aug 9 am-9 pm daily, Sept 9am-7 pm daily. **Linné Museum** (residence in the garden), May 30-Aug 30, Tue-Sun 12-4 pm, May 16 -24 and Sept 5-13, Sat-Sun only 12-4 pm. **Linnés Hammarby**, 12 km south of Uppsala, May 2-Sept 13, park 10 am-8 pm daily, museum and café Tue-Sun 12-4 pm.

TRAIN: To **Stockholm** every 30 minutes.

BUS: To **Gamla Uppsala** by lines 2, 20, 24 and 54 from the center of Uppsala, as well as **Linnés Hammarby** with line 882. Line 49 runs several times daily via **Sala** to **Mora**. Connections to **Kiruna** twice daily.

PLANE: The international **Arlanda Airport** is located 2 km south of Uppsala.

Nature hikes with high school teacher G. Olsson, June 28-Aug 30, Sun noon from the East Train Station (Uppsala Östra), return 6 pm, tel. 0171-21210 or 20779.

FISHING: At **Lake Ekoln**, June 15-Aug 15 by arrangement, tel. 081-221711.

CANOEING: On the **Fyrisån** into the heart of Uppsala, 48-km route. Rentals: **Fjällnora Friluftsområde**, tel. 363444. **Friluftsfrämjandet Uppsala**, Sunnerstastugan, Sunnersta, tel. 276086.

BICYCLE RENTAL: **Cykelstället Uppsala**, Svartbäcksgatan 20, tel. 138740.

NOSTALGIC TOUR: Trips to **Linnés Hammarby** or **Skokloster** by narrow-gauge railway, vintage bus and the steamer M/S Enköping: June 7-Aug 30 Sun only, July 21-26 daily, tel. 121230 or 274800.

SIGTUNA (☎ 08)

Stora Gatan 33, 19322 Sigtuna, tel. 59251447.

Ansgarsliden, Manfred Björkquists Allé 12, tel. 59258200, fax 59258384. **Kristina Hotell & Konferens AB**, Rektor Cullbergs Väg 1, tel. 59256020, fax 59250056. **Sigtuna Stadshotell**, Stora Nygatan 3, tel. 59250100, fax 59251587. **Stora Brännbo**, Stora Brännbovägen 2, tel. 59250105, fax 59255319.

Amandas Krog, Långgränd 7, tel. 59250024. **Båthuset Krog & Bar**, beach promenade, tel. 59256780. **Kopparkitteln**, Stora Gatan 31, tel. 59251095. **Plantagenet Restaurang & Pizzeria**, Stora Gatan 34, tel. 59251700.

CAFÉS: **Tant Brun**, Laurentil Gränd 3, tel. 59250934. **Café Monet**, Strandvägen 36, tel. 59251429. **Våffelbruket**, Sigtuna Hamn, tel. 59250800.

Galleri Trekanten, Stora Gatan 33, tel. 070-8280955, paintings, sculptures. **Gröna Lyktan Antikhandel**, Stora Gatan 35, tel. 59251977, antiques. **Sigtuna Kulturgård**, Stora Nygatan 1, tel. 59251508, arts and crafts, café. **Sigtuna Krukmakeri**, Laurentigränd 7, tel. 59251502, nice jugs and pots.

The **church ruins** can be viewed at any time. **Sankta Maria kyrka**, 9 am-6 pm daily, except during services.

Skokloster, May 1-Sept 15, 11 am-4 pm daily, tours every full hour. **Church**, May 1-Sept 15, 11 am-5 pm daily, tours with advance registration, tel. 018-366077, café, same times as above.

Skokloster Camping, tel. 018-386035, fax 386096.

FISHING: **Fyrväppelings Sportfiske**, camp for sport fishing, daily 7 am-9 pm, tel. 0174-60042.

BUS: Hourly to **Stockholm** and **Uppsala**, to **Skokloster** Tue-Thu and Sat-Sun only at 3 pm (return 5 pm).

BOAT: To Stockholm 4:55 pm daily.

STOCKHOLM – THE METROPOLIS OF THE NORTH

GAMLA STAN
CENTRAL NORRMALM
THE ZOO ISLAND
ISLANDS OF LAKE MÄLAREN
IN THE GARDEN OF SKERRIES

**STOCKHOLM
The Rise of a Capital

"Stockholm is made of stone and water" – so concise and terse was a description of the capital of Sweden in a 19th-century travel guide. The bedrock foundation of the city's 14 islands is hardly noticeable due to the developed areas; but it seems more as if the districts were literally floating on water. When describing Stockholm, a shallow comparison is often made to the Italian lagoon city of Venice, but this is inaccurate because the specifically Nordic element is not taken into account. The extreme contrast between light summers and dark winters creates a special atmosphere which seemingly gives the city two completely different faces: the one a bright and cheerful metropolis, the other cold and gloomy urban sprawl.

There are no written records of the early history of **Stockholm**. The story goes that Stockholm was founded by the dwellers of the pillaged settlement of Sigtuna in the 12th century, who had escaped from their devastated city on logs

Preceding pages: View of Riddarholmen with Birger Jarl Torn, a remnant of the city's old defensive wall. Left: Pastel-colored houses on Västerlånggatan, Gamla Stan.

only to be stranded on an island. Although this story offers a graphic explanation for the city's name – since *stock* and *holm* mean log and isle respectively – it lacks documentation.

Up until recorded history, the archipelago and the islands of the city had gradually risen so much that the sea level of Lake Mälaren stood considerably higher than that of the Baltic Sea. This meant the lake's water was forced to overcome the developing narrows between the increasingly higher emerging islands, resulting in rapids. The medieval trading centers on Lake Mälaren, such as Strängnäs and Sigtuna, had no choice but to load and unload goods at dangerous places to continue trade with the Baltic Sea. It was such a settlement that Birger Jarl described in a letter in 1252; it is considered to be the first written mention of Stockholm. The founding year of the city is regarded as 1252, and Birger Jarl can take credit for founding the city.

The earliest settlement was located on the island of Helgeandsholmen, the present site of the House of Parliament, and was probably protected by a small fortress and watchtower. The trading community grew – rapidly reaching its natural boundaries and then spreading over to the neighboring island of Stadsholmen. A larger fortress was built here at the end of

Stockholm

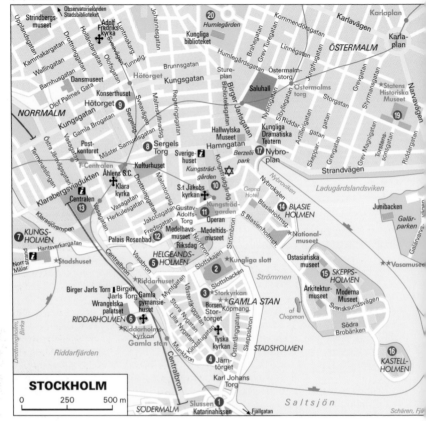

STOCKHOLM

0   250   500 m

the 13th century and named after the union of the three Swedish kingdoms: Svealand, Norrland and Götaland, or *Tre Kronor* (The Three Crowns). The name indicates that these grounds were a king's residence, although Stockholm was not granted a charter as a capital city until the year 1436.

The continuing historic development of the Swedish capital coincides with the rest of the country. As long as the Hanseatic League stifled the country economically, Stockholm also suffered from decisions made by the German merchants, who, in the meantime, had provided half the members of parliament. Whenever Denmark and Sweden wrangled for supremacy in the Kalmar Union,

Stockholm was either besieged, as it was in 1471, or it resulted in mass executions, such as the infamous "Stockholm Bloodbath" of 1520.

Not until Gustavus Vasa's triumphant march into the capital in 1523 can anything be said about continual development, which, in this period of great power and influence, made Stockholm the undisputed capital of the kingdom and allowed its population to increase to 60,000. Two devastating fires, in 1625 and 1697, destroyed the city and fortress. For the reconstruction of Stockholm an ordinance was enacted allowing only the construction of stone houses.

The industrial revolution in Sweden began during the Bernadotte Dynasty.

vate them and to restore them to their former glory. Today, Gamla Stan is a popular and an expensive residential district best explored on foot. Otherwise, the *Tunnelbana* (subway) is the best mode of transportation, which, due to each station's artistic design, is referred to as the longest art gallery in the world. The *Stockholmkortet* is a good-value ticket valid for the subway, buses and entrance to many of the city's museums.

★★GAMLA STAN

★★Gamla Stan, the "Old Town," is what locals call the three downtown islands at the crossing from the Baltic Sea to Lake Mälaren. **Helgeandsholmen**, **Stadsholmen** and **Riddarholmen** are connected by many bridges, hence the epithet *Staden mellan broarna* (City between the Bridges).

Representative buildings of the government and the nobility dominate on Helgeandsholmen and Riddarholmen, while the narrow alleys of Stadsholmen are characterized by middle-class homes. **Skeppsbron** and **Munkbron**, the streets along the outer edges of Stadsholmen, keep the heavy traffic out of the Old Town. Both were built on the former harbor grounds as one can clearly see by the old storehouses with loading cranes. A multitude of narrow alleyways lead from here to the inner part of the island, where Västerlånggatan and Österlånggatan form the north-south connection. The labyrinth of alleys, interior courtyards, passageways and stairs is the heart and soul of Stockholm today. Countless bars, restaurants, boutiques and galleries are ready to please their customers, and the many street musicians and entertainers provide the quarter with an international character.

You can get to the Old Town by going north from the **Slussen ①** subway station (named after the sluice built between Lake Mälaren and the Baltic Sea in

Factories and residential areas were built on Södermalm, Kungsholm and Norrmalm after some of the waterways between the islands were filled in to gain additional land for development. A sewage system and water pipes for fresh water were finally installed in the middle of the 19th century, which enabled the city to get the regularly occurring epidemics under control. The railway to Malmö was built, and Stockholm received its first streetcar and street lights.

Fortunately, one of the building projects of the 19th century turned out to be too expensive: a plan to tear down the buildings in the Old Town and replace them with modern constructions. It was then left up to the 20th century to reno-

Stockholm

1936), first to **Karl Johans Torg**, where there is an equestrian statue commemorating the first king of the Bernadotte Dynasty. The Skeppsbron begins here, with its old merchants' homes from the 17th and 18th centuries clearly showing signs of the land mass having continually been lifted. After 500 meters or so you come to the statue of Gustavus III, which the citizens of Stockholm had erected to memorialize the artistic king; it stood at the staircase of the palace until 1808.

The Royal Palace

The dominant building of the Old Town is *****Kungliga slott** ➋, the Royal Palace. Although the monumental palace has a surprisingly uniform appearance, it is actually a result of a host of compromises: during construction, previous

Above: Changing of the guards – a treasured event at the Royal Palace. Right: The Storkyrkan – the most beautiful example of Swedish Gothic.

building remnants had to be taken into account, there were construction delays due to a fire in 1697 and a lack of funds in the 18th century. Built around a large courtyard, the four-winged Baroque building, inspired by Italian exemplars, developed from a 13th-century fortress. Since the terrain drops off on the north and east sides, stairs were chosen for the entrances; the representative staircase on the east side was reserved for official visitors and the king. The south side (facing Slottsbacken) and the west side have ground-level entrances. The east side of the palace consisted of two smaller wings separated by a garden; such a design was impossible to construct on the west, where the Storkyrkan stood in the way. For this reason, the palace was completed with a semicircular, arched walkway, which, together with the west facade, forms the courtyard where the changing-of-the-guard ceremony takes place at 12 o'clock every day.

Boasting over 608 rooms, it is the world's largest palace in use today. It

Stockholm

serves exclusively as a symbol of prestige these days, and it is open to the public for visits. The west entrance leads to the "Bernadotte Rooms," the guest apartment and to the banquet hall. The entrance on the south side takes you to the chapel and the Hall of State, where ministers would swear their oaths to the king. This is also where Queen Christina's famous silver throne from the 17th century is located, a work from Augsburg, Germany.

There are also some significant museums located inside the palace. The southern entrance on Slottsbacken leads to the **Skattkammaren** (Treasure Chamber), which has an exhibit displaying royal insignias, crowns of the past and other regalia which have not been officially used since 1974. The **Livrustkammaren**, the Royal Armory, is housed in the south wing. Uniforms of Gustavus II Adolphus, Charles II and Gustavus III, the clothing they were wearing at the times of their violent deaths, are also here on display. The **Antikmuseum**, founded by Gustavus III and open to the public as early as 1792, is

still located in the north wing. The **Slottsmuseum** (Palace Museum), which documents the history of the *Tre Kronor* fortification and is part of the old castle itself, is also worth a visit.

*Storkyrkan

Rising above Slottsbacken is the ***Storkyrkan ③** (cathedral); its official name is Nicolai kyrka after its patron saint. The cathedral was first constructed in 1250, but has been rebuilt so many times since then that the exterior appears to be Baroque while the interior exhibits basic Gothic elements. The entrance to the church is on the west side through the former arsenal. The north door is reserved for the Royal Family, such as for the wedding in 1976 and the baptisms of the royal children.

The interior of the Storkyrkan is marvelously furnished and is thereby in accordance with its function as a coronation church. The **Baroque pulpit** and the **Royal Pews** between the pulpit and the choir stairs were created in Sweden according to the plans of Nicodemus Tessin the Younger; the altar is a notable 17th-century imported work from Hamburg. The showpiece of the church is the famous **St. George and the Dragon**, a gift from Sten Sture, for which he is said to have made his vows during the battle at Brunkeberg in 1471. The order went to Lübeck where Bernt Notke carved the impressive oak sculpture. The dramatic battle between Saint George and the dragon symbolizes the Swedes' fight for liberation against Denmark. To present the figures as authentically as possible, the artist used genuine horsehair for the stallion and elk's antlers for the dragon's wings. The **Vädersolstavlan** (Father Sun painting) on the south wall of the church is also worth viewing. It not only shows a pair of suns – the phenomenon of a solar reflection – but also the only preserved 16th-century illustration of the city of Stockholm.

The Alleyways of the Old Town

Källargränd, a short lane, takes you from Slottsbacken to Stortorget. Directly at the beginning of it, there is a small half-open tin hut: Stockholm's oldest public urinal.

The **Stortorget**, the city's large market square, has not only been the main square for the citizens since the founding of the city, but was also the site of executions. This was the stage of the "Stockholm Bloodbath" of 1520, when King Christian II of Denmark had 82 noblemen executed for heresy.

The **Börsen** (Stock Exchange) is the main building on the square; constructed by the architect Erik Palmstedt in the 18th century, it is considered to be the first example of pure classical architecture in

Right: The outdoor cafés at Stortorget provide the center of Gamla Stan with an almost Italian ambience.

Sweden. Bankers still do business on the ground floor; the home of the Swedish Academy, the institution which determines the Nobel Prize winners every year, is located on the building's upper level. This had always been an extremely discrete procedure until 1997, when the naming of Dario Fo so turned the jurors against each other that they even argued in public. Palmstedt was also the creator of the fountain on the Stortorget. Comfortable street cafés and restaurants line the square.

Following **Köpmangatan** eastwards you will walk eventually through an ensemble of old merchant courtyards, some of which date as far back as the 16th century. Gustavus Vasa's sons are said to have quartered their mistresses in luxurious houses here, supposedly connected to the palace by underground walkways. At the intersection with **Österlånggatan** there is bronze replica (1912) of the St. George and the Dragon statue in the Storkyrkan. The street indicates the course followed by the eastern city wall during the Middle Ages. The **Gyldene Frede** (Golden Peace), Stockholm's oldest inn, whose existence can be traced back to 1751, is located at No. 51. The artist Anders Zorn bought the establishment in 1919, the year before he died, and bequeathed it to the Swedish Academy, whose 18 members traditionally meet here for a meal every Thursday. The inn became a popular venue due to Carl Mikael Bellman, an 18th-century ballad singer and poet, a regular customer who would often entertain the patrons.

In the past, iron and copper were traded at **Järntorget** ❹ (Iron Market). The most conspicuous building on the square is **Södra Bancohuset**, founded in the 17th century as a bank for the nobility, today it is the state headquarters of the real estate administration. On the opposite side of the square is **Mårten Trotzigs Gränd**, a 90-centimeter-wide alleyway, the narrowest one in Gamla Stan (Old Town),

which connects with **Västerlånggatan**. This busy shopping street of the Old Town is the western counterpart of Österlånggatan, which also following the course of the city's wall in the Middle Ages. Although window shopping is already interesting due to the often quite humorous displays, you should also take the opportunity to look around and enjoy the gable ornamentation, artistic portals and window frames of the houses.

After about 300 meters the **Kindstugatan** leads to the **Tyska kyrkan** (German Church), officially named, however, St. Gertrud's Church. Originally, it served as an assembly room for the German merchants after they lost their privileges under Gustavus Vasa. Stockholm's German community has continued to attend church services here since the Baroque reconstruction in the 17th century. The pulpit and the royal pews are noteworthy; they are based on designs by Nicodemus Tessin the Elder. The classical concerts held in the church in summer are very popular.

Helgeandsholmen

The northernmost and smallest of Stockholm's three Old Town islands, **Helgeandsholmen ❺** is separated from Stadsholmen by the Stallkanalen. The canal flows on the north side of the palace along the street named **Slottskajen** and ends at **Mynttorg**. Present members of the Swedish parliament have their offices here, in Stockholm's former mint: for this reason it is also called the **Kanslihuset** (Chancellery). By way of the small **Stallbron** you reach the "Island of The Holy Spirit" (Helgeandsholmen), which is dominated by the mighty buildings of the Riksbank (State Bank) and the Riksdag (Parliament).

Sweden had a four-class Riksdag until 1865, but it never held a joint session. After the constitution was reformed, it was necessary to erect a new building for the now two chambers. Not only was the building a demonstration of newly attained power, for it was built in conjunction with the Riksbank in the immediate

Stockholm

vicinity of the palace; but the powerful architectural style was intended to emphasize the self-confidence of parliamentary members. Sweden dissolved the second chamber in 1971, and the Riksbank moved to a new building. This made it possible for the assembly room to be moved to the former bank and the old conference hall could be used for party meetings. All parts of the Riksdag have been connected to the members of parliament's offices by a network of tunnels. During construction, traces of the oldest settlement in Stockholm were found. These artifacts have been carefully preserved in the **Medeltidsmuseet** (Medieval Museum) under the **Norrbron**.

Riddarholmen

From Mynttorg, follow Myntgatan to get to **Riddarhustorget** (Knight's House Square), whose north side is flanked by two ornate pavilions. The **Bondeska Palatset**, the townhouse of the former Minister of Finance Gustav Bonde, was designed by the 17th-century architect Jean de la Vallée. Although extremely thrifty in his attempts to put Charles X's finances to order, privately he appeared exceedingly extravagant. The building served as the town hall from 1713 to 1915, and now houses the Supreme Court (*Högsta Domstolen*).

The neighboring ***Riddarhuset** (Knights' House) – also by De la Vallée – was where the Estate of the Nobility met until they lost their privileges in 1865. The late-Renaissance style, typically a combination of natural stone and brick surfaces, set an example for many manor homes in of Sweden. Today, the palace remains in the hands of Swedish nobility, and a family reunion of sorts is held here every three years. The statues located in

Right: The Blue Hall of the Stadshuset, a representative venue for the annual Nobel Prize winners' banquet.

front of and behind the building depict Gustavus Vasa and Axel Oxenstierna.

By crossing the **Riddarhusbron** you will arrive at the island of **Riddarholmen** ❻, where a statue of the city's founder greets you from a tall column on the square, the **Birger Jarls Torg**. The island belonged to the Franciscans until the Reformation. Afterwards, it was parceled out to the nobility, who then built marvelous palaces on the grounds. Of notable mention are the **Wrangelska palatset**, west of the Birger Jarls Torg, where the royal family resided from 1697 to 1754, and on the foundations of the former Franciscan monastery the so-called **Gamla gymnasiehuset**, the former secondary school, which was first a city palace, and then, from 1841 on, a school.

You cannot overlook the ***Riddarholmskyrkan** with its openwork spire – once a Franciscan friary. Gustavus II Adolphus chose to be interred here among his royal predecessors. His successors had also selected this church as their location of entombment, the last one being Gustavus V who died in 1950. His son, as well as his great-grandson, the present-day king, have contrarily stipulated private burial sites in their wills.

By walking past the Birger Jarls Torg you arrive at the terrace of **Riddarfjärden**, located at the east end of Lake Mälaren. From here you have a magnificent view of Södermalm to the left with the old brewery, and Kungsholmen to the right with the Stadshuset, Stockholm's landmark. The sculpture *Sun Ship*, by Christian Berg, is located directly on the shore; just to the left of it is a luxurious restaurant and hotel, housed in the former yacht of the American billionairess Barbara Hutton. Here, close to the city center yet separated from its noise, you can take a quiet walk to the north end of the island. A tower, the last remnant of the city's fortified walls from the days of Gustavus Vasa, is located here, the **Birger Jarls Torn**.

Kungsholmen

A pedestrian bridge next to the **Centralbron** will take you to the **Klara Mälarstrand**, where boats service various destinations on Lake Mälaren. At this point, the **★Stadshuset** tower, 106 meters high, is a beacon to direct visitors the rest of the way to the island of **Kungsholmen** ❼. The monumental City Hall building of dark brick was designed by Ragnar Östberg and constructed between 1911 and 1923. The facades are diverse in design; cool Functionalism prevails on the landward side, while the arcades on the water side evoke an almost Mediterranean atmosphere. The main entrance to the complex is here. Many renowned Swedish artists were involved in its eventual creation, among them the "painter prince" Prince Eugen, one of Gustavus V's brothers. The so-called burgher courtyard will lead you to the reception rooms of the building. Tours start from the large flight of stairs. Among other things, you will be able to see the **Gyllene salen** (Golden Hall), a room with 600 square meters of floor space decorated entirely with golden mosaic tiles; the **Blue Hall**, boasting an area of 1,600 square meters, is nearly as large as a football field. It is the stage for the annual awards banquet organized by the Swedish king for Nobel Prize winners. The tour also includes a ride up to the top of the tower (106 meters), where you can enjoy a breathtaking view of the "floating city" when weather permits.

There were numerous craftsman's establishments located here in the 19th century, but since then the island has been transformed into more of a solid middle-class residential area. The "sweet side" of town is **Norr Mälarstrand**, whose houses, with beautiful views of Lake Mälaren, are among Stockholm's most coveted. This is also the site of the quay for copious houseboats. At the end of the island in an area called **Rålambshovsparken**, there is a bathing beach, which, due to its proximity to downtown Stockholm, is very popular indeed.

Stockholm

CENTRAL NORRMALM

A functional, new city district developed on **Norrmalm** from the 1940s to the 1970s. **Sergels Torg** ❽ forms its center, beneath which cars, the *Tunnelbana* and pedestrians pass through on various levels. Unfavorable weather might attract you to do some shopping in the underground mall and in the department stores which surround the busy square.

An impressive, tall glass column 37 meters high towers above Sergels Torg and is illuminated at night. Wide stairs lead the way to the large pedestrian square below the junction. A colorful mixture of people gather here in all seasons: musicians, traveling entertainers, missionaries, and skateboarders; unfortunately, though, also the drug dealers and pickpockets typically found in any metropolitan area.

Above: Sergels Torg, traffic and consumer center of Stockholm. Right: The Kungsträd-gården – a green oasis right downtown.

The glass facade of the **Kulturhuset** rises high on the south side. Built in the 1960s, the cultural center is representative of the generous policies regarding culture. There is an Internet café here, and everyone is welcome to take advantage of the manifold offerings from newspapers to theatrical productions – free of charge. The Panorama Café on the upper floor is an inviting venue for observing the hustle and bustle on Sergels Torg while enjoying coffee and cake.

If you leave the square by way of **Klarabergsviadukten**, you should turn onto Drottninggatan at the **Åhléns** department store. For the most part, the street is a pedestrian zone with all of the boutiques and cafés to go along with it. August Strindberg's last apartment was at No. 85 on **Blå Tornet**. Presently, it is a museum where theatrical performances are sometimes held. Drottninggatan ends at the **Observatorielunden**, a wonderfully peaceful park, where the Carl Hårleman Observatory (18th century) and the **Stadsbiblioteket** are located. The

cube-shaped building from 1925, out of which rises a cylinder, is considered to be the first example of Swedish Functionalism. Svearvägen and Kungsgatan lead you back to the downtown area and to **Hötorget** ❾ (Hay Market), the location of the classical **Konserthuset**, where not only music is played, but also where the Nobel Prizes are awarded on December 10 every year. The **Orpheus Fountain** in the center of the square is a work by the Swedish-American sculptor Carl Milles (1875-1955). Hötorget hosts a fruit, vegetable and flower market on weekdays. In addition, there is the new **Saluhall** (Market Hall) underground where you can buy many international specialties. Walking through Sergelsgatan, another pedestrian zone, you return to Sergels Torg.

From there it is only 300 meters to the **Kungsträdgården** ❿, the palace's former herb and vegetable garden with a pleasure grounds, which has been open to the public since the 19th century. The **Sverigehuset** is situated in the northwest corner, housing the **Tourist Information Center**, a booking office and a small but interesting bookshop. The park is a popular meeting place in the city center; in summer there are free cabaret shows here, and the park becomes a skating rink in the winter. A statue of Charles XII is located in the southeast corner of the grounds above the square named after him. August Strindberg, the Swedish dramatist and novelist, asserted that the reign of this early 18th-century king consisted of nothing other than "mistakes, folly and foolishness."

Sankt Jakobs kyrkan is one of the many churches that was razed after the Reformation but rebuilt in the 17th century when the city was lacking houses of worship. The **Operan** ⓫ opposite was built in the neoclassical style in 1891. The previous building on this site was erected under the rule of Gustavus III in the 18th century and provided the stage for the infamous masked ball where the king was assassinated. All of Sweden's top opera stars, such as Birgit Nilsson, started their careers here. The **Café Operan** is legend-

ary: celebrity seekers stand in line until ready to drop waiting to be let in – only to be disappointed to learn that they are merely amongst their own kind.

The park in front of the main entrance is the only part that was realized from Nicodemus Tessin the Younger's 18th-century plans of the palace grounds: **Gustav Adolfs Torg**, with a massive equestrian statue of the king in the center of the square. The **Medelhavsmuseet** (Mediterranean Museum), located on **Fredsgatan** northwest of the square, houses the largest exhibition concerning Cyprus outside the island itself. The museum has King Gustavus VI to thank for the collection, who, as an avid archeologist in his youth, often participated in excavations there.

The government quarter, where all of the ministries were assembled in the 1980s, is located near the waterfront op-

Above: Colorful sculptures by Niki de Saint Phalle greet visitors to the Moderna Museet.
Right: Taking a break from sightseeing stress.

posite the Riksdag. The **Palais Rosenbad** ⑫, the seat of the prime minister, sits directly on the bank of the Norrström on Strömgatan.

Vasagatan will take you to the central train station, which is called the **Centralen** ⑬ in Stockholm. Not only the railway routes converge here, but also the bus and *Tunnelbana* lines. Buses to the Arlanda Airport 30 kilometers away leave from here. Klarabergsviadukten will guide you back to Sergels Torg.

The Museum Islands

There are a few museums huddled closely together located on the three islands connected by bridges in **Strömmen**, the shipping channel to the North Sea.

Blasieholmen ⑭ has only been a peninsula for a hundred years or so, since the sound between it and Norrmalm was filled in. You cannot fail to notice Stockholm's most exclusive accommodation: the **Grand Hotel**. Here you can reserve a room with a view either of the palace or of the Nybroviken. Contrary to the Café Opera, celebrities really do meet at the bar here.

The ***Nationalmuseet** was built directly adjacent to the hotel at the beginning of the 20th century and houses the national art collection, which, until then, had been in the palace. Many of the exhibits, including those of the Flemish masters, came to Sweden during the Thirty Years' War when the country literally had "access" to many European art treasures. Charles Gustav Tessis enlarged the collection in the 18th century with purchases from Paris; Gustavus III later provided further additions. Presently, the museum is divided into three sections: the graphic art collection consists of 120,000 exhibits, the arts and crafts number over 28,000, while the museum's main attraction is the collection of paintings spanning five centuries of European art.

Stockholm

The island of **Skeppsholmen** ⑮, originally called *Lustholmen*, was so named since it was within view of the palace's royal pleasure garden. Today, the entrance to the island is via a narrow bridge near one of the world's most original youth hostels. The **af Chapman**, an English freighter, which served the Swedish navy several years as a training ship, reported for duty as Stockholm's first youth hostel in 1949. Despite recent competition, the ship has remained the city's most popular youth hostel.

Museums are located in the island's former navy buildings. In addition to the **Arkitekturmuseet** and the **Ostasiatiska museet**, boasting an extensive collection from China, there is also the more recent **Moderna Museet**. The museum exclusively exhibits 20th-century art. The colorful sculptures of Niki de Saint Phalle and the scrap creations of Jean Tinguely have found their home in the space between the museums – magnificent contraptions whose only purpose is self-propulsion.

Kastellholmen ⑯ is the property of the Swedish Marines, who have modernized all of the fortresses here and are still finding use for some of them. The island is especially popular for young people, since its location predestined it to be a venue for open-air concerts.

Östermalm: Little Paris

Östermalm is said to be boring and lifeless – at any rate, that is the claim of many Stockholm residents. Envy certainly plays a part in this because Östermalm is, in fact, the most expensive district in the capital city. In the 19th century it was still called *Ladugård* (cowbarn) due to the royal court's cattle grazing here in the pastures. Later it was used as training grounds for the Swedish military before well-to-do Stockholm citizens decided to settle here. The wide avenues and generously built houses reflect how Paris was emulated. Galleries, banks, hotels, museums and embassies characterize the quarter.

A good starting point for exploring the district is **Nybroplan** ⑰ at the end of **Nybroviken**, where many dining vessels are anchored and from where excursion ferries set sail to the skerries off the coast of Stockholm.

Dramaten is the nickname of the **Kungliga Dramatiska Teatern** which composes the entire north side of the square. The beautiful Art Nouveau theater is the successor to an older building from the days of Gustavus III. The theater not only has a large playhouse, but also four experimental stages. It was on such a stage that Ingmar Bergman began his career, which seemed to be at an end after he was discreetly told he was not suited to be a director. After his great success as a director, he returned to the Dramaten as theater manager in the 1960s, and became world-renowned for his interpretations of

Above: Decorated helmet from the Vendel Age, a showpiece at the Statens Historiska Museet. Right: Great fun at Stockholm's Gröna Lund amusement park.

Strindberg. In front of **Berzelii Park** opposite the Dramaten there is a bronze statue of a sewage canal worker peeking out of a manhole. He is so loved in Stockholm that compassionate citizens even provide him with a wool scarf in winter. **Berns Salonger**, one of Stockholm's most famous restaurants, which achieved literary fame due to Strindberg's novel *Röda Rummet* (The Red Room), is also located at the park.

Due to the heavy traffic, going for a stroll on **Strandvägen**, the most beautiful street in the district, can only be recommended early in the morning or late in the evening. The best view, in any case, is from onboard the ferry which runs between Nybroplan and Djurgården. Strandvägen ends at the diplomatic district intersecting with **Nobelparken** ⑱. From here you can follow the signs to the **Kaknästornet**, Stockholm's television tower. The tallest building in Scandinavia (155 meters), with a restaurant and a lookout platform, offers a fantastic view of the city as well as the entire Stockholm archipelago.

From Nobel Park we recommend you follow Storgatan to **Narvavägen**, where the *Statens Historiska Museet ⑲ (Historical Museum) is located. Its collection goes back to the State Treasury, an institution founded in the 17th century, which registers and stores antiquities of all kinds. Over the course of the centuries it has developed into a comprehensive collection of the history of Sweden all the way from the Stone Age up into the Middle Ages. The highlight of a visit to the museum is the **Guldrummet** (Gold Room), located in a bunker in the courtyard. Originally, the room was constructed to protect the museum's treasures in case of a nuclear war; today gold and silver burial offerings – mainly from the Viking Age – are on display behind bullet-proof glass.

Narvavägen ends at **Karlaplan**, a traffic circle where several streets converge –

just like in Paris. You can follow Karlavägen to the **Humlegården** ⑳, the city's former hops-growing area. The **Kungliga biblioteket**, a reference library with an extensive collection, is located in the center of the present-day park. The headquarters of the **Nobel Prize Foundation** is located on the east side of the park at Sturegatan 14. This is where Alfred Nobel's huge fortune is administered and becomes even more fruitful as can be seen by the annually increasing sums of prize money. You can return to Nybroplan by following Stureplan and Birger Jarls gatan.

THE ZOO ISLAND

You can reach the island of **Djurgården** (Zoological Garden) by taking the previously mentioned ferry from Nybroplan or one of the other boats shuttling between Slussen and the island. Until into the 18th century, Djurgården was the royal hunting grounds, where the kings could pursue one of their favorite

sports in the immediate vicinity of the palace. As soon as it was opened to the public, the animal park quickly developed into a local recreational area and a popular destination for excursions. In addition, the world's first open-air museum on the hill of ****Skansen** and **Gröna Lunds Tivoli** ㉑ (amusement park) directly at the ferry docks certainly had something to do with it.

The most conspicuous building on the island is the **Nordiska Museet** ㉒ (Nordic Museum) on Djurgårdsbron. Built in the so-called Vasa style, this form of Renaissance style architecture can only be found in Sweden. The building houses a collection by Arthur Hazelius, who began his hobby by acquiring examples of everyday Nordic art. From wooden plates and room furnishings to complete farmyards, nothing escaped his passion. It proved impossible to exhibit this collection indoors, so the museum joined with the open-air museum of Skansen. This marriage developed into the actual attraction of the museum, not

least because of its animal park with Nordic fauna.

The ****Vasamuseet** ㉓ was established in the immediate vicinity of the Nordic Museum and is totally dedicated to the so-called "Titanic of the Baltic Sea" (see also p. 234).

The **Waldemarsudden** ㉔ situated on the southern tip of the island is especially interesting for art lovers. At the beginning of the 20th century, Prince Eugen, the "painter prince," had an Art Noveau villa with a studio built in a well-kept park; his succession to the throne had already been secured so that he could now dedicate himself solely to his own artistic passion. There is a very nice view of Södermalm and the docks of the Finnish ferries from the park.

The **Rosendals slott** ㉕, Charles XIV and his wife Désirée's residence, was transported from France in its entirety

Above: Södermalm, a workers' community of the 19th century, has since developed into the trendiest part of town.

and is located on the north side of the Djurgården. The mansion is fully furnished and can only be visited on a guided tour.

Södermalm – The Workers' Island

Beginning in the 17th century, foul-smelling and combustible workshops were usually moved to the island of **Södermalm**. When larger factories began establishing themselves in the 19th century, a real workers' community developed here; the apartments even had bathrooms and heating. Today, these apartments are so desirable, especially among young people, that a unique type of subculture has developed on the island of Södermalm. Bizarre shops and discos are perfectly combined with conventional businesses and cozy corner bars which seem to have withstood the changes of time. Unfortunately, some sterile quarters were constructed during the urban renewal building projects of the 1990s – **Medborgarplatsen**, for example, resem-

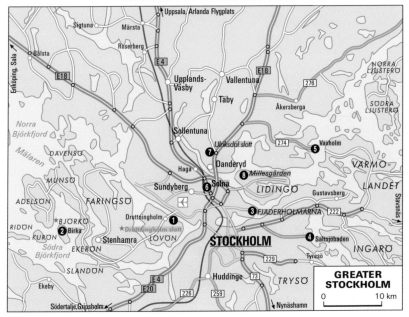

bles the residential ghettos in the north and west of Stockholm.

Globen, as the name implies, is a spherically shaped multipurpose hall 64 meters in diameter; the modern architectural landmark is located south of the island in **Johanneshov**.

The traffic junction of Slussen forms the entrance to the district of Södermalm. You shouldn't miss a ride on the **Katarinahissen** (elevator), which not only overcomes the elevation difference of 36 meters between the lock and the town, but also serves as a lookout platform. A bridge at the upper platform of the elevator leads to the **Morseback** restaurant, where dances are held for the older generation on weekends.

It's considered a "must" to take a walk to the **Fjällgatan** a few hundred meters farther east, where the granite cliffs plunge 30 meters to the Baltic Sea. Here you have the best view of the entire downtown area and of the scattered skerry islands. The Finland-bound ferries dock below the Fjällgatan. On weekends, the largest ferries serve the tiny Finnish **Åland Islands** between Stockholm and Helsinki. Some may wonder at this fact, but it is easily enough explained by revealing how well the ferries are equipped: up to 20 bars and discos stocked with enticingly cheap alcohol are the actual motivation for these excursions; after a brief stay on Finnish soil the tanked passengers climb aboard for their return trip to Stockholm.

ISLANDS OF LAKE MÄLAREN

Ships used to be the only transportation possible between the settlements around Lake Mälaren. While this is no longer the case, of course, traveling to the sights on the lake by boat still remains the most attractive mode of transportation. This also goes for the journey to ***Drottningholm slott ❶** (Queen's Palace) on **Lovön**, although in the meantime, there is a bridge connecting the island with the district of Bromma. Boats run from Klara Mälarstrand to the city and palace hourly.

Drottningholm is without a doubt the most beautiful palace in Sweden. Charles X's widow, Hedvig Eleonora, commissioned Nicodemus Tessin the Elder with the construction which was carried out by his son. These two architects are also responsible for the Baroque garden designed in the French style. The palace took shape around 1750, when Queen Lovisa Ulrika, one of Frederik II's sisters, had Carl Hårleman remodel it. The magnificent staircase, the galleries and the queen's elaborate bedroom, which are open to visitors, came into being at that time. The south wing of the palace is closed to the public, since it is still in use as the residence of the Royal Family and has been since 1981.

The **Palace Theater** is an attraction in itself. Except for the electrical illumination, the backdrops and stage machinery have remained unchanged for 200 years. Still functional, performances are staged here for special occasions. Ingmar Bergman brought renown to the theater when he had a studio replica of it built for his film *The Magic Flute*. The **Theater Museum** has an interesting display of set decorations from the Gustavus era. In keeping with the spirit of the 18th century, **Kina Slott**, a small Chinese palace, was also constructed in the spacious park. An interesting attraction here is a table which is prepared for dinner on the level downstairs and rises to the dining hall at the press of a button; the neighboring café has conventional table service.

It is a two-hour ferry crossing from Klara Mälarstrand to the island of *Björko**. The splendor of the old Viking capital of **Birka** ❷, which was one of the most important trading centers of the north, rapidly diminished after the city's destruction in 970. The Vikings continued to resist the attempts of the Archbishop of Bremen, Ansgar, to convert them to Christianity in the 9th century. A chapel from the 10th century was dedicated to Saint Ansgar. Marked trails on the island lead to the burial grounds and the site of the former city, both of which have been on the UNESCO World Heritage List since 1993.

IN THE **GARDEN OF SKERRIES

The archipelago of Stockholm is about 150 kilometers in length altogether and extends as far as to 70 kilometers into the Baltic Sea. The reported number of islands, most of which are uninhabited, varies between 24,000 and 30,000, depending on your source of information. Only 6,000 people reside here permanently. Naturally, in the summer months, when the 40,000 vacation homes are inhabited, the population increases manifold. This unique **Skårgarden**, the Swedish word for such an island seascape, is a true paradise for those who like water sports, as well as for anyone looking for rest and recuperation. There are numerous possibilities for excursions through the island world, leaving either from Slussen, Nybroplan or Strömkajen, and lasting anywhere from two to ten hours. There are also regular links to larger towns, such as Vaxholm and Saltsjöbaden, as well as to Sandhamn. Special arrangements, like restaurant boats with jazz or dance music, round off the array of tempting offers.

The small island group of **Fjäderholmarna** ❸ is just a 25-minute cruise from Nybroplan. It is a popular excursion destination for those who have to spend the summer in the city. In addition to restaurants, a fish smokehouse and an extremely popular bakery, the islands also offer the **Baltic Aquarium** and the **Skerry Museum**.

Founded by a Swedish industrialist, **Saltsjöbaden** ❹, the chic counterpart to Fjäderholmarna, is in the southeast part of the capital. The city itself is a sailing

Right: The Royal Family lives in the south wing of Drottningholm Palace.

center well equipped with all of the appropriate docking facilities. The most illustrious address on the town square is the **Grand Hotel**, a turn-of-the-century building deservedly crowned with turrets. It is about an hour's boat ride here from Nybroplan.

The trip to **Vaxholm** ❺ in the east of Stockholm takes just as long to reach. The old fortress at the entrance to the capital city harbor dates back to the days of Gustavus Vasa. He even had passages between the islands filled in to force the ships to pass by his fortress, thus enabling him to keep tighter control over the port entrance. The stronghold was abandoned in the 19th century when it became obvious that the ramparts could no longer withstand modern ship artillery. The fort is now a museum. The city area of Vaxholm includes some 62 islands, where many Stockholm residents maintain summer houses. Most all of these are wooden due to an ordinance forbidding the construction of stone houses so as not to mar the picturesque character of the quaint little town. When the restriction was lifted, a citizens' initiative successfully had it reinstated.

Sandhamn, three hours from Nybroplan, is located at the outer edge of the archipelago. A quarantine facility was built here during the cholera epidemic. The piloting station for ships is also located here, if they need help navigating into and out of the harbor.

The inn of Sandhamn maintains a 300-year-old tradition; the local nautical navigators were obliged to provide guests with food and drink. Today, it is the home of the Royal Swedish Sailing Club. The Gotland Regatta begins here every year in July.

Hagaparken – The King's Park

Hagaparken in **Solna** ❻, on the E4, belongs to one of the sights outside Stockholm you can easily reach by car or *Tunnelbana* (subway). The expansive estate was built under the supervision of King Gustavus III in the English garden

Stockholm

style. The king had plans for the construction of a new residence, but these were abandoned after his assassination. Only the pavilion was ever completed. The residence is generally referred to as **Lilla Slott** (Small Palace). Today, the complete, original Rococo furnishings continue to create a lasting impression on those who visit it.

Directly adjacent to the palace, Gustavus IV had the so-called "Queen's Pavilion" erected, which now, as **Haga Slott**, serves as the official guest house of the government. At the entrance you first notice the sentry's copper tent, built for the royal guard at the end of the 18th century in the style of Roman army tents according to a theater painter's sketches. Especially when the weather is nice, Hagaparken is a popular picnic area for suburban residents.

Ulriksdal slott ➐ a 17th-century Renaissance castle of Gustavus VI, the pres-

Above: In the Skårgarden off the coast of Stockholm.

ent-day king's grandfather, is also located on the E4. The complete furnishings, given to the Royal Family by the citizens of Stockholm for the royal wedding in 1923, are open to the public for viewing. More worthwhile, however, might be a visit to **Ulriksdals Wärthus**, without doubt the most celebrated restaurant outside the downtown area.

Millesgården – The Artist's Park

From **Torsvik** (by bus or train from the Ropsten *Tunnelbana* station) it is only a few steps to **Millesgården** ➑, located on the island of **Lidingö**. The sculptor Carl Milles (1875-1955) had a house and a studio built on a precipitous cliff here. He not only used the terraces of the terrain for exhibiting many of is own works, but also for displaying his collection of Roman and Greek sculptures. Milles, who decorated numerous Swedish cities with distinctive fountains and statues, bequeathed his home town with a unique sculpture garden.

STOCKHOLM (☏ 08)

Stockholm Information Service, PO Box 7542, 10393 Stockholm, tel. 7892495. **Excursion bookings, ticket sales:** Sverigehuset Kungsträdgården, Hamngatan 27, 10393 Stockholm, tel. 7892490 or 7892415, e-mail: info@stoinfo.se. The tourist offices also sell the **Stockholmskort**, which is valid for 24, 48 or 72 hours. It entitles you to ride for free on the public transportation system in greater Stockholm, and provides some free boat trips and free admission to most museums. It is relatively expensive and worth it only if you go to at least three museums per day of validity, which is difficult to manage due to the short opening hours. The Stockholmskort is also part of the **Stockholm Package**, which is available in different hotel categories for up to three nights with breakfast at a flat rate. It can be booked in all travel offices – also outside of Sweden.

Hotelcentralen at the main train station, bookings at hotels and youth hostels, tel. 240880.

Hotels in the center **(C)**, near the center **(NC)**, on the outskirts **(O)**: ✪✪✪ **Hotell Diplomat (C)**, Strandvägen 7 C, tel. 6635800, fax 7836634. **Hotel Esplanade (C)**, Strandvägen 7 A, tel. 6630740, fax 6625992, both nice hotels on Stockholm's main boulevard. **Grand Hotel (C)**, Södra Blasieholmshamn 8, tel. 679350, fax 6118686, Stockholm's top address. **Grand Hotel Saltsjöbaden (O)**, tel. 7170020, fax 7179531, fabulous hotel amidst the skerries. **Hasselbacken Hotel & Restaurant (NC)**, Hazeliusbacken 20, tel. 6705000, fax 6638410, quiet hotel on the island of Djurgården. **Lady Hamilton Hotel (C)**, Storkyrkobrinken 5, tel. 234680, fax 4111148, in the Old Town. **Radisson SAS Royal Viking Hotel (C)**, Vasagatan 1, tel. 141000, fax 108180, near Vasa Park. **Sheraton Stockholm Hotel & Towers (C)**, Tegelbacken 6, tel. 142600, fax 217026, the city's new luxury hotel. ✪✪ **Adlon Hotell (NC)**, Vasagatan 42, tel. 4026500, fax 208610, large hotel in the Vasa district. **Aldoria Hotel (NC)**, Sankt Eriks Gatan 38, tel. 6541885, fax 6522963, also in the Vasa district. **First Hotel Amaranten (C)**, tel. 6541060, fax 6526248, near City Hall. **Silja Hotel Ariadne (NC)**, Södra Kajen 37, tel. 6657800, fax 7149705, at the Finland terminal with a view of the harbor. **Hotel Birger Jarl (C)**, Tulegatan 8, tel. 6741000, fax 6737366, quiet hotel in Östermalm. **City Hotel Gamla Stan (C)**, Lilla Nygatan 25, tel. 7237250, fax 7237259, in the Old Town. **City Hotel Kungsgatan (C)**, Kungsgatan 47, tel. 7237220, fax 7237272, near Hötorget. **City Hotel Slöjdgatan (C)**, Slöjdgatan 7, tel. 7237200, fax 7237209, near the Drottninggatan pedestrian zone. **Freys Hotel (C)**, Bryggargatan 12, tel. 50621300, fax 50621313, smaller

hotel near Hötorget. **Stockholm Globe Hotel (NC)**, Arenaslingen 7, tel. 7259000, fax 6490880, near the Globen Hall. **Gustav Vasa Hotel (NC)**, Västmanngatan 61, tel. 343801, fax 307372, smaller hotel near the Vasa district. **First Hotel Reisen (C)**, Skeppsbron 12, tel. 223260, fax 201559, in the Old Town with a view of Strömmen Bay. **Radisson SAS Strand Hotel (C)**, Nybrokajen 9, tel. 6787800, fax 6112436, modern, with a view of the Nybroviken. **Scandic Hotel Continental (C)**, Klara Vättugränd 4, tel. 244020, fax 4113695, near the train station. **Scandic Hotel Slussen (C)**, Guldgränd 8, tel. 7022500, fax 6428358, located above the sluice. **Victory Hotel (C)**, Lilla Nygatan 5, tel. 143090, fax 202177, in the Old Town. ✪ **Alexandra Hotel (NC)**, Magnus Ladulåsgatan 42, tel. 840320, fax 7205353, small hotel in the center of Södermalm. **Hotel Bema (NC)**, Upplandsgatan 13, tel. 232675, fax 205338, nice family hotel in the Vasa district. **Columbus Hotell & Vandrarhem (NC)**, Tjärhovsgatan 11, tel. 6441717, fax 7020764, in the center of Södermalm. **Djuröbaden (O)**, Gamla Prästgården, tel. 57151800, fax 57150500, small, quiet pension in the outer skerries. **Good Morning Hotels Stockholm Syd (O)**, Västertorpsvägen 131, tel. 180140, fax 976427, in the suburb of Hägersten, but with Tunnelbana connection. **Mälardrottningen Hotel och Restaurang (C)**, Riddarholmen, tel. 243600, fax 243676, boat with few cabins, very nice location. **Pilgrimshem Hotell & Vandrarhem (O)**, Bållstavägen 100, tel. 6275555, fax 98239, in Brommen not far from Drottningholm, Tunnelbana and bus connections. **Rosinge Hotel (NC)**, Sigtunagatan 6, tel. 336770, fax 942449, nice hotel in the Vasa district. **Sandströms Hotell (NC)**, Sankt Eriks Gatan 75, tel. 307476, fax 307476, Vasa district. **SkepparHolmen Hotell (O)**, Franckes väg, tel. 7476500, fax 7479192, in Saltsjö-Boo amidst the skerries. **Hotell Tre Små Rum (NC)**, Höberggatan 81, tel. 6412371, fax 6428808, in Södermalm. **Welcome Hotel (O)**, Norrbyvägen 30, tel. 7042520, fax 7048130, in Bromma, good connection to the city.

YOUTH HOSTELS: **af Chapman (C)**, Skeppsholmen, tel. 6795015, fax 6119855, old sail training ship, open year round. **Mälaren, Den Röda Båten (C)**, Södar Mälarstrand, Kajplats 6, tel./fax 6641114, old Mälaren boat, open year round. **M/S Rygerfjord (C)**, Söder Mälarstrand, Kajplats 12, tel. 840830, like Röda Båten. **Långholmens Vandrarhem (NC)**, Gamla Kronohäket, tel. 6680500, fax 7208575, hostels in a former prison on an island in Lake Mälaren, open year round. **Vandrarhem Skeppsholen**, tel. 6795017, fax 6117155. **City Back Packers**, Barnhusgatan 16, tel./fax 206920.

⚠ Angby Camping, Blackebergsvägen 24, Bromma, tel. 370420, with Tunnelbana connection. **Långholms Husbycamping**, in Långholmen, tel. 070-7526335, only for mobile homes, near the city. **Askrike Camping**, tel. 54135013, in Vaxholm, amidst the skerries.

✗ FAMOUS RESTAURANTS: Gyldene Freden, Österlanggatan 51, tel. 109046, classic Swedish cuisine. **Berns Salonger**, Berzelii Park 9 tel. 6140550, classic Swedish cuisine, also dinner shows. **Morseback**, Morseback Torg 3, tel. 08-6419020, reservations necessary. **Operakällaren**, Operahuset, tel. 6765000, reservations necessary, Mon-Fri from 10 am, Sat-Sun from 4 pm, Swedish cuisine with a French twist. **Coq Blanc**, Regeringsgatan 111, tel. 4116153, reservations necessary, from 10 am, the in-crowd meets here, international cuisine with a French touch.

SWEDISH CUISINE: **Café Blå Porten**, Djurgårdsvägen 64, tel. 6627162. **Solliden**, Djurgårdsslätten 49-51, tel. 6601055. **Bistro Ruby**, Österlånggatan 14, tel. 249760. **Fem Små Hus**, Nygränd 10, tel. 108775. **Salt**, Hantverkergatan 34, tel. 6521100, music. **Frey's Hörna**, Bryggargatan 12, tel. 246640. **Sturehof**, Stureplan 2, tel. 6798750. **Blå Dörren**, Södermalmstorg 6, tel. 7430743. **Nils-Emils Bakficka**, Folungsgatan 126, tel. 6413387. **Zinkens Krog**, Ringvägen 14, tel. 6682856. **Fish stand at the Slussen Tunnelbana station**, delicious crisp bread with herring (Strömming), 11 am to 6 pm daily. **Bistro Talluden**, Karlsbegs Strand 4, tel. 7300615. **Husmannen**, Roslagsgatan 6, tel. 100153. **Mistral**, Södra Kajen 37 (Västrahamn), tel. 6657800, good buffet. **Ulriksdals Värdhus**, at the Ulriksdal Castle, tel. 850815.

INTERNATIONAL CUISINE: **Lidingöbro Värdshus**, Kaknäsvägen 62-72, tel. 6620694, fish restaurant. **Maharajah**, Gamla Stan (Old Town), Stora Nygatan 20, tel. 210404, Indian. **La Cantina**, Stortorget 16, tel. 200671, Italian. **Michelangelo**, Västerlånggatan 62, tel. 215099, Italian. **Dragon Palace**, Kornhamns Torg 55, tel. 205340, Chinese. **Hermitagen**, Stora Nygatan 11, tel. 4119500, vegetarian. **Magnus Ladulås**, Österlåggatan 26, tel. 211957, crazy, trendy restaurant. **Dolce Vita**, Kungsholmsgatan 16, tel. 6506080, Italian. **Hong Kong**, Kungsbrostrand 23, tel. 6537720, Chinese. **Mammas & Tapas**, Scheelegatan 3, tel. 6535390, Spanish. **Long Horn Smoke House**, Flemingatan 27, tel. 6511661, steak house. **Stockholm Fisk**, Vasagatan 1, tel. 140606, fish restaurant. **Wedholms**, Nybrokajen 17, tel. 6117874, fish restaurant. **Naglo**, Gustav Adolfs Torg 20, tel. 102757, international. **Tandoori**, Upplandsgatan 6, tel. 141032, Indian. **Sloppys**, Hamngatan 2, tel. 6119235, international, also bar and nightclub. **The Loft**, Regeringsgatan 66, tel. 4111991, Irish. **Åhléns Café**, Åhléns Varuhus, Klaraberggatan, tel. 76766053, good restaurant in a department store. **Kol & Kox**, Olofsgatan 7 A, tel. 7245860, Italian. **Bamboo Palace**, Kungsgatan 17, tel. 218241, Japanese. **Bamboo City**, Drottninggatan 28, tel. 243655, Chinese, Mongolian. **Café Piastowska**, Tegnérgatan 5, tel. 212508, Polish. **Mike's Entertainment**, Blekholmsterrassen 15, tel. 6988080, restaurant with shows. **Bean's & Bear's**, Regneringsgatan 91, tel. 4115850, vegetarian. **Elias Taverna**, Södermanngatan 8, tel. 4427450, Greek. **Krishna**, Ringvägen 125, tel. 6448810, Indian. **Karsson & Co**, Renstirnas Gate 30, tel. 7022229, light meals. **Carl's Kök**, Luntmakergatan 90, tel. 6123780, light meals. **Shushi Bar Sapporo**, Hornsgatan 94, tel. 849740, Japanese. **Dionysos**, Bondegatan 56, tel. 6419113, Greek.

CAFÈS: **Cafe Opera**, Operahuset, tel. 6765807, come here to "see and be seen." **Diplomat Teahouse**, Strandvägen 7 C, tel. 6635800, beautiful terrace on Strandvägen. **Café inside the Kulturhuset**, Sergels Torg, tel. 211035, nice view of the square, free newspapers – also foreign ones. **Stortorgets Kaffestuga**, Stortorget 22, tel. 7205981.

🕙 PUBS: Södermalm: Bottle & Glass, Hornsgatan 136, tel. 845610, there's always something happening here. **Half Way Inn**, Swedenborgsgatan 6, tel. 76419443, somewhat on the crazy side. **Vasastaden: Pub Anchor**, Sveavägen 90, tel. 152000, live rock 'n' roll music.

🍸 Henry's Bar, Hantverkaregatan 8, tel. 6519311, classic bar. **Bar in the Grand Hotel**, moderate prices. **Bar Ruby**, Österlånggatan 14, tel. 205776, always full and quite loud. **Sidetrack**, Wollmar Yxkullsgatan 7, tel. 6411688, gay bar. **La Isla**, Friedhelmsplan 7, tel. 6546043, salsa club. **Karlson & Co**, Kungsgatan 56, tel. 54512140, necktie required, minimum age 27 – unfortunately just a boring disco.

🎵 BZ Discotek, Berzelii Park 9, tel. 6795620, entry only if you have the "right look." **Daily's Bar**, Kungsträdgården, tel. 215655. **Monky Bar**, Sankt Eriks Gatan, tel. 6501183. **Åland Ferries**, June 6-Aug 16 daily from 7 pm, on Finnlandkajen, these are only interesting on weekends.

🛍 Drottningsgatan, Hamngatan, market halls at **Hötorget, Östermalmstorget** and Medborgarplatsen. **NK department store** on Hamngatan has wonderful designer items. Nice Swedish porcelain can be found at **Gustavsberg Fabriksbod & Keramik Centrum**, Odelbergsvägen 5 B, tel. 57035658. Arts and crafts goods are from all over Sweden are available at the **Skansen Open-Air Museum**.

GAMLA STAN: Palace, changing of the guard, Mon-Sat 12:10 pm, Sun and holidays 1:10 pm, with music. **Representational rooms, Imperial Hall**, June-Aug 10 am-4 pm daily, Sept-May Tue-Sun 12-3 pm. **Treasury**, the **Museum of Antiquities of Gustav III**, same opening hours. The **Royal Armory**, May 1-Aug 31, 11 am-4 pm daily, Sept-April closed Mon. **Storakyrkan**, 10 am-6 pm daily, except during services and concert rehearsals, entrance fee. **Tyska Kyrka** (German Church), Mon-Fri 12-4 pm. **Medeltidsmuseet** (Medieval Museum), July-Aug Fri-Mon 11 am-4 pm, Tue-Thu 11 am-6 pm, Sept-June Fri-Sun and Tue-Wed 11 am-4 pm, Thu 11 am-6 pm. **Riddarhus** (Knights' House), Mon-Fri 11:30 am-12:30 pm. **Riddarholmskyrkan**, June-Aug Mon-Sat 11 am-4 pm, Sun 12 pm-4 pm, May and Sept Tue and Sat-Sun 12-3 pm. **Stadshuset** (City Hall), only on guided tours, June-Aug 10 and 11 am, 12 and 2 pm daily, Sept 10 am, 12 and 2 pm daily, Oct-May 10 am and 12 pm.
KUNGSHOLMEN: **Tower Museum** in **City Hall**, May-Sept 10 am-4:30 daily.
NORRMALM: **Kulturhuset** (House of Culture), Tue-Thu 11 am-7 pm, Fri 11 am-6 pm, Sat-Sun 12 pm-5 pm, Internet café: **Café Access, www.cafeaccess.se. Blå Tornet** (Strindberg Museum), Sept-May Tue 11 am-7 pm, Wed-Fri 11 am-4 pm, Sat-Sun 12-4 pm, June-Aug Tue-Fri 11 am-4 pm, Sat-Sun 12-4 pm. **City Library,** Sept-May Mon-Fri 10 am-6 pm. **Observatory**, formerly open only to groups, possible exception upon inquiry at the tourist office. **Concert Hall** and **Opera**, events and ticket reservations at the tourist office in Sverigehus. **Sankt Jacob Kyrkan**, 9 am-6 pm daily, except during services. **Medelhavsmuseet** (Mediterranean Museum), Tue 11 am-9 pm, Wed-Sun 11 am-4 pm.
MUSEUM ISLANDS: **National Museum**, Tue and Thu, 11 am-8 pm, Wed and Fri-Sun 11 am-5 pm. **Architecture Museum**, Feb 14-Dec 30, Tue-Thu 11 am-8 pm, Fri-Sun 11 am-5 pm. **East Asian Museum**, Tue 12-8 pm, Wed-Sun 12-5 pm. **Modern Museum**, Feb 14-Dec 30 Tue-Thu 11 am-10 pm, Fri-Sun 11 am-6 pm.
ÖSTERMALM: **Dramatiska Teatern**, guided tours offered June 8-Aug 15, Mon-Sat 3 pm, in July and August also in English. Otherwise only Sat 3 pm. **Kaknästornet** (Television Tower), bus line 69, Sept-April 10 am-9 pm daily, May-Aug 9 am-10 pm daily. **Historika Museet** (Historical Museum), Tue-Sun 11 am-5 pm, Thu 11 am-8 pm.
DJURGÅRDEN: **Skansen Open-Air Museum**, Nov 1-Feb 28, 9 am-4 pm daily, March-April and Sept-Oct 9 am-5 pm daily, May 9 am-8 pm daily, June-Aug 9 am-10 pm. **Gröna Lunds Tivoli**, May-Aug Tue-Sun 12-10 pm, Sat-Sun to midnight. **Nordiska Museet**, Tue-Sun 11 am-5 pm, Thu 11 am-8 pm. **Vasa Museet**, Aug 21-

June 9, 10 am-5 pm daily, Thu 10 am-8 pm, June 10-Aug 20, 9:30 am-7 pm daily. **Waldemarsudde**, Sept-May Tue-Sun 11 am-4 pm, June-Aug Tue-Sun 11 am-5 pm. **Rosendals slott**, tours: June-Aug Tue-Sun 12, 1, 2 and 3 pm, Sept only Sat-Sun
SÖDERMALM: **Katarinahissen** elevator operates Mon-Sat 7:30 am-10 pm, Sun 10 am-10 pm.
OUTSIDE OF STOCKHOLM: **Drottningholm slott**, open daily May 11 am-4:30 pm, June-Aug 10 am-4:30 pm, Sept 12-3:30 pm. **Theater Drottningholm**, daily May 12-4:30 pm, June-Aug 11 am-4:30 pm, Sept 1-3:30 pm. **Kina Slott** (Chinese Palace), daily April and Oct 1 pm-3:30 pm, May-Aug daily 11 am-4:30 pm, Sept 12-3:30 pm daily. **Fjädarholmarna, Baltic Aquarium**, **Skerry Museum**, June 8-Aug 16, Mon-Sun 10 am-6 pm, otherwise Tue-Sun 10 am-4:30 pm. **Vaxholm Fortress**, May 15-Aug 31, 12-4:45 daily. **Lilla Slott** (Gustav III's Paviljong på Haga), tours: June-Aug Tue-Sun 12, 1, 2 and 3 pm, Sept Sat-Sun only. **Ulriksdal slott**, tours: May 19-Aug 30 Tue-Sun 1:40 and 3:40 pm, May 2-17 and Sept 15-27 Sept Sat/Sun only. **Millesgården**, Oct-April Tue-Sun 12-4 pm, May-Sept 10 am-5 pm daily.
BY AIR: **Arlanda Airport, Arrivals**: Terminal 2, tel. 7976103, terminal 4, tel. 7976090, **Departures**: Terminal 5, international, tel. 7976100. **Domestic flights**: Bromma Airport,tel. 7976800.
BY BOAT: **Vaxholm**, June 6-Aug 16 daily 12, 3 and 7 pm from Nybroplan, return daily 1:30, 4:30 and 8:20 pm.
Sandhamn, June 6-Aug 16, daily 10 am from Nybroplan, return 3 pm.
Gustavsberg, June 30-Aug 1, Tue-Sat 11 am from Nybroplan, return 3 pm.
Sigtuna, June 23-Aug 6, Tue-Sun 10 am from Stadhusbron, return 4:55 pm.
Björkö/Birka, May 1-Sept 27, daily 10 am from Stadhusbron, return from Birka 3:45 pm, June 6-Aug 16 also 9 am from Stadhusbron, return 12:45 pm.
Drottningholm, May 1-Sept 13, daily 9:30, 10, 11 and 11:30 am, 12, 1, 13:30, 2, 3, 3:30 and 4 pm from Stadhusbron, return daily 10:30 and 11:50 am, 12:50, 1:20, 1:50, 2:50, 3:20, 3:50, 4:50, 5:20 and 6 pm, June 6-Aug 16 also 5 and 6 pm from Stadhusbron, return 7:30 pm.
June: Day of the Skerry Boat; Stockholm Marathon; Midsummer in Skansen; the royal couple visits Skansen on the **national holiday** (June 6); **Riddardagar**, Renaissance festival in Gripsholm.
July: **Stockholm Jazz Festival** on Skeppsholmen; **theater performances** in Gripsholm Castle.
August: Eleven-day **Stockholm Water Festival**, with cultural events, prizes and food stands.

Stockholm

CENTRAL SWEDEN – WORLD OF THE RED TIMBER HOUSES

GÄVLE / FALUN
BORLÄNGE / MORA
SILJANSLEDEN
SÖDERHAMN
HUDIKSVALL

CENTRAL SWEDEN

The region between Stockholm and Sundsvall is generally known as Central Sweden. Geographically speaking, that designation is also plausible; although historically speaking, Uppland and Dalarna still belong to the Svear Empire. Gästrikland, Hälsingland, and Härjedalen are already parts of Norrland (North Land), as these seemingly endless vast open spaces beyond the Gävle-Mora axis have been called since the Middle Ages.

The countryside between Uppsala and Sundsvall in the east and the Norwegian border to the west is densely wooded. Agriculture is only possible in the river valleys and on some of the plains, otherwise, cattle raising dominates; this formerly consisting mainly of dairy farms. The farther north and west you go, the higher the mountains are. These range from only 200 meters in southern Gästrikland to almost 1,800 meters in northern Härjedalen.

The larger towns are concentrated on the Baltic Sea coast and around Lake Siljan, the geographical as well as historic center of Dalarna. Economically, the

Preceding pages: Midsummer Eve festival in Rättvik on Lake Siljan. Left: People of all ages celebrate together.

south is marked by mining and the metal industries, while the north profits from its extensive forests.

Northern Uppland

The E4 continues northwards from **Uppsala** through a relatively unvarying forest region. It is therefore recommended to begin with the rural Route 290 for the first 45 kilometers, and then continue via Route 292 from **Dannemora** in order to pick up the E4 near Tierp for the return journey. Route 290 initially follows the course of the Fyrisån River, and after 22 kilometers reaches **Salsta slott** ❶, a Renaissance castle from the 17th century, now housing the forestry administration's offices.

In the 15th century iron ore was already being mined in the Dannemora area, where water power harnessed from the rivers could be used to drive the massive forging hammers. In **Österbybruk** there are still buildings remaining from a *bruksamhälle* (metal-workers community). In addition to the 18th-century manor house and the garden designed by Carl Hårleman, you can view the workers' dwellings, each of which accommodated four families. As is also the case with the workshops and the smithy, these were built around 1800.

Central Sweden

**Örby slott ❷ lies 10 kilometers to the west. This castle was the stage for one of the many feuds carried on by Gustavus Vasa's sons while vying for the Swedish throne. Erik XIV first held his brother John III captive in Gripsholm Castle, John then had Erik locked up in Örby and presumably poisoned (1568). The mighty tower dwelling is the oldest part of the grounds and dates back to their grandfather, Gustavus Vasa. Today, the castle belongs to the heirs of an iron and steel dynasty and can be toured only in part.

Örbyhus, nine kilometers to the south, is the location of the small town of **Vendel**, which gave its name to an entire epoch (A.D. 500-800). The town was still connected to Lake Mälaren at that time and must have been significantly important. A total of 14 burial mounds constructed in the shape of ships and a multitude of burial objects, such as artifacts with the typical Vendel "tendrils" design, were found on the southern slope below the church. The giant burial mound of **Ottarshögen**, the final resting place of the Svear ruler Ottar, is also from the Vendel Age. The burial findings are on display at the Historical Museum in Stockholm; the small museum in Vendel has only a collection of replicas.

On the E4 in **Tierp kyrkeby ❸** there is a rubble-stone church from the 14th century. Its late-Gothic frescos (ca. 1470) lent the name "Tierpstil" for this style of painting found in more than 20 churches in northern Sweden and Finland.

Mehedeby marks where the E4 crosses the Storfjorden, the fjord into which Sweden's longest river flows, the **Dalälven**. A few kilometers down river in **Älvkarleby ❹**, the mighty river, abundant with fish, was dammed in 1915 to build Sweden's largest hydroelectric station, thus cutting off the waterfall. Only on *Fallens Dag* (Waterfall Day) in June is the river unleashed to return to its old bed. The area off the coast of Älvkarleby is a favorite location among fishermen for sea trout.

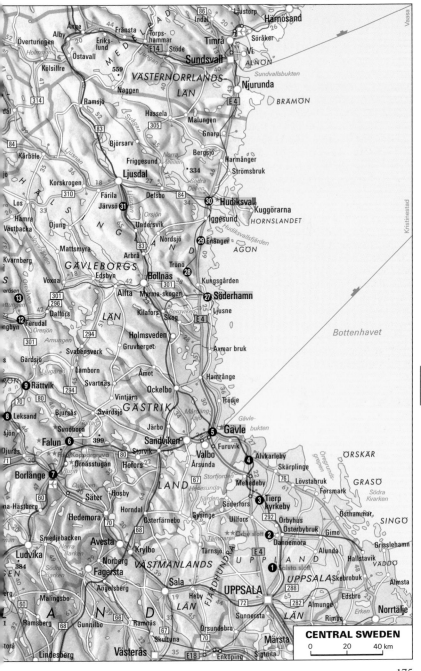

CENTRAL SWEDEN

0   20   40 km

*GÄVLE

Gästrikland was called *X-Län* for a long time in Sweden because of the "X" on the inhabitants' license plates. Today, the license plate prefix is only on cars registered some time ago. Gästrikland has an area of 4,600 square kilometers and comprises the southernmost part of Norrland. The provincial capital *Gävle ❺ was the first town in Norrland to be granted a charter (1446). The old seaport on the Gulf of Bothnia is today an industrial city of 80,000 inhabitants.

The spacious tree-lined avenues traversing the city were laid after the big fire of 1869. North of **Gavleån** the trees ring the **Esplanaden**, a long, narrow park with a theater in the north and the town hall near the southern end. The sculpture *Hyperborean Goddess* (Goddess from Beyond the North Wind) was placed on the square there, presumably to show the visitors that Gävle belongs to Norrland.

By crossing Drottninggatan and the newly redesigned **Stortorget**, you arrive at the **Trefaldighetskyrkan** (Church of the Holy Trinity), which took on its present appearance in the 17th century. The high altar, resembling the silver altar in Stockholm, and the 12th-century baptismal font are worth seeing.

The **castle** is located south of Gavleån. This is the northernmost of all Vasa castles and is now the governor's residence. From the castle it is just a few steps to **Gamla Gefle**, the Old Town – passing a Henry Moore sculpture on the way. Houses and farmsteads from the 18th and 19th centuries have been preserved in this idyllic timber-built town. One of them is the house where Joel Hägglund was born, who emigrated to America at the beginning of the 20th century. He was an active pioneer of the American trade union movement under the name of Joe Hill un-

til executed for murder following a dubious trial.

Also recommended is the **Länsmuseet** on Södra Strandgatan, boasting the oldest wooden boat in Sweden from the 1st century A.D. and a nice collection of Swedish art. Those more technically inclined should find a visit to the **Sveriges Järnvägsmuseum** interesting. The National Railway Museum is located directly off an exit of the E4 and was moved here from Stockholm in 1970. The collection is so comprehensive that well-to-do railroad enthusiasts can even have trains set up however they want here and then be taken for a ride in them.

Next, you can take an excursion to **Bönan** and **Utvalsnäs**, two old fishing villages where smoked herring is produced and sold.

Dalarna – Land of the Little Wooden Horses

Route 60 takes you 100 kilometers inland from Gävle to Lake Siljan in the heart of **Dalarna** (The Valleys). The Ovansilja, a thinly populated, densely wooded area where small farmers had to eke out an existence in the past, extends northwest of the lake. There are only a few larger towns in this region. Nedansilja, on the other hand, is known for mining, which has a long tradition here. Even the Vikings were acquainted with this "iron land."

When the mine owners in the 17th century wanted to flaunt their wealth by building prestigious houses, they had to accept the fact that brick houses, a status symbol at that time, were too expensive even for them. Instead, they built wooden houses and simply painted them red. Making paint from iron oxide had been discovered at least a century before; it was called *Falurött* (after the mining town of Falun). Later on it was discovered that not only did this material provide a brilliant color, but it also preserved

Right: Hand-crafted Dalarna horses – a favorite souvenir item from Nusnäs.

the wood incredibly well. The demand for *Falurött* grew so rapidly that the profession of "red paint man" developed: these craftsmen traveled from town to town conjuring up the desired paint with all kinds of hocus pocus.

The farmers, on the other hand, had completely different worries of their own. Since the farmers were constantly parceling their land as inheritance, the farms became so small and unprofitable that the heirs were forced to look for an additional source of income. The countryside blessed them with a little mascot: the *Dalahästar* (Dalarna horse). The peasants carved and wove little every-day items and toys, and traveling merchants crossed the land selling the products in the cities. When a woodcarver got the idea to paint the small wooden horses with *Falurött* and to decorate them with folk-art designs typical of their local region, the omnipresent souvenir of today was born.

In addition to selling wooden horses, Dalarna is also closely associated with another tradition: the many wandering minstrels who play tunes at various festivals. In the 19th century, numerous inhabitants of rural Dalarna would go to the cities looking for employment, playing music to attract attention. On the side, they would peddle their wares from home. The saying "When two Dalarnans stand together, three fiddles play" was coined back then, and is still a commonly used phrase today.

*FALUN

After driving from Gävle on an 86-kilometer stretch beautifully rich in woodland and lakes, you reach ***Falun ❻**, the capital of Dalarna, with a population of 50,000. Founded in 1280, the Mining Company of Falun is the oldest stock corporation in the world. The heyday of mining was in the 16th and 17th centuries, when the local mine was the world's largest copper producer and its export yields strengthened Sweden's powerful position in Europe.

Central Sweden

Mining methods at the time were totally unsophisticated. Whenever a copper vein was discovered, the miners came with fire and water and exploited the source until it was exhausted. This created huge caverns in the copper mountain which increasingly began to resemble Swiss cheese until, in 1687, the inevitable happened – a cave-in. Luckily no lives were lost, because the accident happened on Midsummer Day, a national holiday. **Stora Stöten**, "Great Earth Fall," is the name of the 65-meter-deep funnel-shaped pit resulting from the collapse. Mining started again after the accident, but due to overseas competition, it never reached its previous level of intensity.

The Mine and the City

The mine of **Stora Kopparberg** (Great Copper Mine) is located on Route 60 at

Above: Carl Larsson (self-portrait, 1900). Right: Larssongården in Sundborn on Lake Toftan influenced Swedish interior design.

the exit to the city of Borlänge. The old mine, ****Falu Koppargruva**, and the **Stora Museum** in the former administration building convey long-lasting impressions of nearly a millennium of mining history.

At the entrance to the mine grounds you see the old wire-drawing building where the steel cables for the hauling plant were braided. Ox hide was still being used for making ropes on into the 19th century. The oxen necessary for the process were driven along the long trail from Småland to Dalarna and then slaughtered on site. More or less resourceful miners had the brilliant idea of using the ox meat to make sausages. The *Falukorv*, a type of sausage, can be found at any *gatukök* (snack bar) today.

Before entering the mine elevator, visitors are provided with rain capes and helmets. It is a good idea to bring a sweater and some sturdy shoes since, at a depth of 60 meters, the tunnel is damp and hardly warmer than 5°C. The adventuresome shaft and tunnel construction, buckets for transporting personnel, and the numerous caved-in shafts are still impressive. In 1719, a miner who had been buried alive was found in one of them; because he had lain in vitriolic water the entire time, he was so well preserved that an old woman was able to identify him as her fiancé who had gone missing 40 years earlier. E.T.A. Hoffmann wrote of this incident in his novella *The Mines of Falun*.

Despite the many city fires, some of the old workers' districts in Falun have survived the course of time. Fine examples of these are **Elsborg**, a "new district" from the 18th century which replaced the workers' pitiful huts, and **Gamla Herrgården**, where there are still streets from the Middle Ages. The environmental pollution of the 18th century is hardly imaginable today: the sulfur vapors of the copper smelting were so pungent that all of the vegetation in the surrounding area of Falun died out.

The Stortoget in Falun also forms the town center, whose focal point is the 17th-century **Kristine kyrka**, since the church is positioned diagonally to the main square of the city's otherwise right-angled layout of the 18th century. The **Stora Kopparbergs kyrka** at the north train station is, however, considerably older. The miners' church is located amidst the remains of an old workers' community and partially dates back to the 14th century. The interior is decorated with ornamental paintings in the Dalarna style. This form of country art is also the central theme of the **Dalarna Museum** next to the Stortorget.

Falun is also known as Sweden's largest winter-sports area, since it is located – by Scandinavian standards – practically on Stockholm's doorstep (240 kilometers away). Since the 1920s, the city has been making every effort to be chosen host to the winter Olympic Games; and the necessary facilities have long been completed. In 1994, it was believed they had finally achieved their goal because tradi-tionally it was Scandinavia's turn again. But much to the disappointment of the Falun citizenry Lillehammer, Norway was favored.

Linné and Larsson

Located six kilometers east of Falun is **Svedens Gård**, a former cavalry captain's estate from the 18th century, when the provinces were to provide and sustain army contingents. In 1739, Carl von Linné and the daughter of the doctor residing there celebrated their nuptials in the still preserved guest house. The furnishings and the hand-painted wallpaper of **Linnés bröllopsstuga** (wedding hut) show the sophisticated style of home décor in the 18th century.

The name of the painter and illustrator Carl Larsson (1853-1919) is inseparable from the town of Falun. He lived in ***Sundborn** – 15 kilometers northeast of Falun on **Lake Toftan** – in a house he designed himself. The interior furnishings he and his wife designed were docu-

Central Sweden

mented by numerous watercolor paintings he presented to the public through various publications. Larsson thus became the most-copied interior designer in Sweden. The fact that he was an excellent portrait artist as well can be witnessed in the collection in the old parsonage located next to the church.

BORLÄNGE

Although you can reach Rättvik on Lake Siljan by way of Route 80, 46 kilometers past Falun the stretch via Borlänge (routes 60 and 70), though twice as long, has much more to offer. After 12 kilometers on this road you reach the **Ornäs** exit and an estate of the same name. Its guest house, ***Ornässtugan**, one of the best-preserved wooden medieval houses in Sweden, has been a museum since 1750.

Above: The inhabitants of Rättvik sail to church in decorated boats from June to August. Right: The fiddle is the favored instrument in Dalarna.

It is said to have served as a refuge for Gustavus Vasa when he fled from the Danes in 1520.

The city of **Borlänge ❼** is a modern industrial city in the middle of the historic mining area of Bergslagen. The city did not begin to flourish until it was linked to the railroad network in 1880. The paper and steel industries employ a good part of the city's 47,000 inhabitants. The local **Geologiska museet** houses the largest mineral collection in Sweden. The **Framtidsmuseet** (Museum of the Future) makes science and technology intelligible. Towering over the area at the southern edge of city is a gigantic modern dome-shaped building, the **Kupolen** shopping and convention center.

The old industrial areas of Bergslagen have been transformed into lively commemorative sites. Just 50 kilometers south of Borlänge, at the northern end of the Strömsholm Canal (see p. 130) and near Smedjebacken, several disused mines and other mining facilities have been combined to create the *Ekomuseum*.

Each of these museums sheds light on a particular aspect of mining history.

Our journey takes us from Borlänge to Lake Siljan and, shortly afterwards, to the confluence of the Österdal and Västerdal rivers, the Dalälven. Route 70 crosses the Österdalälven next to an old **raft bridge** at Österfors, five kilometers farther on.

The North and East Shores of *Siljan

The Österdalälven flows from the southeast tip of **Lake Siljan** near **Leksand ❽**. The community of 14,000 huddles around a church considerably older than the town itself. Up into the modern age there were only separate farmsteads which were united through church parishes. These communities built their churches in the immediate vicinity of the shore to be easily reached by boat in the summer and by sled in the winter. The *kyrkbåtarna* (church boats) remain among the most interesting attractions of the region, particularly on Midsummer Day, when a church-boat race is held. Up to 10,000 onlookers are here when the maypole is raised for the summer solstice festival.

The **church** of Leksand, whose oldest elements date from the 12th century, is located on a burial grounds from the Viking Age. The number of galleries in the church is astonishing, allowing a capacity of 2,000. A fixed seating arrangement determined where the women, men, soldiers, children and the choir were to sit, whereby the choir gallery characteristically bears the name "wailing loft."

Many visitors are attracted to the numerous music festivals of the region, such as the one in Leksand where hundreds of fiddlers in traditional costume gather during the first week of July. The **Summerland Adventure Park** provides additional entertainment. Together with the district of **Tällberg**, farther north on the lake, well over 1,000 hotel rooms are available. **Plintsberg** and the observation tower on the **Vidablick** near the junction of routes 70 and 80 offer spectacular views of the lake.

Central Sweden

Second to Leksand, **Rättvik** ❾ is the largest tourist town on the east side of Lake Siljan. The highlights here are also the folk musicians (last week in July) and the church-boat race. The old tradition of traveling to church on decorated boots is carried on every Sunday from June to August, departing from the dock at the cultural center. Near the dock you can find the 87 **Kyrkostallen** (church stalls), where the farmers sheltered their horses when attending church in the winter and sometimes spent the night there themselves. The **Vasastenen**, located directly on the lake, commemorates Gustavus Vasa's futile speech to the citizens of Dalarna imploring them to revolt against the Danes.

There are many open-air museums, lovingly built and furnished, in the villages on Lake Siljan, such as **Gammelgård** in Rättvik and Leksand's **Hemsbygd gården**.

In **Nusnäs** ❿, a few kilometers before reaching Mora (to the left of Route 70), the tradition of making little Dalarna horses has been kept alive. The machine-cut raw product takes final shape in numerous family businesses and is painted with local country patterns. There are also owls and geese in the array of products, and instead of the traditional red, the souvenirs are also available in blue, white and black. You can tour the workshops – and of course purchase their wares – even if the 1880 price of 25 Öre for a Dalarna horse has risen in the meantime.

MORA

With a population of 20,000, **Mora** ⓫ is the largest town on Lake Siljan. Located on a promontory near the spot where the Österdalälven flows into the lake, it is, like Leksand, the center of an old church parish. The *Inlandsbana*

Right: A serene late afternoon view of Lake Siljan.

leaves from here for Gällivare (see also p. 217).

Mora became world famous for the "Vasa Run" cross-country ski race, which has been held annually on the first Sunday in March since 1924. It commemorates Gustavus Vasa's legendary getaway in 1521: After narrowly escaping the "Stockholm Bloodbath" of 1520 (see p. 17), he wanted to organize an army of farmers in Dalarna to rise against Danish rule, but they refused to follow in allegiance. Since his persecutors were already close on his heels, Gustavus Vasa fled towards Norway. Then, however, word of the Danes raising taxes spread to the people of Dalarna like wildfire, and the opinion among the farmers changed in favor of Gustavus Vasa. They sent two skiers who caught up with the future king in **Sälen**. Overjoyed with this development, Vasa returned to Mora in record time, led his army in battle and utterly destroyed the Danish forces.

Today, the fastest skiers can cover the distance of 85 kilometers in eight to nine hours; the slowest participants arrive in Mora quite exhausted several days later. In the past, it was a moral obligation of every male Swedish citizen to have participated in this race at least once in his lifetime; though today this is no longer the case. At least 30 percent of the participants nowadays are women.

Mora also became known for its painter, etcher and sculptor Anders Zorn (1860-1920). After he had become very successful and wealthy in Europe and America – he had, for instance, portrayed several American presidents – he returned to Mora. You can visit his retreat, the **Zorngården**. He had his residence, an old farm house, remodeled in the style of a cottage: an *eldhus* (fire house, i.e., kitchen building), served as his studio – the oldest *eldhus* preserved in Dalarna, by the way. Zorn's fountain sculpture *Morgonbad* found a place in front of his residence itself. The **Zornmuseet**, opened in

Central Sweden

1939, not only displays a selection of Zorn's own works (watercolors, oils, graphic art and sculptures), but also his personal collection – including paintings by Velasquez. The statue of Engelbrekt Engelbrektsson, the popular hero from Dalarna, was donated by Carl Milles.

Zorn was concerned about the preservation of the farming culture, and so he acquired a complete farm in Mora, as well as other traditional buildings and objects from all over Dalarna, now on display at **Zorns Gammelgård**, an open-air museum.

South of Siljan

Heading south from Mora, Route 242 leads along Lake Siljan to Leksand. Two bridges allow crossover to the island of **Sollerön**, where there was a Viking settlement 6,000 years ago. The Vikings maintained a large burial grounds here which was uncovered near **Bengtsarvet**. The findings were taken to Falun and are on display at the Länsmuseum (Provin-

cial Museum) there. The last existing shipyard for church boats is located on Sollerön.

The **Gesundaberget** (514 meters), opposite the island on the mainland, is prepared for ski runs in the winter. At the valley station of the chair lift there is a small hotel and restaurant open only from mid-June to mid-August. Children always enjoy **Tomteland** (Gnome Land), a collection of workshops where Santa Claus and his helpers make Christmas presents in the summer – and sell them to parents year round.

*SILJANSLEDEN

Lake Siljan, **Lake Orsasjön** in the northwest and lakes **Skattungen** and **Oresjön** in the northeast – clearly joined by rivers and depressions – create a distinct circular shape. The major roads north of Siljan make this arch more apparent: leaving from Mora going clockwise, routes 45 (to Orsa), 296 (Skattungbyn, Furudal) and 301 (Furudal-

Rättvik). Those visiting the Nature Museum in Rättivik are given an explanation of this puzzling circular-shaped depression with a perimeter of ca. 100 kilometers: approximately 400 million years ago, a meteorite is believed to have crashed to earth in the center of the circle – the impact resulting in the obvious ring we see today.With a radius of 20 kilometers we can only try to imagine how powerful the force of the collision must have been. The enormous impact of the giant extraterrestrial object heated the earth's surface so much that it literally evaporated. Such a meteorite itself can therefore never be found; merely the deformations in the landscape bear witness to its having existed.

This pre-marked circle was reason enough for the communities around Lake Siljan to lay a course around it. The marked *Siljansleden offers hikers and

Above: Midsummer celebrations at Tällberg on Lake Siljan. Right: In the Grönklitt Bear Park.

cyclists paths around the lake varying from 200 to 300 kilometers in length and lead through unspoiled landscapes with diverse rest stops – without demanding ascents.

Taking the 301 from Rättvik, after 10 kilometers you arrive at **Norrboda Kyrkbyn**, a mining town gathered around a church. Shortly after passing through town, you will see a well-marked trail leading to the nature reserve of **Styggforsen**, with a 36-meter-high waterfall and clearly visible geological strata. The incredible forces of the impact of the meteorite shoved the earth layers from horizontal to vertical. The masses of water eroded the softer rock and left a narrow canyon behind, a popular source of many sagas and tales. It is said that a ledge protruding into the gorge endured until three old spinsters gathered on it. There are supposedly trolls and other mythical creatures living there, possessing all the possible personality traits from unparalleled virtue to unmatched evil.

The continuing round-trip tour of the ring continues through beautiful unspoiled landscapes leaving us with favorable impressions of the seemingly endless expanses of countryside in north-western Sweden. Just some 15 kilometers north of **Furudal** ⑫ the *Siljansleden* hiking trail reaches the *fäbod* (dairy farm) of **Ärteråsen** ⑬, which has been in operation since the 17th century. In the hamlet of **Skräddar-Djurberga** (15 kilometers north of **Skattungbyn** on the 296) the dairy maids keep a relatively large stock of animals; naturally, you can sample the fresh, nutritious homemade products there on location. Everyone should try *mesmör* at least once: this sweet cheese, often spread on bread in Sweden, is made by boiling milk in a big pot over an open fire for several hours, or long enough for the lactose to caramelize.

Orsa ⑭, a resort located on the shores of a lake of the same name, appears modern at first, but it boasts a small 14th-

century church with nice 16th-century frescoes. A special attraction is the popular recreation area of **Fryksås** ⓯. In addition to numerous water sports, the area offers fishing and a variety of other free-time activities. There is also the nearby **Grönklitt Björnparken**, a vast outdoor enclosure where you can watch bears, lynx and wolves from safety observation ramps – most likely the only opportunity for many nature lovers to see these animals in their natural habitat. Former dairy-farming cabins here are rented out to vacationers.

To the Headwaters of the Dalälven

Route 70 from Mora to the Norwegian border passes through very sparsely populated forests. The only larger community is Älvdalen, 35 kilometers away. After 23 kilometers there is a byroad branching off to **Evertsberg** ⓰, a town located on the course of the "Vasa Run." The skiers will hardly have time for a look at the **church**, which has one of the most beautiful late-Gothic altars from Nuremberg. It remains an unsolved mystery which roundabout way the masterpiece took through the forests of Sweden to finally end up here.

The town of **Älvdalen** ⓱ also has a church from the 15th century which is only used in the summer because it cannot be heated. The **Tiondehärbre** (tithe storage), the oldest timber-built house in Sweden, dating back to the 13th century, is worth seeing. This is where the local farmers were required to pay one tenth of the value of their yielded harvest as church tax.

Porphyry, a colored volcanic rock primarily used in the Baroque period for burial stones and urns, was mined in Älvdalen for quite some time. The quarry has been abandoned, but a **porphyry grinding shop** here produces jewelry and decorative items for the home.

As a defense against the Norwegians, the **öda skansen** was erected just a few kilometers north of Älvdalen in 1675. The provost of Älvdalen, though, had put

Central Sweden

the Norwegian villages of **Särna** ⑱ and Idre under the Swedish Crown in a surprise coup 20 years before. A monument commemorating this event is located next to the church of Särna. The town of Särna on the Österdalälven has, in the meantime, evolved to compete not only with Idre, but also with the famous and exclusive winter-sports town of **Sälen** ⑲ (90 kilometers farther south, in the upper reaches of the Västerdalälven). **Särnafjäll** has developed into one of the largest winter-sports areas in Sweden.

Located on the small road between Särna and Fulufjället there is a parking area called **Björbäckstugan**. A popular trail will lead you on an approximately one-hour hike to the ***Njupeskärs vattenfall**, Sweden's highest waterfall (93 meters). From here, there are other hiking possibilities in the nature reserve of **Fulufjället**.

Above: Haymaking in Härjedalen. Right: A great many beavers have settled in Töfsingdalens National Park.

Another vacation village is located in **Idre** ⑳. The mountains here reach elevations of more than 1,000 meters, and the view from the ascending road leaves a lasting impression of the wide open spaces of the north. The effect intensifies as you continue on Route 295 to the ski resort of **Grövelsjön** ㉑.

Here in the area bordering Norway, there are three more nature reserves, **Rogen**, **Långfjället** and **Nipfjället**, which together with **Töfsingdalens National Park** and the Norwegian national parks of **Femundsmarka** and **Gutulia** form a vast natural landscape. It is used on both sides of the border by hikers and canoeists alike. You should allow a week for the hike from Grövelsjön to Lake Femunden.

Nearby Lake Rogen, surrounded by the Rogen Nature Reserve, is a paradise for any canoe enthusiast. Those who would like to totally escape civilization are recommended to visit Töfsingdalens National Park, which requires a 13-hour walk to reach. Golden eagles still nest

186　　　　**Map pp. 174-175, Info pp. 190-191**

there, and many beavers have found homes in the lakes of Töfsingån as well.

Pilgrimage in Dalarna's Forests

Riksvägen 45, covering the distance from Mora to the far north, is the longest royal highway in Sweden. At the same time, it is also the shortest connection between Gothenburg and the North Cape, and bears the name *Inlandsvägen*. Leaving from Mora, the road heads to the north – straight through the forest at times. In the border zone of the Dalarna and **Härjedalen** regions, there is yet another area where the Finns immigrated in the 16th century. The **Hamra National Park** was established here east of Route 45. The park is only 28 hectares in area, and its main purpose is to protect endangered plants; elk, lynx and deer live here as well. Part of the park is also laid out with footpaths.

After another 40 kilometers we arrive at **Sveg ㉒**, with 4,000 inhabitants the largest community, and also the county seat of Härjedalen. There are shops, a gas station and a church – the present-day "attractions" of a town which, in the 9th century, had a *ting* (place of assembly) located where the church now stands.

With a population density of only one person per square kilometer, the entire region of Härjedalen is the most thinly populated area in all of Sweden. It is mainly covered with forests. The tree line for conifers here is at 750 meters above sea level, but many mountains are much higher than that, so bare peaks rise up out of the forest. At 1,796 meters, the **Helagsfjället** is Sweden's highest mountain south of the Arctic Circle.

In Sveg we arrive at the old trade route from the Gulf of Bothnia to Trondheim – now *Riksvägen* 84. It served as the medieval pilgrimage route to the grave of Saint Olav in former Nidaros. The close proximity to this important Norwegian pilgrimage site is without a doubt responsible for Härjedalen becoming the first region in Sweden where Christianity gained a foothold.

Central Sweden

The oldest church of the area can be found in **Lillhärdal** ㉓, 25 kilometers southwest of Sveg. It dates back to the 14th century and possesses one of the oldest statues of the Virgin Mary in Sweden (13th century).

After heading west 14 kilometers from Sveg on *Riksvägen* 84 we arrive at **Remsgården**, a typical country farm in **Glissjöberg** ㉔. In the main building there are well-preserved frescoes from the 18th century. Additionally, you can pay a visit to the restored Härjedalen sawmill of **Remssågen**. Route 315 branches off from Highway 84 to the north five kilometers east of Glissjöberg. After another 40 kilometers, in Vemdalen, we are pleasantly surprised by an octagonal Rococo church with finely carved furnishings by local artists.

Leaving **Hedeviken** ㉕ (on the west side) to the south via Route 312, you arrive at the **Nyvallen** dairy hut in **Sånfjället National Park**. After 12 kilometers, the 312 curves to the east north of Sånfjället and ends after about three kilometers in the town of Nyvallen itself. The park was established in 1910 to save the declining bear population.

From **Funäsdalen** ㉖ on the 84 you come to the high plateau of **Flatruet**, which rises to 1,154 meters. It is really quite amazing that the numerous rock drawings found here near **Ruändan** (depicting mainly animals) are probably four to five thousand years old. You can reach Ruändan via the highest mountain road in Sweden: heading northwards from Funäsdalen towards Ljungdalen via **Mittådalen** and **Messlingen**.

Beginning in **Ljungdalen**, at the end of the mountain road, a 19-kilometer hiking trail leads to Helagsstugorna. This mountain hut is an ideal place from where you can begin hikes to Helagsfjället and to the **Sylarna Mountains**.

Right: Anders Zorn's "Midsummer Dance" was painted in 1903.

SÖDERHAMN AND HUDIKSVALL

Those traveling farther north generally take the E4. Passing **Mårdängsjö**, a bird sanctuary on a lake with a nice rest area, you come to the region of **Hälsingland**. It is a predominately wooded area where agriculture is only possible in the valleys of Ljusnan and Voxnaälven. Despite owning large areas of forest, the farmers still needed an additional source of income. They found a solution in the 12th century with the cultivation and processing of flax. When the Swedish state began to provide lasting support for this secondary occupation in the 18th century, it moved up to become recognized as the primary occupation in the area. The farmers then became wealthy and provided themselves with fabulous wooden houses, which the envious referred to as *bondesslott* (peasant palaces).

Fishing had long been the economic basis for survival on the coast, but not until World War II did it become an industry. To help curb migration to the cities, the Swedish state entices companies to the area by offering subsidies in return for investing here. This way, employment is brought to the people and not vice versa.

Larger cities did not develop in Hälsingland until relatively late, and when they did it was exclusively on the coast. To populate the inland regions, Charles IX and Gustavus II Adolphus had no choice but to promise new settlers years of tax exemption and free seed allotments to lure them to the area.

Söderhamn ㉗ was originally a small fishing village and remained one until 1620, when the king had Swedish firearms production moved here. After some disastrous fires, however, the factories eventually moved to Eskilstuna. Today, Söderhamn is a center for the logging industry. The best view of the city is available from **Oscarsborg fästning**. The drilling workshop, where the rifle and gun barrels were made, now serves as the

Söderhamn Museum. Due to the huge donations made by the person it was named after, the **Ulrica Eleonora kyrka** of 1685 could be built of stone.

Northwest of Söderhamn in the town of **Tröno** ㉘ there are even two churches. The **Gamla Kyrkan** of **Trönbyn** from the 12th century is the oldest stone church of Norrland, and is enclosed by a completely preserved churchyard wall. The **Nya Kyrkan** is impressive due to its reliquary produced in the workshops in Limoges. The enamel shrine depicts the murder of Thomas à Becket in the Canterbury Cathedral.

Between Söderhamn and Hudiksvall, in the town of **Enånger** ㉙, the **Gamla kyrkan** (15th century) has two wooden triptychs carved by the craftsman Haaken Gullesson. He ran a workshop here in the 16th century and supplied most churches in the area with furnishings, e.g., in **Njutången**, **Hälsingtuna** and **Forsa**.

*Hudiksvall ㉚ is the oldest city in Hälsingland. It served as a trading center for the people of Norrland and was granted a town charter in 1528 to better control the merchants. The city was burned to the ground by the Russians in 1721. Only on **Strömmigssund** are there a few old preserved harbor storerooms. The "Fishing Town" on Hamngatan is a collection of beautiful wooden buildings. The **Trönesska gården** and the **Brunska apotek** on Storgatan are 19th-century constructions. The **Hälsinglands Museum** on the Storgatan has a grave from the Stone Age, as well as *bonader* (folk art) and bright traditional costume dress.

From Hudiksvall it is nearly 80 kilometers to **Järvsö** ㉛ on Ljusnan (Route 84 to Ljusdal, then 10 kilometers to the south). It is wonderfully situated and upholds its traditions. One of the largest country churches in Sweden is on an island in the middle of the river and can seat 1,800.

The *Hälsingehambon* ends in Järvsö. Some 800 couples begin their roundelay at Sweden's largest folk dance event on **Hårgaberget** on the morning of Midsummer Day, and dance via **Bollnäs** and **Arbrå** to Järvsö into the evening.

Central Sweden

ÖSTERBYBRUK (☎ 0295)

_i_ 78143 Österbybruk, tel. 21492.

⊟ ⑤ Värdshuset Gammel Tammen, tel. 21200. **Österbybruks Vandrarhem SFT**, tel. 21570, fax 20050.

▲ Simbads Camping, tel. 20630, mobile phone: 070-5577492, May 15-Sept 1.

✕ A simple restaurant is part of **Värdshuset Gammel Tammen**. **Café Hembygsgården** is only open Sat-Sun 12-5 pm.

▥ Metallurgical Museum (Vallonssmedjan) May 1-31, Sept 5-6 and 12-13, 12-4 pm daily, June-Aug 11 am-5 pm daily.

▥ Salsta Castle, Department of Forestry, can only be viewed from the outside. **Örby slott**, tours: May 9-June 22 and Aug 8-Sept 13, Sun 1 pm, June 23-Aug 7, Tue-Sun 1 pm. **Museum Vendel**, May-Aug, Tue-Sun 11 am-4 pm, otherwise only Sat-Sun 11 am-4 pm. **Church of Tierp**, 9 am-6 pm daily, except during services.

▣ Organ concerts in the church every Sun in July.

GÄVLE (☎ 026)

_i_ Kirkogatan 14, 80135 Gävle, tel. 188390.

⊟ ⑤⑤ Provobis Grand Central Hotel, Nygatan 45, tel. 129060, fax 124499. **Scandic Hotel Gävle**, Johanneslötsvägen 6, tel. 188060, fax 141860. ⑤ **Hotell Gävle**, Staketgatan 44, tel. 515470, fax 517510. **Gamla Gefle**, Södra Rådmansgatan 1, tel./fax 621745, old cozy Villa.

✕ Bistro Konvaljen, in the Scandic Hotel. **Engeltofta**, Bönavägen 118, tel. 96063, summer restaurant with live music and its own bathing beach.

▥ Trefaldighetskyrkan, 9 am-6 pm daily, except during services. **Gamla Gefle**, stores and studio Tue-Sun 10 am-6 pm. **Länsmuseum**, June-Aug 10 am-4 pm daily, otherwise only Sat-Sun 10 am-4 pm. **Järnvägsmuseum**, June-Aug 1-4 pm, otherwise only Sat-Sun 1-4 pm.

FALUN (☎ 023)

_i_ Stora Torget, 79183 Falun, tel. 83637.

⊟ ⑤⑤ First Hotel Grand, Trotzgatan 9-11, tel. 18700, fax 14143. **Scandic Hotel Lunget**, Svärtsjögatan 51, tel. 22160, fax 12845. ⑤ **Brigittagården**, Uddnäsvägen 58, tel. 32048, fax 32471. **Hotel Bergmästeren**, Bergskolgränd 7, tel. 63600, fax 22524. _YOUTH HOSTELS:_ **Vandrarhem Helsinggården**, Helsinggårdensveien 71, tel. 10560.

▲ Lungnet Camping, Lungnetsleden, tel. 83563, with swimming pool.

✕ Rådhuskällaren, Stora Torget, tel. 25400, sophisticated home cooking. **Vass Brita**, Bergmannsgatan 23, tel. 13881. **Hammars Konditori**, Åsgatan 28, tel. 39039, Café and pastry shop in an old forge.

▥ Stora Kopparber mine, tours: May-Aug 10 am-4:30 pm daily. **Grubenmuseum**, same opening hours. **Kristina Kyrka** and **Kopparbergskyrka**, 9 am-6 pm daily, except during services. **Dalarnamuseum**, May 15-Aug 31, Mon-Fri 10 am-5 pm, Wed to 9 pm, Sat-Sun 12 pm-5 pm, otherwise only Sat-Sun 10 am-4 pm.

▥ Sveden Gård, May-Sept 11 am-4 pm daily, otherwise only Sat/Sun 11 am-4 pm. **Sundborn**, May-Sept 10 am-5 pm daily, otherwise by appointment, tel. 60053.

▣ Lunget: A ski area is available here, where world championships have already taken place.

BORLÄNGE (☎ 0243)

_i_ Borgnäsvägen 25, 78133 Borlänge, tel. 18125.

⊟ ⑤⑤ Provobis Hotel Galaxen, Jussi Björlings Väg 25, tel. 80010, fax 16230. **Hotel Brage**, Stationsgatan 1, tel. 224150, fax 87100, with a discotheque. ⑤ **Ulfshyttans Herrgård**, Ulfshyttan, tel. 251300, fax 251111, small, in a nice location.

▲ Mellstra Camping, tel. 328255, 5 km north of route 70 directy on Dalaälv.

✕ Many restaurants in the **Kupolen** mall – from fastfood to Italian, Mon-Fri 10 am-8 pm, Sat 10 am-4 pm.

▥ Geologiska Museum, June-Aug 11 am-5 pm daily.

▥ Ornässtuga, April 1-Oct 28, Mon-Sat 10 am-6 pm, Sun 1 pm-5 pm.

LEKSAND (☎ 0247)

_i_ Norsgatan, 79327 Leksand, tel. 80300.

⊟ ⑤⑤⑤ Hotell Dalecarlia, Tällberg, tel. 89100, fax 50240. ⑤⑤ **Green Hotel**, Tällberg, tel. 50250, fax 50130. **Hotell Klockargården**, Siljansvägen 6, Tällberg, tel. 50260, fax 50216, 20 different hotels, some with fireplace or four-poster. **Tällbergsgården Pensionat**, Holgattu 1, Tällberg, tel. 50850, fax 50200, fantastic view and a Smörgåsbord to recommend. **Masesgårdens hälsohem**, Gryntnäs 61, Leksand, tel. 12231, fax 12251.

▲ Västervikbadet, tel. 34201, with 10 _HUTS_.

✕ Björkbergets Turist & Konferens, Björkberget, Siljanäs, tel. 23122, fish and game specialties.

▥ Church of Leksand, 9 am-6 pm daily, except during services ad choir rehearsals. **Hembygdsgården**, shops: June-Aug, Tue-Sun 10 am-6 pm.

☻ Third week in June: **Midsummer Festival**. First week in July: **Musician Festival**.

RÄTTVIK (☎ 0248)

ℹ️ Torget, 79522 Rättvik, tel. 70200.

🛏️ 🆂🆂 **Gårdebygården**, Hol Daniels Väg 6, tel. 10007, fax 10257, beautiful location. 🆂 **Stiftsgården Rättvik**, tel. 51020, fax 12754. **SFT Vandrarhem**, Centralgatan, tel. 10566, fax 70394.

🅰️ **Rättvik Camping**, tel. 51690, fax 51689, directly on the lake, also *BICYCLE* and *BOAT RENTALS*. **Rättviksparkens**, tel. 11606, with 80 *HUTS*.

❌ **Hotel Gårdebygården** serves regional specialties and international cuisine, also on the terrace.

🏛️ **Gammelgård**, June 18-Aug 13, Mon-Sat 11 am-6 pm, Sun 12-6 pm, tours: 1 and 2:30 pm. **Vidablick Observation Tower**, café, June 4-Aug 7, 11 am-9 pm daily, May 12-June 3 and Aug 8-21, 11 am-4 pm daily.

📅 Third week in June: **Midsummer Church-boat Races**. Last week in July: **Rättvik Folklore Festival**, with thousands of musicians and dancers.

MORA (☎ 0250)

ℹ️ Ångbåtskajen, 79230 Mora, tel. 26550.

🛏️ 🆂🆂 **Mora Hotell**, Strandgatan 12, tel. 71750, fax 18981. 🆂 **Hotell Moraparken**, Parkvägen 1, tel. 17800, fax 18583.

🅰️ **Mora Campingplatz**, Hantverksgatan, tel./fax 15352, also has 35 *HUTS*.

❌ **Terraces** in the **Mora Hotel**, good and reasonable.

🏛️ **Zorngården**, Mon-Sat 9 am-5 pm, Sun/holidays 11 am-5 pm, July also Thu 9 am-9 pm. **Zorns Gammelgård**, tours: Mon-Sat 10 am-4:15 pm, Sun/holidays 11 am-4:15 pm.

🎭 **Tomteland**, Gesundaberget, Sollerön, tel. 21200, open June 10-Aug 13 and Nov 25-Jan 7, 10 am-5 pm daily.

🚂 First Sunday in March: **Vasalauf**. Take the **Inlandsbana** to **Östersund**, schedules available from the tourist office. Two-day *TROLLY RIDES* with tents, for reservations contact: Vansbro Turistbyrå, tel. 0281-75230.

ORSA (☎ 0250)

🛏️ 🆂 **Hotel Vandrarhem Grönklitt**, tel. 46200, also *HUTS* in **Björnpark Grönklitt**, park: June-Aug 9 am to sunset.

ÄLVDALEN (☎ 0251)

ℹ️ Dalgatan 47, 79631 Älvdalen, tel. 80290

🛏️ 🆂 **Hotell Älvdalen**, Dalgatan 77, tel. 10500.

🏛️ **Church** of **Evertsberg**, June 15-Aug 15, 11 am-4 pm daily. **Porphyry Museum**, June 10-Aug 15 Mon-Sat 10 am-2 pm, Sun 12-4 pm. **Tiondehärbre**, can only be viewed from the outside.

🚲 Wilderness station of **Navadalen**: simple vacation *HUTS* at a fair price, with sauna, on the lake. Also *CANOE RENTALS* and over 200 km of *HIKING TRAILS*, maps. For info contact the tourist office.

IDRE (☎ 0253)

ℹ️ Kommunalhuset, 79091 Idre, tel. 20710.

🛏️ 🆂 **Idre Fjäll**, Hotel Hüttendorf, tel. 41000, fax 40158, facility with 100 rooms and 600 *HUTS*.

🎭 Mountain tours, also in winter, info: tourist office.

⛷️ *SKIING:* 32 lifts, 30 slopes, 55 km of cross-country trails. *GOLF:* 18 holes, considered to be Dalarna's most challenging course. Info: tourist office.

SVEG (☎ 0680)

ℹ️ Härjedalsportens Turistförening, 84200 Sveg, tel. 10775.

🛏️ 🆂 **Hotel Härjedalen**, Vallervägen 11, tel. 10338.

🅰️ **Sveg Camping**, tel. 13025, fax 10337, central, on the Ljusnan.

🏛️ **Flågelsjö**, tours : June 15-Aug 15 Sat-Sun 12 and 2 pm. **Gammelremsgården**, June 15-Aug 15, 11 am-6 pm daily.

🚲 *MOUNTAIN BIKING:* **Topsport**, Funäsdalen tel. 0684-21435, mountain tours, safaris and canoeing. **Strandgården**, Tänndalen, tel. 0684-23027. *CANOEING:* **Hede Sport Camping**, tel. 0684-11020. *SAFARIS:* **Hedevikens Fritid**, Hede, tel. 0684-12139.

SÖDERHAMN (☎ 0270)

ℹ️ Björnäsvägen 2, 82640 Söderhamn, tel. 75353.

🛏️ 🆂🆂 **Scandic Hotel Söderhamn**, Montörsbacken 4, tel. 18020, fax 18901 🆂 **First Hotel Statt**, Oxtorsgatan 17, tel. 41410, fax 135124.

🏛️ **Söderhamn Museum**, June-Aug, Mon-Sun 10 am-4 pm, otherwise Sat-Sun same times. **Ulrica Eleonora kyrka** and churches of **Tröno** and **Enånger**, 10 am-6 pm daily.

HUDIKSVALL (☎ 0650)

ℹ️ Möljen, 82480 Hudiksvall, tel. 19000.

🛏️ 🆂 **Hotell Hudik**, Norra Kyrkogatan, tel. 15040, fax 12345. **First Hotel Statt**, Storgatan 36, tel. 15060, fax 96095.

🚲 Penultimate Saturday in June: **Hälsingehambon** in Järvsö.

Central Sweden

NORTHERN PROVINCES ON THE GULF OF BOTHNIA

SUNDSVALL

ÖRNSKÖLDSVIK

UMEÅ

LULEÅ

HAPARANDA

THE "BIRCH BOULEVARD" E4

On the journey from central Sweden towards the north and the Gulf of Bothnia, the E4 skirts the coastline. There is a total of 660 kilometers between Sundsvall in Medelpad and Haparanda in Norrbotten on the Swedish-Finnish border. With only a few exceptions, the coastal region remains flat and swampy, and birch trees line the road in many places, lending the epithet "Birch Boulevard" to this route. On the way, you cross through the landscapes of Medelpad, Ångermanland, Västerbotten and Norrbotten, sparsely populated regions that are primarily covered with woods and forests. Only at the river basins where the rivers flow into the Baltic Sea will you find larger settlements. These were founded for the export of lumber, which was the most important source of income for centuries. Fishing plays only a minor role, since here in the far north the harbors are frozen over for months at a time, and the fishing season is short-lived. Pastural agriculture dominates here; only in the coastal valleys is modest farming possible.

Preceding pages: If you want to see a timid elk in the wild, you'll need a lot of luck – or patience. Left: Canoeing on the Ångermanälv.

The abundance of natural waterways and the resulting availability of inexpensive hydroelectricity have attracted many high-consumption businesses to the Gulf of Bothnia. The recent trend has been to export less lumber and export more finished products, such as prefabricated wooden houses and furniture; scrap wood is used to manufacture plywood and paper. Tourism plays an ever-increasing role here; today one fourth of all income earned comes from tourism.

Medelpad – Land of the Pilgrim

Ever since the Middle Ages, **Medelpad** (Middle Path) has been the name of the countryside around Sundsvall because an important pilgrim's route to Trondheim in Norway began here. This stretch of road that is now marked by the E14 running between Sundsvall and Trondheim was a fairly easy route for the pilgrims. It therefore became the most frequently used pilgrimage route between Sweden and the west coast of Norway as early as the 11th century. There was also another advantage at the time: in the Middle Ages, the land mass lay much lower than it does today and the waters of the Gulf extended farther inland.

Back then, pilgrims could sail all the way to **Borgsjö ❶**, 80 kilometers west of

Northern Provinces

Sundsvall, landing at Saint Olav's Port, which was built for them. Only then did they trudge through the endless forests. They allowed a good 30 days to negotiate the 350-kilometer stretch to Trondheim; in all, it took the pilgrims three to four months to complete the pilgrimage.

Even after the Reformation, it was still not at all uncommon for a Swede to undertake a pilgrimage to the important shrines of Scandinavian saints at least once in his or her lifetime. This custom continued even after the land mass had risen, and the harbor of Borgsjö lay high and dry, thus forcing the pilgrims to take the much longer route from Sundsvall to Trondheim.

Ljungdalen, the Ljungan Valley, where the E14 winds 70 kilometers along the river, is a vacation paradise. Especially canoeists, sport fishermen and golfers get their money's worth here. There are two golf courses at **Skottsund** and **Öjestrand** at the mouth of the Ljungan River. Not even beach vacationers will be left out, since the long, sunny summer days may warm the shallow waters of the Baltic inlets up to 20°C. **Njurunda ❷** has a beautiful sand beach.

THE CITY OF STONE – *SUNDSVALL

*Sundsvall ❸, with 94,000 inhabitants, is the second-largest city in northern Sweden and is also the administrative seat for Medelpad. The original settlement was chartered in 1624 under Gustavus II Adolphus. The monarch called for the establishment of a number of cities on the Swedish coast, as well as on the Finnish coast along the Gulf of Bothnia. On the one hand, he wanted to bind the northern and eastern regions of the kingdom firmly to the central core, while on the other hand, he wanted to create the means of controlling trade – by granting charters – to secure tax revenues flowing back to the royal treasury.

However, despite its charter and convenient location on Alnösund, Sundsvall for a long time remained only a modest center, trading with the Finnish west coast and the north country which was becoming increasingly important. Not until the 19th century, when the first sawmills were built, did things begin to boom. Over 40 sawmills were in operation in no time. The sawmill owners bought up woodland from the farmers, who then turned to the mills for employment, sometimes under miserable conditions. The lumber barons, on the other hand, became so rich that their affluent lifestyles caused a sensation throughout Sweden. In 1879, this situation led to the first great strike in Sweden, with 5,000 workers tak-

MEDELPAD/
ÄNGERMANLAND

0   20   40 km

ing part in the uprising. Only with military intervention could the strike be brought to an end.

In 1888, Sundsvall burned to the ground, but enough funds were available to rebuild the city, originally of wood, out of stone. The recently established district of Stockholm called Östermalm served as a model for the reconstruction. The squared residential areas were constructed around the city park, **Esplanaden**, and the Storgatan, leading to a large marketplace in the center. Prior to the great fire, part of the Stortorget contained a lake that was used as a reservoir by fire fighters. Without much ado, 5,000 tree trunks were rammed into the marshy ground to provide a foundation for the

Rådhuset (City Hall). A statue honoring King Gustavus II Adolphus was placed in front of the building.

A good example of the wealth of the lumber barons at that time is the **Hotel Knaust** on Storgatan. Here, parties were given with sumptuous glitter and glamour; today the former splendor is reflected only in the pretentious staircase, since the hotel now houses the Patent Office. Also on Storgatan you can find the newest city landmark, the **Kulturmagasinet**, a conglomeration of four harbor warehouses enclosed by glass facades and covered by a common roof to encompass a spacious cultural center. The library, the Medelpad Archives and the Municipal Museum are housed here. In

Northern Provinces

addition, the Kulturmagasinet offers an ever-changing program, with poetry readings and opera performances. In the **Café Skonerten** you can enjoy a good meal at a reasonable price.

During the first week in July, the Storgatan pedestrian zone is transformed into a huge center of festivity, because then Sundsvall becomes the scene of the largest street party in all of Norrland. Parades, musical events and crowds of people set the mood of the town, where a type of carnival – a Mardi Gras of the North – seems to have broken out.

Gustav Adolfs kyrka on the western side of Storgatan dates back to the 19th century. The local artist Ivar Lindecrantz decorated the facade with wooden sculptures. On the **Norra Stadsberget**, a bit outside the city limits, there is an open-air museum. On the **Södra Berget** is a large

Above: Flat and swampy – the countryside of Medelpad near Sundsvall. Right: The ferry from Sundsvall to Finnland is a favorite weekend meeting place for young people.

winter sports resort built around the **Hotel Södra Berget**. Slalom runs and cross-country trails challenge even experienced skiers. The newest summer attraction consists of so-called "adventure loops" – obstacle courses that are mastered partly by climbing and partly by hanging freely from steel cables.

The harbor remains an important trading center where locally produced wood and metal goods are shipped worldwide. Also significant is the ferry harbor. The trip to Vaasa in Finland takes only seven hours; the ferry is also a favorite meeting place for local youth. You can count on weekdays being much quieter and therefore easier to book a ferry voyage.

The **Alnösund** separates Sundsvall from the island of **Alnön**, but a thousand-meter-long bridge has provided access since 1964. The island was inhabited as much as 4,000 years ago, and today serves the citizens of Sundsvall as a nearby recreation area. An interesting geological and botanical nature reserve at the north end, bathing beaches in the

198

south and weekend cottages are the main attractions. Also worth seeing on the island is the **Gamla Kyrka** of **Alvik**. The early 13th-century towerless stone construction boasts absolutely beautiful vaulted ceiling frescoes from the 16th century. In the Middle Ages, the church served as a place of worship for only 12 families who had designed and built the church themselves. The Gamla Kyrka is today a favorite choice for weddings. The ancient wooden baptismal font from the 12th century is still in use in the **Nya Kyrka** across the way.

The **Indalsälven River** empties into the northern part of Alnösund and is a popular spot for canoeists at its lower course. For over 50 kilometers, between the hydroelectric plant at Järkvissle and the town of Bergeforsen, the river is hemmed in by steep mountain cliffs. Views of the gorge can also be enjoyed by driving along Route 86. Unusual for Sweden is the Indalsälven estuary, a widely fanned delta – where many species of birds flock to breed.

Salmon lovers always enjoy a detour to the hydroelectric dam at **Bergeforsen** ❹ because of the salmon hatchery that can be visited there.

The longest marathon run in Sweden, over 110 kilometers, follows along the Indalsälven, where relays as well as individual races are held in June. The starting line is **Hammarstrand** at the foot of **Mount Kullsta**, the finish line is at Bergeforsen. From Mount Kullsta there is a marvelous view of the Indalsälven; it is hard to believe that 200 years ago the river was still a lake. When a rafting canal for timber transport was completed here, and the locks were opened for the first time, the waters of the lake quickly drained into the canal, lowering the water level 15 meters in only a few hours.

Timrå ❺, a northern suburb of Sundsvall, is the location of yet another golf course situated directly on the coast. The spacious areas allow golf courses to be created fairly inexpensively, and the "green sport" has become very popular as a result. Guests are always welcome.

Northern Provinces

*Härnösand – The Athens of the North

Continuing north, the world's biggest "Y" stands near the Sundsvall airport. Bengt Lindström created the 700-ton multicolored colossus and decorated it with three tons of paint. The monumental letter memorializes the area's earlier license plate prefix.

In the province of **Ångermanland** lies ***Härnösand** ❻ (pop. 27,000). The first settlement, located on an island in the Härnösund, was targeted by John III to become the spiritual and administrative center of Norrland after he granted the town a charter in 1585. Härnösand proved incapable of the task, although the first secondary school in Norrland had already been established here in 1647. In 1721, the Russians burned the city to the ground. Reconstruction is said to have been due to Gustavus III's efforts; the

Above: Rustic fresco in the fabulous Gamla Kyrka in Alvik on the island of Alnön.

facade of the **Rådhuset** owes its classical style to him. Since this style was also used afterwards in the construction of the **Domkyrkan**, as well as of many private residences a century later, the inhabitants quickly conferred their city with the catchy title of "The Athens of the North."

On the mainland, connected to the Old Town of Härnö Island by means of the Nybro, an open-air museum was established: ***Murberget**, the second-oldest in the country after Stockholm's "Skansen." Over 80 houses are collected around a fieldstone church, whose similarity to the ancient church of Alnö is unmistakable. Visitors to the historic tavern should try their skill at the medieval wooden bowling alley. In 1994, the **Länsmuseum** was added; in the basement are displays of local artifacts, weapons and models illustrating the city's history. The upper story contains a bizarre collection of sailors' souvenirs: match boxes, bottle caps and razor blades from all corners of the seven seas – items the seamen's heirs didn't know what to do with.

Built for the E4 in 1997, a two-kilometer-long viaduct crosses the **Ångermansund** at the mouth of the river **Ångermanälv**. The bridge is part of the "Thirty Bridge Project" intended to level the route between Härnösand and Örnsköldsvik and reduce driving time.

Into the Ådal Valley

If you don't necessarily want to take the fastest route northwards, an excursion starting at Härnösand in the valley of Ångermanälv, or **Ådal** as the locals say, is highly recommended. Continue on the E4 to Högsjö and then follow Route 90 along the left bank of the river to **Lunde** ❼ and Kramfors. Upriver – between Kramfors and the Angermanälv estuary – flows the longest stretch of navigable river in all of Sweden. In summer, excursion boats shuttle up and down the river.

In the 19th century in **Kramsfors** ❽, Christoffer Kramm put the first steam-powered saw into operation, which is on display at the **Museum of Local History**. Ådal is remembered as the scene of a bloody event, the *Ådalsstrejk* of 1931. In the middle of the Great Depression, the sawmill workers rebelled. When negotiations with the owners broke down, the government sent out the militia; five lives were lost in the confrontation. This appalling event resulted shortly afterwards in establishing the democratic right to strike for the Swedish worker, and also led to the Saltsjöbaden Agreement, which laid down the provisions governing positive cooperation between employers and employees.

The town of **Sollefteå** ❾ lies 40 kilometers farther upstream. To honor the historic tradition of transporting timber to the sawmills by river, a **Raftman's Memorial** has been placed on a stone pillar in the middle of the Ångermanälv. The river is also an extremely popular haunt for salmon fishermen, and even in the middle of the city you can catch a beauty.

Forty kilometers northwest of the city is the **Nämforsen**, a mighty waterfall; nearby, Stone Age rock drawings have been found, the northernmost in Sweden.

Junsele ❿, situated in the northern Ådal Valley, 25 kilometers farther along Route 90, and **Ramsele** ⓫ in the adjacent **Faxdal**, are both famous vacation resorts, attracting hikers and skiers alike. Since the winter days are very short here, the slopes and cross-country trails are illuminated. Nonetheless, Junsele's main tourist attraction is the **Djurpark** (zoo), boasting white tigers.

The High Coast

Between Härnösand and Örnsköldsvik the mountains extend right up to the sea, hence the name **Höga Kusten** (High Coast). The newly-built stretch of the E4 is located 30 kilometers north of Härnösands, between **Högsjö** and **Skog**; it shortens the drive by skirting the old bridge that crosses over the sound farther west near Lunde.

Winding along and following the complete route to Örnsköldsvik, the **Höga Kustleden** trekking trail, over 130 kilometers long, provides a hiking experience rich in variety and compass. The trail passes through many fishing villages that have earned culinary fame – undisputed and rightly so – through the production of *surströmming* (pickled herring) and *tunnbröd* (wafer bread).

The High Coast also offers one of the most singular overnight stays imaginable: on the island of **Högbonden**, lying offshore of the fishing village of **Bönhamn**, the residence of the lighthouse keeper, perched on a 70- meter-high cliff top, has been converted to a youth hostel offering 28 beds. Since the ferry from Bönhamn sails to the island four times daily, a day trip could also be easily undertaken. On a clear day, the view from the lighthouse reaches a good hundred kilometers over the High Coast.

Northern Provinces

Back on the mainland south of Bönhamn, the tiny fishing village of **Fällsvik** is nestled in a nature reserve, **Rosidan** ⑫, a favorite destination for sun-worshipers who enjoy basking on the smoothly polished boulders here. In **Häggvik**, Swedish artist Anders Åberg founded the **Mannaminne** (Mankind Memorial Museum). After this, almost too chic to mention, is the fishing village of **Norrfällsviken** ⑬, lying farther to the north, which owes its existence exclusively to tourism. Leisure time activities, a public beach with pool, tennis courts and a golf course characterize the town.

In the church crypt of **Ullånger** ⑭, on the E4, you will find an enamel-clad shrine manufactured in Limoges which is well worth seeing. Just three kilometers north of **Docksta**, a small road leads west to **Skuleberg** ⑮ (293 meters). Only six meters below the peak, in the "King's

Above: Along the coast, many families earn extra income from fishing. Right: Skuleskogen National Park is renowned for its arctic flora.

Cave," traces of a Stone Age settlement were discovered, as well as indications that the cave entrance must have been located close to the beach. The land mass must have risen almost 300 meters in the last 10,000 years. Today, you can reach the peak by climbing a steep trail or by taking the cable car. At the cable car station in the valley there is the **Skule Naturum** exhibit concerning the local geology, flora and fauna and the **Skuleskogen National Park**. The park covers the area between the E4 and the highest elevations of the *Höga Kusten*, and is known for its abundant plant life including arctic flora. Some 30 kilometers of marked trails cross through the park. Inside there are remains of 500-year-old trees. The nine-kilometer stretch called *Kustleden* is strenuous at times but worthwhile. **Slåttdalskrevan**, a gorge 200 meters long and 40 meters deep, is at the end of the trail. Parking can be found in the northern section near **Näske** and in the south near **Käl** (on the way to **Sund**); good starting points for hiking tours.

From **Köpmanholmen** , north of the national park, you can go to the island of **Ulvön**, an ideal destination for a day trip. At the old fishing harbor of **Ulvöhamn** , the fishermens' huts and boat shelters are crowded together. In the last few years hotels, restaurants and cafés have opened up, making a longer relaxing stay possible. The ferry to Ulvön provides the means for an excursion to the island of **Trysunda**, far out to sea in the outlying archipelago. The village of Trysunda is considered to be the best-preserved fishing village on the High Coast. If you want to spend more time here, you can stay at Sweden's smallest youth hostel – offering only eight beds.

ÖRNSKÖLDSVIK

Örnsköldsvik , with 58,000 inhabitants, is the provincial capital of Ångermanland. First founded in 1842, the city was named after its governor who, in the 18th century, did great service to the development of Norrland. In addition to being the educational and administrative center for the province, Örnsköldsvik draws shoppers from all over the surrounding countryside. During weekly shopping trips, customers pack shopping carts full of goods; it is no wonder when you consider that in the sparsely populated environs, stores are scarce. In the remote countryside, gas stations supply the local inhabitants with provisions.

In Norrland you have to do without bakeries selling fresh bread daily: just as in the past, the farmers could not possibly take the time to bake every day; but finally it occurred to somebody to produce a long-keeping dry bread. Nowadays *knäckebröd* enjoys worldwide fame; the round slices were lined up on wooded sticks, and the hole in the middle of each slice reminds us today of the old storage method.

Örnsköldsvik's city center is grouped around the lumber shipping harbor. In an old building nearby, the **Culture Factory** has been established, where in its museums you can learn about the development

Northern Provinces

of forestry, woodworking and paper production. If you wish, you can even produce paper yourself and take a piece as a
souvenir.

On rainy days, the **Paradisbadet** provides fun and relaxation. A 98-meter-
long pipeline water slide winds around
the swimming pool. The bathing paradise
is located directly on the E4. The slopes
of **Varvsberg** boast a number of ski
jumps, which testifies to the area's use as
a training center for ski jumpers. From
the restaurant perched on the mountain
you can enjoy the view of the archipelago
off the coast, where the tourist trade has
just begun to develop. The most important area for winter sports is located 90
kilometers west of here near **Solberget**
on Route 348. A modern alpine center including six downhill runs and three ski
lifts has been conjured up here out of
nothing – and snow is guaranteed.

In ***Gene Fornby**, south of Örnsköldsvik, replicas of farmsteads from
the Iron Age have been built on the site of
an ancient burial ground in the woods.

Örnsköldsvik is the place to go for
sports fishermen. Since 1991, the town
has been proclaimed Sweden's number
one fishermen's paradise. Since then, the
fishing guide *Fiske Ö-vik* has been published here. The guide reveals the best
fishing spots in the region, as well the
best times of the year for salmon or ice
fishing. And for the canoeing enthusiast,
there is the **Nätraån River**, 10 kilometers
south of Örnsköldsvik.

If you are on the stretch between
Örnsköldsvik and Umeå and are looking
for refreshment, you're definitely better
off finding a spot on the quiet coast near
Husum, **Rundvik** or **Nordmaling** than
stopping at one of the rest areas on "Birch
Boulevard."

In **Olofsfors** ⑲, a water-powered forge
is used to demonstrate the operations of a

*Right: In dim light, the fish are said to bite all
the better.*

restored ironworks from the 18th century.
Hörnefors ⑳ was the site of the last battle to have taken place on Swedish soil: in
1809, the Swedish army rose against the
Russian troops who had marched across
the frozen Gulf of Bothnia and occupied
Umeå. Since Russia took the victory,
Sweden was forced to surrender Finland
to Russian rule.

****UMEÅ – CITY OF BIRCH TREES**

**Umeå ㉑ is the capital of the region
of **Västerbotten**, which already belongs
to the northern part of Norrland. For a
long time it was the gateway to "Swedish
Alaska," as northern Sweden is often
called. The location on the Ume älv was
an important meeting point for raftsmen,
lumberjacks, traders and hunters when it
was granted a city charter in 1646. A noticeable upswing for the city occurred
with the appearance of the first steam-
powered saws, and the boom continued
even after the great fire on Midsummer
Day in 1888. In the reconstruction, extra-
wide streets were laid out to act as firebreaks,
and then lined with birch trees whose fo-
liage would help check flying embers and
sparks – lending the epithet "City of
Birch Trees." The foundation of the university in 1963 was the most important
impetus in municipal development, leading to an almost overnight decrease in the
population's average age to under 35
years. Since then, the character of this
city of 100,000 has been largely determined by its students.

In front of the 19th-century train station, a public square was laid out in the
shape of a semicircle and adorned with a
modern glass sculpture entitled *Green
Fire*. From the train station, Rådhusgatan
leads to the **Rådhustorget**, the marketplace and also the heart of the city. Only a
single building from the 19th century is
still standing here: the brick Neo-Renais-
sance City Hall; a bust of Gustavus Vasa,
the city's founder is in front of the it.

Compared to other Swedish cities, the quarter has a lot of bars and restaurants that are quite lively in the summer months, even long past midnight.

The river down below the Rådhustorget, the **Ume älv**, sports at this point a large fountain that windsurfers use as a turning point. Behind the 19th-century Neo-Gothic city church there is a memorial marking the common grave of a Swedish colonel and a Russian Cossack who fell in the battle of 1809.

The city park has been enlarged to include the **Gammlia** open-air museum. Typical edifices of the Västerbotten region are on display here, including a church that was built on the island of **Holmön** from the planks of a stranded ship. The Västerbotten **Länsmuseum** is also here, with an exhibit featuring skiing; it also claims to have the world's oldest "snowboard."

Holmsund ㉒ at the mouth of the Ume älv is Umeå's harbor. Ferries sail from here, reaching Vaasa in Finland in three hours. The E12 connects Umeå with Mo i Rana on the west coast of Norway; the 435-kilometer stretch passes through virtually uninhabited wilderness.

A special attraction is the hydroelectric plant of ***Stornorrfors** near **Sörfors** ㉓: producing 2.3 megawatts of power, it is Sweden's largest. The dam includes a salmon ladder which provides a path for the fish to migrate upstream. A salmon hatchery is located just to the rear of it, which releases 100,000 young salmon into the river annually. At the yearly opening of the weirs on the first Sunday in July, thousands of spectators flock to the old weir bridge to marvel at the cascading torrents.

One of the greatest challenges for canoeing enthusiasts is a 370-kilometer pristine water course – one of very few in Sweden – the ****Vindelälven**; starting in Ammarnäs on the eastern side of the Vindelfjälls and ending at **Vannäs** ㉔, where the river converges with the Ume älv, about 20 kilometers west of Umeå. Experienced canoeists allow 20 days for the entire stretch.

Northern Provinces

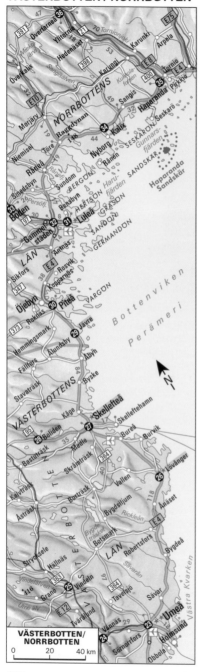

The village of **Vindeln** ㉕, 60 kilometers northwest of Umeå, profits from the fine reputation of its river unspoiled by human hand; and to round off its variety of winter-fun activities, it also offers dog-sled excursions.

In ***Lövanger** ㉖, 100 kilometers north of Umeå, you can visit the "church towns" of Norrland. The area's farmers, who had to travel from far and wide to attend church services, could find long-term accommodations here. The villages fulfilled a social function as well: only here were the farmers able to exchange goods with their "neighbors," do business or foster relationships leading to marriage. The "church huts" of Lövanger can be rented today as vacation cottages.

*Skellefteå ㉗ is yet another seaport on the Gulf of Bothnia which owes its significance to the lumber industry. The village was first mentioned in an official 14th-century document, but it was not granted a charter until 1845. The town had only 200 inhabitants then; now there are 74,000. The wealth of Skellefteå is reflected in the **Landsförsamlingskyrkan** (Provincial Assembly Church) on the banks of the Skellefte älv. The church was remodeled in the classical style in the 18th century. For the area, the naturally well-illuminated House of God possesses an unusually high number of artistic treasures. The Skellefteå Madonna, carved from walnut, hails from the 12th century and was probably created in Germany. The triptych altar is a magnificent piece produced in the workshop of Bernt Notkes in Lübeck. Not far from the church lies **Bonnstan**, the "church village" with 116 well-preserved huts where farmers lived during the "provincial assembly." Nowadays the huts are used as weekend cottages.

At the beginning of the 20th century, due to rich deposits of precious metals in the backwoods, Skellefteå became a center for metal processing. In 1942, between **Kristineberg** and **Boliden** ㉘ (125

and 35 kilometers from Skellefteå respectively), a 96-kilometer-long **cable car** line was laid to transport ore to the processing plant. The mines and the processing plant have since been abandoned, but a 14-kilometer cable car ride between **Örträsk** and **Mensträsk** serves as an unhurried means of transporting tourists.

Fifty kilometers north of Skellefteå, near **Jävre ㉙**, Sweden's northernmost Iron Age archeological site is located. The **Arkeologstigen**, a combination road and hiking trail, leads to the excavations. The small town of **Piteå ㉚** has been in its present location only since the 15th century. After a major fire, the former inhabitants abandoned the silted-up harbor of **Öjebyn** and resettled a few kilometers to the east closer to the sea. The church and the church village, however, remained in Öjebyn. Today, Piteå is famed for its long, fine, sand beaches, earning the coastline

Right: The wooden cabins of the church village of Skellefteå are congenial weekend cottages.

the title "Riviera of the North." After long periods of sunny weather, the water can reach temperatures of up to 20°C. Two excellent swimming areas are the **Piteå-havsbad** and **Bykeshavsbad**, a 50-kilometer drive on the E4.

*LULEÅ

*Luleå ㉛**, the provincial capital of Norrbotten, has 70,000 inhabitants. The city boomed in 1888, when the railway was opened for the transportation of ore from Kiruna to the Gulf of Bothnia; Luleå rose to become Sweden's largest seaport for exportation. However, the harbor is closed for at least four months a year when the Baltic Sea is frozen over. The Neo-Gothic **church** was erected in 1893; soon afterwards, Luleå was promoted to an Episcopal see. The northernmost Swedish diocese encompasses approximately one-third of the province's total area. The **Länsmuseum**, displaying a large collection of artifacts from the Sami culture in Norrbotten, is worth a visit.

Northern Provinces

However, the most important tourist site is located 10 kilometers south of the city in *Gammelstaden ㉜. Old Luleå, founded in the 14th century and abandoned in the 17th, boasts the largest church village in Sweden, with a total of 450 huts. The town was included on UNESCO's World Heritage List in1996. The huts, still used for special occasions, are grouped around the largest hall church of the north. Consecrated in 1491 and built on massive granite blocks, the church was not only intended as a house of worship, but also as a stronghold; a fact apparent in the structure today. The white-plastered fieldstone church offers a few artistic and historic rarities, including a triptych from 1500 produced in Antwerp and a choir decorated with frescoes – which are probably the northernmost in the world. The church is older than the city itself, which was first chartered under Gustavus II Adolphus.

Above: Feeding reindeer near Luleä. Right: Övertorneä's 17th-century wooden church.

At the time, no one could imagine that the land mass would rise so quickly. Already a generation after the city's founding, the harbor had begun to silt up, and so the city and the harbor were relocated nearer to the mouth of the Lule älv. The old "harbor" has since been reclaimed by Mother Nature. The silted up bay became such a popular breeding place for a great number of bird species that it has been set aside as a nature reserve.

Along with culture and nature, technology has not at all been neglected in the modern-day Luleä. From the nature reserve a long walk takes you to the College of Technology and the **Teknikens hus**, a real El Dorado for learning about technical devices and systems by using the hands-on method. While in the Teknikens hus "taking part" is part of the program, a visit to the modern **SSAB** (Svensk Stal AB) steel works allows only visual participation. A visit can be arranged through the local tourist office.

The garrison city of **Boden** ㉝, 30 kilometers northwest of Luleä, is the largest

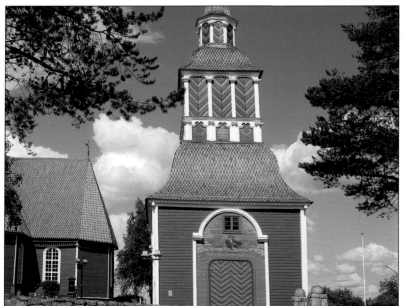

railroad junction in the north. The Stockholm-Haparanda line meets here with the freight trains transporting ore between Narvik, Kiruna and Luleå.

Via **Kalix** ㉞, another small town whose livelihood is woodworking, the E4 reaches **Haparanda** ㉟, marking the northernmost point of the Gulf of Bothnia. After peace negotiations between Russia and Sweden defined the Torne älv as the border in 1809, the old city of **Tornio**, among others, fell to Russia. However, since the Swedish inhabitants had no desire to live under czarist rule, they erected a new settlement on the western bank of the Torne älv. The development potential this resettlement allowed can be seen by the incredibly oversized train station. Today the city primarily owes its existence to woodworking, which, since the existence of the EU, has even spread across the former Finnish border, now merely an interior frontier.

Near Haparanda, the rapids of the **Kukkolaforsen** swirl and surge. The big annual fishermen's festival of Iksöndagen is celebrated on the river banks on the last Sunday in July. Fish are caught the traditional way; from tottering wooden planks with nets fastened to meter-long poles.

A few isles south of Haparanda were designated as a national park: **Haparanda Sandskär**. The park consists mostly of dunes, birch woods and a large aspen forest. Flocks of birds stop at the islands on their annual migration. There is a bird-tagging station here (reachable by private boat from Haparanda or Kalix).

Normally, starting at Haparanda, you would continue north on the Finnish side of the border, taking the E8 and the E75; you can also choose to take Royal Highway 400, following the Torne älv, to reach the wide-open spaces of Lapland. After 80 kilometers of driving through fascinating scenery, you will reach the northernmost tourist site on this journey – the church of **Övertorneå** ㊱. This is considered to be the best-preserved 17th-century church in the north, and it has one of the oldest still-functioning church organs in all of Sweden.

Northern Provinces

SUNDSVALL (☎ 060)

i Torget, 85230 Sundsvall, tel. 614235.

◉◉◉ Scandic Hotel Sundsvall City, Espanaden 29, tel. 171600, fax 122032. **◉◉ Hotel Baltic**, Sjögatan 5, tel. 155935, fax 124560. **Scandic Hotel Sundsvall Nord**, Värdshusbacken 6, tel. 566860, fax 566954. **Hotel Södra Berget**, Södra Stadsberget, tel. 23000, fax 151034. **◉ Grand Hotel**, Nybrogatan 13, tel. 157205, fax 616484. **Prize Hotel**, Sjögatan 11, tel. 150720, fax 123456.

▲ Granli Camping, 5 km north of Sundsvall, directly on the sea. tel. 613569.

✕ Seaport, Strandgatan 10, tel. 121800, connoisseur restaurant, dancing on weekends. **Elvira Madigan**, guest haven, tel. 125140, restaurant ship, dinner is served on board during the tour. **Café Skonerten** in the Kulturmagasinet, tel. 191800.

▥ Kulturmagasinet, Mon-Fri 10 am-6 pm, Sat until 4 pm, Sun 11 am-2 pm or for events, tel. 191800. **Gustav Adolfs Kyrka**, 9 am-6 pm except during services.

▶ Discotheque Oscar, Vängåven, is *the* meeting place for Sundsvall, Fri-Sat 9 pm-2 am.

▦ Tingshuset, Östra Långgatan, sells **arts and crafts**. Lovis Konst, on the corner of Bankgatan, carries **woven** and **wrought-iron products**. Rolf Libergs troll paintings are available in his **gallery** at Nybrogatan 5.

▨ Church on the island of **Alnön**, May 10-Aug 31, 11 am-6 pm daily. Beware: Sat weddings or baptisms. **Bergforsen, salmon breeding station**, June-Aug 12-3:30 pm daily.

◂ The **steamship Primus** runs between the inner harbor and Tjuvholmen every 40 minutes in summer. *RAFTING:* On the Ljungan, tel. 31867. *CANOEING:* On the Indalsälv, tel. 0661-614235. **Boda Borg Adventure Park**, tel. 0691-12200, training camp for aspiring stuntmen. *SKIING:* The Södra Berget ski area has world-class standards, tel. 123000. *FISHING:* Fishing permit with the respective fish stock available on the Internet: www.algonet.sel-fishhole/fishhole.htm. First week in August: The **Craftsmens' Fair** on Norra Stadsberget takes you back to the 19th century.

▣ First week in July: **Sundsvall Street Festival** on the esplanade, the wildest carnival of the north.

HÄRNÖSAND (☎ 0611)

i Järnvägsgatan 2, 87145 Härnösand, tel. 88140.

◉◉ Scandic Partner Hotel Stadt Harnösand, Skeppsbron 9, tel. 10510, fax 26790. **◉ Royal Hotell & Restaurang**, Strandgatan 12, tel. 20455, fax 26790. **Route 66 Restaurant & Motel**, Industrigatan 14, tel. 19560, fax 18780.

▲ Sälstenscamping, tel. 16150, 2 km north of the center on Härnön.

✕ Restaurant **Spjutegårdens** in Murberget open-air museum. On Sundays a substantial Smörgåsbord, tel. 11090.

▥ Domkyrkan, daily 9 am-6 pm, except during services. **Murberget Open-air Museum,** daily. **Länsmuseum**, June 20-Aug 31, 11 am-5 pm daily.

▦ Typical Nordic **arts and crafts** sold at Hantverk, Östbäcksgatan 1.

KRAMFORS (☎ 0612)

i Ängsgatan 4, 87200 Kramfors, tel. 10900.

◉◉ First Hotel Kramm, Torgatan 4, tel. 13160, fax 13542. **◉ Frånö Hotell**, Riksvägen 25, tel. 30520, fax 30585.

SOLLEFTEÅ (☎ 0620)

i Torggatan 4, 88130 Sollefteå, tel. 82563.

◉◉ Stad Hotell Halstaberget, tel. 12320, fax 16424, 4 km south of town. **Österås Hälsohem**, tel. 23090, Österås, beautiful area where there is a high regard for a natural way of life.

▲ Sollefteå Camping, on Angermanälv, tel. 17370, with sauna, *ROW BOATS* and *TENNIS COURT.*

▦ A large selection of **arts and crafts** at Majoren (House of the Senses), tel. 15900, open daily.

◂ *RAFTING TRIPS:* Ångermanälv, tel. 13388. *FISHING:* In the Sollefteå area, tel. 82536. **Adventure weekend** in a **Lapp tent** in Junsele, tel. 0621-71099. **Stone-Age weekend** on the Ångermanälv, tel. 10630.

HIGH COAST

i Mitsverige Turism, PO Box 77, 87122 Härnösand, tel. 0611-29030.

◉ SFT Vandrarhem Högbonden, Ullånger, tel. 0613-23005. **Norrfällsviken** leisure time facility, tel. 0631-21432, fax 30001. **Hotel Café Mårsen**, tel. 0660-34093, fax 21382. **SFT Vandrarhem Trysunda**, tel. 0660-43038.

▥ Skule Naturum, June 15-Aug 15, 10 am-5 pm, with café.

◂ Häggvik, Mannaminne leisure time park, tel. 0631-20290, June 15-Aug 31, 10 am-6 pm daily, otherwise 11 am-4 pm daily. *VACATION HOMES* for rent. Visit an **artists' colony**, info: Mitsverige Turism.

▨ HIKING in Skuleberget, tel. 0613-40115.

▣ *BOAT:* **Bönhamn-Högbonden**, June 9-Aug 20, 11 am, 2 and 5 pm daily, the trip takes 10 minutes.

Köpmannholmen-Ulvön, June 10-Aug 15 Mon-Sat 10 am and 5 pm, return 7:30 am and 3 pm; Sun 10 am and 6:30 pm, return same as weekdays. A two-hour journey, **Trysunda** is located at the half-way point.

ÖRNSKÖLDSVIK (☎ 0660)

ℹ Nygatan 18, 89188 Örnsköldsvik, tel. 12537
🛏 **☺☺** **Scandic Hotel Örnsköldsvik**, Hästmarksvägen 4, tel. 82870, fax 19198. **Hotell Focus**, Lasarettsgatan 9, tel. 82100, fax 83867. **First Hotell Statt**, Lasarettsgatan 2, tel. 10110, fax 83791. **☺ Strand City Hotell**, Nygatan 2, tel. 010610, fax 211305.
▲ Mosjöns Camping, 18 km north on the E4, tel. 0663-20089, fax 22164, *FISHING* is possible.
✖ Restaurant **Varsberg**, tel. 28654.
🏛 **Culture Factory**, June 15-Aug 15, Tue-Sun 10 am-5 pm, otherwise only Sat-Sun 11 am-4 pm. **Paradisbadet**, Mon-Fri 10 am-6 pm, Sat-Sun to 10 pm. The open-air museum of **Gene Fornby**, tel. 53710, June 22-Aug 11 daily 10 am-5 pm.
🚢 **Steamship trips** through the **skerries**, tel. 12537. *CANOEING* on the Nätraån, tel. 0661-30331. *FISHING:* **Fiske Ö-vik**, tel. 12537. *SKIING:* **Ski center Solberget**, tel. 0661-50170 and 50171.

UMEÅ (☎ 090)

ℹ Renmarkstorget 15, 90326 Umeå, tel. 161616.
🛏 **☺☺** **Comfort Home Hotel Uman**, Storgatan 52, tel. 127220, fax 127420. **First Hotel Grand**, Storgatan 46, tel. 778870, fax 133055. **Scandic Hotel Umeå**, Yrkesvägen 8, tel. 135250, fax 138021. **☺ Hotel Björken**, Patientvägen 1, tel. 108700, fax 108999. **Comfort Hotel Umeå**, Norrlandsgatan 5, tel. 125800, fax 141075. **Hotel Wasa**, Vasagatan 10, tel. 778540, fax 778549. **Vandrarhem Åliden**, Pedagogengränd 1 C, tel. 194300.
▲ Umeåcamping, tel. 161660, located on the sea, north of the city on route E4, has 56 *HUTS*.
✖ **Theatercaféet**, **Restaurant**, Vasaplan, tel. 156321. **Sävargården** im Grammlia Museum, good Swedish home cooking. **Viktor**, Skolgatan 64, tel. 23648, seafood Swedish style, i.e., with sugar and cream. **Brännlands Wärdhus**, Brännland, tel. 30085, regional specialties.
🏛 **Grammlia** open-air museum, June 15-Aug 20, 10 am-5 pm daily. **Västerbotten Länsmuseum**, Tue-Sun 10 am-4 pm, Wed to 9 pm. **Stornorrfors** hydroelectric plant, 10 am-12:30 pm daily. **Salmon farming**, 1-3 pm daily.
🚗 *CANOE AND DOGSLED TOURS:* Tourist office Umeå or Vindel Turism, tel. 0933-11014.

LÖVÅNGER (☎ 0913)

🛏 *CHURCH HUTS, HOTELS:* Kungsvägen, tel. 10395, fax 10672.

SKELLEFTEÅ (☎ 0910)

ℹ Kanalgatan 56, 93134 Skellefteå, tel. 58880.
🛏 **☺☺** **Scandic Hotel Skellefteå**, Kanalgatan 75, tel. 38300, fax 778411. **First Hotell Statt**, Stationsgatan 8, tel. 14140, fax 12628. **☺ Vandrarhem Anderstorpsgården**, tel. 37283.
▲ Skellefteå Camping, tel. 18855, north of the city on the E4, 78 *HUTS*.
✖ Restaurant in **Statt Hotell**, Stationsgatan 8, tel. 14140.
🏛 **Landsförsamlingskyrkan**, 9 am-5 pm daily, except during services, tours sometimes in the summer.
🚠 Cable car **Örträsk-Mensträsk**, operates from June 15-Aug 15.

PITEÅ (☎ 0911)

ℹ Norliagatan 1, 94131 Piteå, tel. 93390.
🛏 **☺ Hotel Belona**, Furunäset, tel. 77950.
▲ **Pite Havsbad**, tel. 32300, 10 km south of Piteå, with room for 700, 150 *HUTS*.
☝ Last week in June: **Large market** with music and dancing until the wee hours.

LULEÅ (☎ 0920)

ℹ Storgatan 43, 97185 Luleå, tel. 293746.
🛏 **☺☺** **Nordkalotten Hotel & Konferens**, Lulviksvägen, tel. 89350, fax 19909, beautiful, built in the Nordic style. **Scandic Hotel Luelå**, Banvägen 3, tel. 228360, fax 69472. **☺ Furufjärdens Gästgård**, Gussövägen, tel. 74700, fax 74710.
✖ **Margaretas Wärdshus**, Luleå Gammelstad, Lulevägen 2, tel. 54290, amidst a church village.
🏛 **Länsmuseum**, Mon-Thu 10 am-8 pm, Fri-Sun 12-4 pm.
Gammelstaden, June to mid-August 9 am-6 pm daily.

HAPARANDA (☎ 0922)

ℹ Norra Esplanaden, 95331 Haparanda, tel. 11585.
🛏 **☺☺** **Haparanda Stadshotell**, Torget 7, tel. 10223, fax 10223. **☺ Kukkolaforsen Turist & Konferens**, Kukkolaforsen, tel. 31000, fax 31030.
🏛 **Church** of **Övertorneå**, 10 am-4 pm daily.
☝ Last week of July: **Big Fishermen's Festival** in Kukkola with stands, music and dancing.

Northern Provinces

SWEDISH LAPLAND

ÖSTERSUND

ARVIDSJAUR

GÄLLIVARE

KIRUNA

SAMI – PEOPLE OF THE SWAMP

Today the three northern Swedish provinces of Jämtland, Norrbotten and Lapland are the settled territory of the Lapps. The term is considered degrading; they call themselves "Sami" (People of the Swamp). The origins of this ethnic group are obscure. The Sami probably migrated from the east around the beginning of the Christian era, in any case long before the arrival of the Vikings, and settled throughout all of northern Scandinavia. With the growing interest of the Germanic tribes for the northernmost parts of Scandinavia, the Sami were forced farther and farther from the coast lands, and ever deeper into the inhospitable central regions. They yielded to the pressure of the invaders, thus suffering the loss of their fishing and hunting grounds and their farmlands until, finally, only the nomadic life of the reindeer herder was left to them.

Today, the Sami are only a minority in the land which was once theirs – from a total of 45,000, only 10,000 of them live in Sweden. The Sami population is concentrated in a north-south orientation; the farther north you go, the more plentiful the Sami settlements.

After hundreds of years of enduring the exploitation of their rich northern territory, of being judged as annoying troublemakers, and later being forced to accept Christianity and to become tax-paying citizens, only recently have the Sami and their traditions undergone a new assessment – slowly but surely the world has accepted them as being worthy of preservation. Museums, libraries and schools have been established to ensure the survival of this ancient culture. Moreover, since 1996, all of Lapland enjoys UNESCO protection as a cultural and natural heritage site.

To artificially protect the lifestyle of the Sami has proved problematic; one needs only to look at reindeer herding to see how fundamental are the changes in the life of this people. In the past, the entire family clan followed the herds to summer grazing areas in the north and then, in the colder season, returned to winter quarters. Today, only a handful of specialists follow the herds, using four-wheel drive vehicles and even helicopters, while keeping contact with each other over radio phones.

Materials for Sami arts and crafts include the few things available to the craftsman: wood, moss and every con-

Preceding pages: The Rapaälv in Sarek National Park often changes it's course. Left: Impressions in ice – the spectacular Tännfors.

Swedish Lapland

Map p. 216, Info p. 227

215

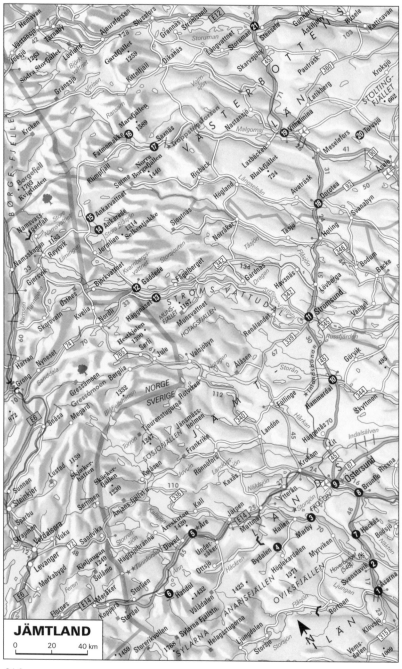

JÄMTLAND

0   20   40 km

ceivable part of the reindeer. Today, production is almost exclusively aimed at the tourist consumer.

The language of the Sami, which belongs to the Finno-Ugric family, is nature-oriented and rich in vocabulary; over 100 different words exist just for the term "snow," for example. However, the countless dialects, sometimes only spoken by a handful of families, complicate communication so drastically, that often the Scandinavian languages are used instead.

JÄMTLAND
An Untouched Paradise

The southernmost population of Sami can be found in **Jämtland**. In this last European natural region south of the Polar Circle, not even two percent of the land is cultivated. The eastern area is blanketed by forests – in the west, mountains reaching heights of up to 1,800 meters present an almost Alpine character.

Two important travel routes cross Jämtland: Route 45, the so-called **Inlandsvägen** that runs from Halmstad in southern Sweden through Karesuando and on to the Finnish border, and the E14 between Sundsvall and Trondheim, following the ancient pilgrimage route of Saint Olav (see p. 195). Route 45 is paralleled during the 1,060-kilometer stretch between Mora and Gällivare by the *Inlandsbana. It took 40 years for this railway to be driven through the wilderness; it finally opened in 1936. The railway's original purpose, to transport ore from Kiruna to southern Sweden during the winter months, could not be realized, since foundations and bridges were too weak to accommodate the weight, and transportation via Narvik on the Norwegian coast proved more cost-effective.

Today, from Midsummer to the middle of August, the *Inlandsbana* accommodates tourists with regular passenger trains or nostalgic trains pulled by steam locomotives. The *Wilderness Express* can

also be chartered. The tour from Mora to Gällivare takes two days, including even unscheduled stops at tourist sites. While train, engineer and tour guide spend a night in Östersund, passengers have to decide whether to pitch their tents on a favorable spot near the tracks, or to search for a room for the night.

The main routes from Jämtland intersect Östersund near *Lake Storsjön. The lake covers 450 kilometers and marks the geographical center of the province. Northbound on the Inlandsvägen and before reaching the lake by **Åsarna ❶**, you cross over the **Ljungan River**, loved by hiker and canoeist alike. At this point, the river creates a waterfall. Cross-country skiers will enjoy the meticulously prepared trails in the winter months.

In **Svenstavik ❷**, Route 321 follows the western shore of the lake to a view of **Mount Hoverberget** (548 meters) with its 170-meter-long cave.

In **Marby ❸**, the café in **Gammelgården**, next to the ruins of a 14th-century church, offers a welcome break. From the village of **Hallen**, a byroad ascends to **Bydalsfjäll**, and then to **Bydalen ❹**. Long-distance hikes can be undertaken from here, passing through **Oviksfjäll** and **Anarisfjäll** and reaching even the Sylarna Mountains.

The most famous winter sport resort of Jämtlands is *Åre ❺, which is located directly on the E14, halfway between the western rim of Lake Storsjön and the Norwegian border. The quaint wooden hotels built during the last century endow the village with a special charm. From the center of town the old mountain railway, built in 1906, can be taken up to the **Åreskutan**, Åres' local peak which reaches a height of 1,420 meters.

Visitors who are pressed for time can take the more modern cable car, built in 1979. The old **church** is also worth a visit, one of the stations on St. Olav's pilgrimage route. The church contains a medieval statue of St. Olav, whose lost crown was replaced by a three-cornered hat in the 18th century.

Near **Duved**, nine kilometers west, the ****Tännfors** crashes into the valley below. The waterfall, 60 meters wide and 32 meters high, is impressive enough in summer, but in winter the frozen cascade formations are truly breathtaking.

Trekkers heading for the **Sylarna Mountains** or Anarisfjäll start hiking south of **Handöl ❻** at the **Storulvåns Fjällstation**.

*ÖSTERSUND
The City of Gustavus III

Following the Inlandsvägen from Svenstavik along the eastern shore of Lake Storsjön, you will soon reach **Hackås ❼**, Jämtland's oldest settlement, proven to be settled two thousand years ago and Christianized one thousand years ago. In the church, remains of construction work dating back to the 11th century can be identified. Two historic trails lead to Iron Age burial mounds and a farmhouse that has remained in the same family since the 14th century. Only five kilometers farther north, near **Brunflo ❽**, an ancient fortification tower catches the eye. Today it is used as the bell tower for a modern church.

*Östersund ❾ has 60,000 residents, making it the only official city in Jämtland. King Gustavus III had the city built on terraces on the shore of Lake Storsjön. His love for stage acting explains why construction of the theater was completed two years before the church.

The main attraction in Östersund is ***Jamtli Historieland**, an open-air museum with 60 houses and farmyards, including a pilgrim's hut from the 16th century. The **Länsmuseum** is located on the same site, with a collection of Sami cultural artifacts as well as other items.

Right: The skiing area near Vemdalsskallet in Jämtland is extremely popular.

The island of **Frösön** was named after the Germanic fertility goddess Fröja and was already settled in the Bronze Age. Today a bridge connects the island to Östersund. Sweden's northernmost rune stone can be found here, located on the probable site of an important *tingstäde* (assembly) site, bearing witness to the pre-Christian era of the region.

The steamship *Thomée*, which has provided excursion service on Lake Storsjön since 1875, offers a relaxing trip around the island. You need a lot of luck and a bit of imagination during the trip to spot the fabled *Storsjöoduret* (Storsjö Monster). Those who missed out can purchase a replica in wood or a stuffed animal in the local souvenir shops.

Endless Forests

From Östersund, Route 45 heading north crosses through immense forests. Scenic views, rest areas and tourist sites are rare, so that after a 70-kilometer drive, the ancient church of **Hammerdal ❿** offers a welcome change. In **Strömsund ⓫**, 30 kilometers further on, the Inlandsvägen crosses an extensive chain of lakes between **Russfjärden** and **Dragan**. Experienced canoeists allow more than a week's time for a tour through the area of **Ströms Vattudal**, starting at the Norwegian border and ending at Strömsund.

Be sure to turn off on Route 343 from Strömsund, since this section of the 500-kilometer-long *Vildmarksvägen* leads to impressive natural wonders, to Kahlfjäll and to settlements of Sami culture.

The town of **Gäddede ⓬** nestles only six kilometers before the Norwegian border. From here it is only 30 kilometers to the **Hällingsåfallet** waterfall and northern Europe's longest canyon near **Häggnäset ⓭**. North of Gäddede, on **Lake Stora Blasjön**, is the village of **Ankarede ⓮**, with a Sami chapel and a church. Sweden's longest dripstone cave was discovered here in 1985: the five-

kilometer-long **Korallgrottan** near **An-karvattnet ⑮**. This route continues to follow the **Bjurälven River**, which has carved out numerous grottos and caves, and sometimes even flows underground.

From the rest area near **Stekenjåkk**, next to the abandoned silver mine, a three-kilometer-long hiking trail ascends to the Sami huts of **Sjärnjåkktorna** at a height of 820 meters. The Sami deliberately chose the treeless peak as their summer quarters, since the wind keeps the mosquitoes away and from Fjäll they have an excellent view of the reindeer herds below.

Unless you take the detour north of Kultsjön to the Sami village of **Fatmomakke ⑯** – an important meeting place at the crossing of two reindeer migration routes – you'll descend eastwards into the valley, following the **Kultsjön** to the vacation village of **Saxnäs ⑰**. From the bridge, nearly 10 kilometers east of Saxnäs, you can enjoy a view of the impressive ***Trappstegsforsen** waterfall, descending in steps.

Remaining on the northbound Inlandsvägen from Strömsund, you will reach **Dorotea ⑱**, founded in the 19th century. Dorotea and her sister village Vilhelmina bear the given names of Gustavus IV Adolphus' wife. The exterior of Dorotea's church was designed by Evert Milles; the interior décor pays homage to the talents of his famous brother Carl.

The remains of a church village can be visited in **Vilhelmina ⑲**. Today, the huts of the village serve as shops and holiday cottages. A worthwhile trip is a detour from Vilhelmina to the mills of **Torvsjö ⑳**, the oldest water-powered construction in Lapland. The Sagavägen River was employed, which after flowing eight kilometers towards the south and following the E90, turns away towards the east. Ten kilometers before reaching Stenselkroken, the next possible entrance ramp to the E90, Torvsjö appears once again.

From Vilhelmina, the Inlandsvägen continues northward. In **Storuman ㉑**, the route crosses the **Blå Vägen** (Blue Trail) a former trading route between

Swedish Lapland

Norwegian Mo i Rana and Umeå, which today has been widened to accommodate the heavy traffic on the E12. Unfortunately, tourists can no longer stay at the hotel at the train station, a splendid building from the turn of the century that has now been converted into a library.

One hundred and forty kilometers west of Storuman, the E12 reaches **Tärnaby** and **Hemavan**, next to the nature reserve of **Vindelfjällen**, where the famous *Kungsleden* hiking trail begins (see pp. 221-222 and 226).

*ARVIDSJAUR

*Arvidsjaur ㉒, 155 kilometers northeast of Storuman on Route 45, was the first Christian congregation in Sami territory (founded in 1605). Here, the Sami used ***Lappstan**, the only existing

Above: A woman in the traditional costume of the Sami. Right: The Sami have lived from reindeer herding since time immemorial (Padjelanta National Park).

church village with *ajtte* (storehouses). Every year in August, the grounds are the scene of a grand church festival that, due to its folklore-orientated character, has become a first-rate attraction for tourists. Arvidsjaur offers an excellent starting point for a relaxing but active vacation, with hiking, rafting in the **Pite älv** (a good 50 kilometers to the north), or trolly trips on the railway tracks to **Jörn**.

In Arvidsjaur, the Inlandsvägen intersects with Riksvägen 95, an old silver route leading from Norwegian Bodø to Luleå on the Gulf of Bothnia. Along this route, Swedish silversmiths reached Sami territory, took their precious metal on commission, and crafted it to the renowned "Lapp Silver." The mastery of the artists who fashioned this jewelry is undisputed. The designs chosen reveal, however, their interest in saving most of the precious silver for themselves: by using thin metal sheets and designs with large spaces, they were able to pocket most of the commissioned silver without the Sami realizing the fraud. The history of "Lapp Silver" is wonderfully documented in the town of **Arjeplog** ㉓, 80 kilometers northwest of Arvidsjaur, in the ****Silbermuseet**. The village, situated between two large lakes – **Hornavan** and **Uddjaure** – is a monument to the past, but in winter, with temperatures below minus 30°C, it is transformed into a testing grounds for the automobiles of the future. On frozen-over Lake Hornavan, the latest European models are tested for suitability under the toughest conditions.

Driving through Arjeplog, you reach the national park of **Pieljekaise**, about 60 kilometers away, which was created to protect the virgin birch forests. Starting points for park excursions, where in the summer flowers bloom in rainbow colors, include **Jäkkvik** ㉔ on Route 95 north of the park, **Hällbacken** ㉕ and **Adolfsström** ㉖ on a byroad south of the park. The Jäkkvik-Adolfsström hiking trail is a section of the *Kungsleden*.

The Land of the Midnight Sun

Route 45 crosses the **Arctic Circle** 150 kilometers north of Arvidsjaur. There is a modern polar station here with a café, as well as a souvenir shop where souvenir collectors can acquire, for a small donation, the obligatory Arctic Circle seal and certificate.

***Jokkmokk** ㉗ is located just north of the Arctic Circle. The earliest archeological finds of the area date back to 4000 B.C. Today's trading post bears the name of a Sami family that maintains its winter quarters here and still pursues trade. Charles IX first legalized the trading post at the beginning of the 17th century – to assure his right to tax collection.

Alcohol plays an unfortunate role in the trading relations between the Sami and the Swedes. The import of alcohol to Lapland was strictly forbidden in the 18th and 19th centuries to prevent the Sami from becoming victims of vice. This failed to solve the problem; instead it forced the price of schnapps to increase to

such heights that smugglers enjoyed a real heyday.

For the last 400 years, a market has been held in Jokkmokk on the first weekend in February. Thousands of eager visitors journey here every year to take part in the festivities. In the modern ****Ajtte Svenskt Fjälloch Samemuseum** there is a multimedia show held to present the Sami traditions. The 18th-century church of **Gamla Samekyrkan**, which burned to the ground in 1972, has been faithfully reconstructed, including the churchyard fence with its conspicuous man-sized niches; these were to hold caskets when winter grave-digging was impossible due to the frozen ground.

The Outdoor El Dorado

From Jokkmokk, a small road winds 100 kilometers westward to **Kvikkjokk** ㉘. This is a stretch of the Carl Linné Trail that was blazed between Luleå and the Norwegian border. In Kvikkjokk, you meet up with the ***Kungsleden** (Royal

Swedish Lapland

Trail), Sweden's most renowned hiking trail, which leads 200 kilometers to the north, reaching Abisko, and just under 300 kilometers to the south, to Hemavan. The trail is well marked and provided with a multitude of mountain huts and shelters; it's not just a footpath. Trekkers should be in good shape and equipped for all eventualities, since it can snow here even in the middle of summer. Many fjords with freezing-cold currents have to be crossed; map-reading and compass skills are vital. Most of the more than 30,000 hikers on the Kungsleden are experienced in wilderness trekking. The northern half is the most popular. From this route, a three- to four-day detour can be made to Sweden's highest mountain, the 2,111-meter ***Kebnekaise (㊴)**. However, the easier approach starts from the **Kebnekaise-Fjällstation**, a 13-kilometer hike from **Nikkaluokta (㊳)** near Kiruna (see p. 226).

You can hike the Kungsleden in summer as well as winter. It joins other hiking trails, for example the **Padjelantaleden**, passing through the national park of **Padjelanta**, or the **Nordkalottleden**, an 800-kilometer-long trail that crosses the borders between Sweden, Norway and Finland no fewer than 14 times.

The national parks of **Sarek**, **Stora Sjöfallet** and Padjelanta border each other and cover an area totaling 5,300 square kilometers. Padjelanta is easily accessible by road and practically dishonors its designation as a "national park" in that the construction of a hydroelectric plant required serious intervention in the natural environment, especially with the creation of **Lake Akkajaure**, a reservoir. Still, the peaks and glaciers of the Akka massif are incredibly beautiful. Sarek Park is an immense wilderness without trails, and true nature lovers would do well to leave it alone. Known, but almost

Right: The wide-open spaces near Lake Tjaktajaure on the Kungsleden.

inaccessible, lies the former glacial valley of **Rapadalen**, with many wild tributary rivers. One stretch of the Kungsleden passes by **Lake Laitaure**, fed by the **Rapaälven River**.

GÄLLIVARE

About 25 kilometers north of Jokkmokk, the Inlandsvägen leads to the entrance of the national park of **Muddus**: 430 square kilometers of virgin tundra, mostly supporting pines, some of which are hundreds of years old, as well as "dry pine" (a non-elastic deadwood conserved through a long natural process; in great demand for construction work, although difficult to work with). Over the water-impermeable granite strata, moors were formed, and in the park's center, **Lake Muddusjaure**, where numerous species of birds flock to breed. The bear population is also quite high.

In **Porjus ㉙**, on Route 45, an enormous power plant was carved out of the mountain to tap the potential energy of the Lule älv rapids. Since the Inlandsbana was not yet available to transport materials for the project, hundreds of day laborers carried construction materials from ***Gällivare ㉚** to Porjus. The best workmen were reported to have needed only one day to carry 100 kilograms 50 kilometers. A small exhibit documents this almost superhuman feat.

*Dundret, the 823-meter local peak of Gällivare, comes into view only 13 kilometers south of the city. Here a modern ski resort has been established. The entire hotel complex was crafted by Finnish carpenters with "dry pine," since not a single Swedish craftsman could be found who knew how to work with this material.

Gällivare had been a small center of Sami inhabitants before the village became completely dependent on the mining industry. The "One Öre Church," built in 1751, could be financed after the king had requested a donation of this amount

from every Swedish citizen. The underground mining of high-quality iron ore from the **Malmberget** district six kilometers away began in 1888 after the completion of the railway line. The land above the pit was left undeveloped for fear of cave-ins, leaving a visible open area between the two sections of the city. The planless construction in Malmberget is quite obvious; here in **Kåkstan**, the city of barracks, locals feel a nostalgic attachment to the clapboard construction of days gone by. Even a "Sobriety Café," a monument to the prohibition days in Lapland, has been opened for business.

Just 13 kilometers east of Gällivare, the Inlandsvägen and E10 *(Nordkalottvägen* Luleå-Narvik) share the same stretch of road for 66 kilometers before separating again at Svappavaara. In **Muorjevaara** ❸, on the way you can try your luck at panning for gold. The Inlandsvägen continues northward 128 kilometers after **Svappavaara** ❸ through the lonely forests and moors of Lapland to Karesuando. The Sami settlement of

Idivuoma ❸ is home to the largest reindeer-slaughtering enterprise in the north.

Karesuando ❸, directly on the Finnish border, marks the northern end of the Inlandsvägen. On the other bank of the **Muonio River** the journey can be continued into Finland via the E8. The local church can accommodate twice the number of today's inhabitants, now 300.

Here, even in summer, permafrost is the rule, and the mosquitoes are so aggressive they can bite through clothing.

★KIRUNA
The Mountain of Iron

Before continuing on the E10 west of Svappavaara to reach Kiruna after a 48-kilometer drive, you should be sure to visit the Sami settlement of **Jukkasjärvi** ❸. The 400-year-old trading center, 10 kilometers north of the main road, boasts an interesting **wooden church** from the 18th century that was decorated in 1958 with colorful wood reliefs by Bror Hjorth. They bring to life the teachings of

Swedish Lapland

Lars Levi Laestadius (1800-61). As founder of the Judgment Day Movement, he preached fervently against alcoholism and promiscuity. It is true that these social ills still exist in Sweden today, but nevertheless the Judgment Day Movement has continued to be an important religious and political influence on the nation. Interesting to view are the plaques that travelers of the 18th century left hanging in the church to illustrate their own personal experiences in the "Wild North."

In Jukkasjärvi, an 80-kilometer rubber raft ride on the rapids of the **Torne älv** is highly recommended for the brave and daring. For those interested in modern technology, the secrets of civilian space travel are unraveled on the rocket testing grounds (*raketskjufält*), 10,000 square kilometers in size, in **Esrange ㊱**, 30 kilometers northeast of Jukkasjärvi.

*★**Kiruna ㊲** is a city of 26,000 and also the administrative seat of the huge commune of Kiruna, where only 3,000 people live outside the city limits. Having a total area of 20,000 square kilometers, this means the outlying areas are practically uninhabited. Even though the iron ore deposits of *★**Mount Kirunavaara** had been renowned since the 18th century, the lack of a means of transportation meant exploitation would be unprofitable. Only after construction of the hundred-kilometer -long railway from Kiruna to Narvik in 1902 could the mining of the richest iron ore deposits in the world begin (the ore has an iron content of 70 percent). Kirunavaara owes its characteristic terraced appearance to the building property left over after the original open-pit mining. Only underground mining takes place here today – a relief for the workers during the long, cold winters. The mine shafts and tunnels penetrate almost 500 meters into the mountain.

In the so-called **Tourist Tunnel**, large enough for the dinged-up buses, you can learn about old and new mining methods. In contrast, the peak of the iron mountain

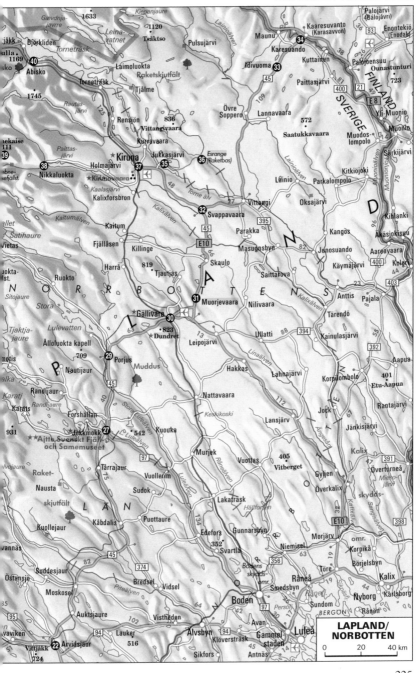

**LAPLAND/
NORBOTTEN**

0   20   40 km

offers only a view of bare, uninhabited landscape. In Kiruna, the rusty tower of the **Stadshuset** immediately catches your eye. According to the architect's concept, the mutual dependence of the city and iron is symbolized here. Modeled after a Sami hut, the **church** of the city, which was planned in 1912, appears to be somewhat lacking in contour. Many artists, including Prince Eugene, worked fervently on the interior décor of the church, expressing their thanks to the workers of the pits so very important to Sweden.

Buses stop go several times a day to **Nikkaluokta** ㊳, 68 kilometers west of Kiruna (see p. 224). **Kebnekaise** ㊴ (2,111 meters), Sweden's highest mountain, is just west of there. If the bus is too slow for you, you can take a helicopter.

Until 1984, no road existed between Kiruna and **Narvik**. You could only continue traveling by riding the trains transporting ore. The new E10 reaches Narvik

after 150 kilometers via **Abisko** ㊵, the beginning (you could also say the end) of the Kungsleden. The *Nordkalottleden* hiking trail, near the village, follows a section of the *rallarvägen*, the access for the railroad maintenance workers for the Kiruna-Narvik line. A chair lift ascends the 1,169-meter **Mount Njulla**, from whose summit, theoretically, you can see the Midnight Sun from May 27 to July 14. Here you can also see the impressive site of Lapporten, a striking u-shaped notch between two distant 1,500-meter-peaks.

The **Abiskodalen** in the national park of **Abisko** is the driest place in Sweden, with only 300 mm annual precipitation. This is due to the **Skanden Mountains**, which shield the region from rain clouds (great chances for a sunny start to a day's hiking on the Kungsleden).

Riksgränsen, 35 kilometers farther along on the west side of the massif off the Atlantic coast, is the area claiming Sweden's highest levels of precipitation. Therefore, a year-round ski resort has developed, with snow guaranteed.

Above: The richest iron ore deposits in the world are found in Kirunavaara.

Map pp. 224-225

ÅRE (☎ 0647)

i 83013 Åre, tel. 17720.

😊😊 **Sunwing Åre**, Tottvägen, tel. 15000, fax 15270, hotel with substantial nightlife. **First Resort Trillevallens Högfjällhotel**, Vällisterfjället, Undersåker, tel. 36090, fax 36013. 😊 **Hotell Årevidden**, Björnänge, tel. 17170, fax 17171.

🏇 *HORSEBACK RIDING:* **Åre Ridcenter**, tel. 34012. *HANG-GLIDING, DOG SLEDDING:* **Åreguiderana**, tel. 52270. *SKI TOURS* and equipment: **Skidåkarna**, tel. 50405.

ÖSTERSUND (☎ 063)

i Rådhusgatan 44, 83182 Östersund, tel. 144001.

😊😊😊 **SAS Radisson Hotel Östersund**, Prästgatan 16, tel. 127740, fax 106729. 😊😊 **First Hotel Gamla Teatern**, Thoméegränd 20, tel. 11600, fax 131499. **First Express Östersund**, Korfältets Centrum, tel. 127660, fax 107671. **Scandic Hotel Östersund**, Krondikesvägen 97, tel. 127560, fax 104098. 😊 **Hotel Aston**, Köpmangatan 40, tel. 510851, fax 105027. **Hotel Zäta**, Prästgatan 32, tel. 517860, fax 107782.

🏕 **Östersunds Camping**, tel. 144615, 3 km south of town, with swimming pool.

🍴 The restaurant in the **Jamtli Museum** has an excellent Smörgåsbord on Sundays. **Loftet**, Kyrkgatan 49, tel. 129022, pretty view of the Storsjön. **Gustav III** in Hotel Östersund, Kyrkgatan, tel. 117640.

🏛 **Jamtli Jämtlands Länsmuseum**, June 15-Aug 15, 11 am-5 pm daily, otherwise only Tue 11 am-8 pm and Wed-Sun 11 am-5 pm. **Jamtli** open-air museum, May 15-Aug 15, 11 am-5 pm daily.

🛥 Schedule of the steamer **Thomée**: tourist office.

🚂 *TRAIN:* Inlandsbana from Östersund, tel. 108672, fax 108670.

📅 Second week in June: **Farmhouse Festival**.

DOROTEA (☎ 0942)

i Torget, 91726 Dorothea, tel. 14063.

😊 **Hotell Dorotea**, Bergsvägen 2, tel. 10810, fax 10612.

🏛 **Church** of **Dorotea**, 10 am-5 pm daily.

VILHELMINA (☎ 0940)

i Volgsjövägen 29, 91232 Vilhelmina, tel. 15270.

😊 **Lilla Hotellet**, Granvägen 1, tel. 15059, fax 15042. **Lundquist Stugmotell**, Volgsjövägen 64, tel. 10264, fax 10357.

ARVIDSJAUR (☎ 0960)

i Garvaregatan 4, 93332 Arvidsjaur, tel. 17500.

😊😊 **Hotell Laponia**, Storgatan 45, tel. 55500, fax 55599.

🏕 **Giela's Camping**, directly on the lake, tel. 13420, also *HUT RENTALS.*

🏛 **Sami Church Village**, open all summer. **Arjeplog** silver museum, June 15-Aug 15, daily 9 am-6 pm.

🛶 *CANOE* and *TROLLY TOURS,* information: tourist office. Second week in August: **Church Hut Festival**.

JOKKMOKK (☎ 0971)

i Stortorget, 962 Jokkmokk, tel.. 12696.

😊😊 **Hotel Jokkmokk**, Solgatan 45, tel. 55320, fax 55625.

🏛 **Ajtte Sami Museum**, June 15-Aug 15, 11 am-5 pm daily, otherwise Tue-Sun 12-3 pm. **Porjus** hydroelectric station , tours: June 1-Aug 15, 10 am-12 pm and 1:30-4 pm daily

🥾 **Fjäll hikes** from Kvikkjokk, tel. 21022.

📅 First week in February: large **Sami market**.

GÄLLIVARE (☎ 0970)

i Storgatan 16, 98221 Gällivare, tel. 16660.

😊😊 **Nya Dundret**, tel. 14560, fax 14827, the hotel with the best view. 😊 **Gällivare Värdshus**, Vid Badhuset, tel. 16200, fax 15545.

KIRUNA (☎ 0980)

i Folkets Hus, 98122 Kiruna, tel. 18880.

😊😊 **Scandic Hotel Ferrum**, Lars Jansonsgatan 15, tel. 18600, fax 14505. **Hotel Vinterpalatset**, Järnvägsgatan 18, tel. 83170, fax 13050. 😊 **Gullrist Lägenhetshotell**, Bromsgatan 12, tel. 10937, fax 14700. **Kebne Hotell**, Konduktörsgatan 7, tel. 68180, fax 68181.

🍴 **Kiruna Samegård**, Brytargatan 14, tel. 17029, reindeer and snow bunting specialties.

🏛 Tour of the **Ore Mine** leaves from tourist office, June 15-Aug 15, 10 am-4 pm daily.

🎨 **Wennbergs Samjöjd**, tel. 10079, Sami craft work.

JUKKASJÄRVI (☎ 0980)

🏨 **Arctic Hall**, world's largest ice hotel, room for 32, open only in winter, room temperature a constant 4°C. Information: tourist office of Kiruna.

🏛 **Local History Museum**, June 15-Aug 15, 10 am-4 pm daily.

Swedish Lapland

THE GÖTA CANAL

Ever since the days of Gustavus II Adolphus, the Swedes had dreamed of a waterway connecting Stockholm with the Atlantic and one that would make the lengthy, dangerous and round-about trip around the southern tip of Schonen superfluous. Already at that time, an ingenious plan was devised to connect the numerous lakes and rivers of central Sweden by means of a canal. Waterfalls, river rapids and the differences in elevations of the lakes – unsolvable obstacles to 17th-century technology – stood in the way of the project's realization.

Not until the 19th century did they succeed in achieving this ambitious plan. Following the loss of Finland to Russia in 1807, the Swedish Parliament was prepared to provide funds for the improvement of the country's infrastructure. Since the canal was also militarily significant, mostly soldiers were employed in the construction – a workforce which, at times, totaled up to 60,000 workers. General Baltazar von Platen, who also worked out the plans for the canal, supervised the construction project.

It took from 1810 to 1832 to lay the 87 kilometers of canal and to construct the 65 locks necessary to compensate for the differences in elevation of the numerous rivers and lakes involved. In the end, a 385-kilometer waterway could finally be put into operation. Yet unforeseen technical problems had not only led to construction delays, but also to the total costs far exceeding the original budget many times over. To spur the soldiers working on the construction to top performance during 15-hour shifts, an extra liter of cognac was added to their weekly food rations.

Preceding pages: A mystery play to commemorate the conquest of Visby by Waldemar Atterdag in 1361 (on the beach of Visby, Gotland, during Medieval Week). Right: Explore Sweden by steamship on the Göta Canal.

Even today in Sweden it is said that the canal was built on schnapps.

From Gothenburg to Trollhättan the waterway first followed the Göta älv River, then crossed Lake Vänern for a good 100 kilometers, ascended 91 meters to Lake Vättern only to descend lock by lock to reach the Baltic Sea near the town of Mem, not far from Söderköping. The last 215 kilometers to Stockholm across the Baltic and through the skerries cannot, of course, be included as a part of the Göta Canal. The most spectacular stretches of the inland journey lie between lakes Vänern and Vättern, as well as between lakes Boren and Roxen, where up to seven locks are involved in raising and lowering the water level 20 meters at a time.

Unfortunately, this masterpiece of 19th-century technology was never able to live up to its full potential. Just a mere 30 years following the grand opening of the canal, the railway line between Stockholm and Gothenburg had finally been completed. In no time at all, the railway took over the transportation of most passengers and goods, running smoothly even during severe winters when the canal was frozen over. As far as transporting goods is concerned, the Göta Canal has no significance today with the exception of the stretch between Gothenburg and Lake Vänern – the Trollhätte Canal. As early as the 1920s, considerations were made concerning the closure of the canal to ships, however, with the arrival of the first tourists the trend changed, and the number of passengers increased again.

Still in all, the Göta Canal Steamship Company managed to celebrate its 130th anniversary in 1999. Of the three canal ships (*Diana, Wilhelm Tham* and *Juno* – today exclusively passenger ferries), the 125-year-old *Juno* is the oldest cabin ferry in the world.

Between mid-May and early September the passenger ferries run on a regular schedule. Although the boats have been

modernized, they still possess a certain nostalgic flair. The 300 G.R.T. vessels offer berths for between 60 and 70 passengers. Constructed to lock specifications, the ferries are long and narrow, as are the cabins, which means you need to decide what you want to stow there – luggage or yourself. However, every guest is compensated with a window seat in the ship's restaurant, where the tables are set with damask tablecloths and real silverware. As might be expected, the cuisine leaves nothing to be desired.

The voyages can take either four or six days depending on the tour chosen, and includes all of the sightseeing excursions in the purchase price. The most interesting port of call, offered as a part of almost every tour package starting at Gothenburg or Stockholm, include Lödöse, Trollhättan (Canal Museum), Läckö Castle, Lyrestad, Forsvik, Vadstena, Vreta Cloister, Söderköping, Trosa and also the Viking center of Birka on the island of Björkö in Lake Mälaren (see page 243 for tour promoters).

Due to the great demand, it is easily understandable that the voyages on the "blue ribbon through Sweden," as the Göta Canal is often called, can be completely booked-up during the high season. Early reservations are therefore absolutely necessary. The only exceptions are on-deck tickets for short-distance passengers taking day trips when the ferry is not filled to capacity. Those having boats of their own may use the canal for a fee at any time.

The Göta Canal has also begun to attract a growing number of bicyclists and hikers ever since the old towpaths were rediscovered. You can follow the canal, and can also combine stretches with on-deck tickets at your convenience. A boat ride on the Göta Canal is certainly one of the highlights of a trip to Sweden. Even writers of detective novels and murder mysteries such as Maj Sjöwall and Per Wahlöö could not resist the lure of the canal, and in *Death on the Göta Canal* the stage was set for a spectacular murder mystery.

The Göta Canal

231

ASTRID LINDGREN

If you took a popularity poll in Sweden, this aging lady would come out even ahead of the members of the Royal Family. Her fans, who are not only children, can be found throughout the entire world. We are talking about Astrid Lindgren, one of the most famous authors of children's and young people's books, whose published works number in the millions and appear in 57 countries. The countless prizes and honors bestowed upon her include, for example, the Hans Christian Andersen Medal – regarded as the "little Nobel Prize for Children's Literature." The daughter of a south Sweden farmer from Småland broke into the children's literature scene in Sweden with her very first book – *Pippi Longstocking* (1944).

Pippi, a red-headed girl who lives in the Villa Villekulla with a monkey and a horse, possesses unbelievable physical strength for someone her age and has no understanding whatsoever for authority. She puts police officers on rooftops, sleeps head-to-foot in bed and couldn't care less about school. No wonder many adults reacted with outrage to this rebellious super-child and regarded her as a bad example for their own children. Incidentally, five German publishers rejected the book before it was finally published by Oetinger in 1948. Yet there is more to Pippi than what meets the eye; she manages to give a completely new meaning to the relatively uninteresting lives of the neighborhood children, and is always Johnny-on-the-spot when the weak or disadvantaged are in need of help. Astrid Lindgren wrote, in 1959, that if anything, she intended to show in *Pippi Longstocking* "that a person can possess power without abusing it." *Pippi Longstocking* continues to be her greatest international success.

Right: Astrid Lindgren (1990) – children all over the world love her books.

Astrid Lindgren's work covers a wide spectrum: in addition to realistic children's novels, there are children's detective stories, mysteries, fantasies and fairy tales, as well as screenplays.

Many books mirror the childhood Lindgren spent in the farmhouse of Näs near the town of Vimmerby. In *The Children of Noisy Village*, which appeared in 1947, she set a monument for those carefree times in "a place that exists no more." Other works including *Madita* and *Emil from Lönneberga* (1963), whose hero's name was changed to Michel in the German version out of consideration for Erich Kästner's *Emil and the Detective*, also belong to this category. These stories convey a feeling and understanding towards life that seemingly knows neither national nor cultural boundaries. Noisy Village can certainly be considered home to all children.

However, some critics have their problems with Astrid Lindgren. While *Pippi Longstocking* has been reproached as being anti-authoritarian, other works of hers are criticized as being too idealistic. Yet when she breaks away from the ideal world pattern, she is begrudged once again: *The Brothers Lionheart* (1973), proclaimed by Astrid Lindgren as her "consolation novel," was condemned as unsuitable for children. It was not up to her as an author of children's books to deal with such themes as death, reincarnation and the fight for freedom.

Despite it all, Astrid Lindgren has never really been bothered much by the criticism she has received. She still took a determined stand against the overprotective, sugary-sweet confines of traditional children's literature. She sees it as her duty to offer standards of conduct to modern-day children who often lack the necessary direction and are often overtaxed in this modern world. In spite of all the criticism, she shows an infallible sensitivity to the wishes and expectations of her young readers.

In her last great children's novel, *Ronia the Robber's Daughter* (1981), she again struck a new chord: using the unbridled life of a robber, a children's love story based on Romeo and Juliet, a nature-experiencing theme and, most importantly, non-aggression as a means against violence. Her maxim has always been – "I'm always on the children's side."

She has frequently created confusion by leaving her domain and unexpectedly meddling in Swedish politics. In 1976, she wrote an extremely critical political fairy tale about an old female troll: *Pomperipossa in the World of Money* appeared in the daily newspaper *Expressen*. Using clarity and simplicity, the author uncovered the deplorable state of affairs in government taxation and financial policies, brought the Minister of Finance to account and, as a result, caused the Social Democrats to lose the vote for the first time in decades.

Shortly before reaching the age of 80, she joined the Swedish movement against nuclear energy and began to fight for improving the protection of animals. With her powerful *My Cow Wants to Have Fun, Too* and numerous other articles in the *Expressen* she uncovered the catastrophic repercussions of applying industrial methods to the raising of animals; for years she battled ministers and agricultural dignitaries drawing attention to herself yet again. In honor of her 80th birthday, the Prime Minister dedicated a new animal protection law bearing her name: "Lex Lindgren." Since then, Astrid has been a "national institution."

Fame has not gone to her head; like her spiritual daughter Pippi, she uses her influence to support those who need her help. And in Sweden, everyone listens to what she has to say. Every television station covered her 90th birthday on November 14, 1997, while Lindgren, long weary of publicity and the same monotonous questions of the reporters, retreated from the onrush of the media to her country house on the island of Furnusund. "I find myself quite uninteresting," she had already commented years before.

Astrid Lindgren

233

The Vasa – The 17th-Century Titanic

"Next to God himself, the well-being of our kingdom rests on our fleet." This is a quote from Gustavus II Adolphus, who in the year 1625 ordered the construction of a warship that should dwarf all preceding vessels – the *Vasa*.

Some 400 workers began with the construction in Stockholm's naval shipyard, over 1,000 oaks had been felled and 64 heavy cannons had been cast in bronze. Hundreds of carvings were created representing the coat of arms of the ancient Vasa dynasties and that of the "Northern Lion," as Gustavus II Adolphus was called, along with 20 Roman emperors as decoration proclaiming the self-confidence and status-consciousness of the king. The *Vasa* became Sweden's most expensive and magnificent warship of the 17th century and, exhibiting a length of

Above: After many unsuccessful salvage attempts, the Vasa can now be marveled at in the Vasa Museet.

69 meters and a mast over 50 meters high, it was also the largest. The battery deck provided room for a 400-man crew, and the luxurious berths of the higher officers were filled-to-bursting with gold-plated sculptures.

After two years of construction, the vessel was finally launched. The *Vasa* was first moored just across the harbor from the royal castle, and cannons, equipment and ballast were loaded on board.

The long-awaited day came at last on August 10, 1629. A large crowd had gathered on the shores to bid the grand *Vasa* farewell on her maiden voyage – unknowingly, they were to become eyewitnesses to a major catastrophe. The ship had to be awkwardly towed for the first 100 meters. Upon reaching the location of present-day Slussen, four of the ten sails were set, the cannons fired a salute, and the *Vasa* set off on her first – and last – voyage. After less than one nautical mile a gust of wind caught the vessel. She tipped over, water gushed into the cannon ports, and the pride of the Swedish Navy had capsized and sank while still in the harbor.

In addition to a crew of about 100, there were numerous women and children on board who were to disembark after the festivities. Only about half of these shipwreck victims survived.

The search for those responsible for the disaster was initiated immediately, it produced, however, no results. The captain was arrested – nothing, though, could be held against him. He himself blamed the shipbuilder. It turned out that the Vasa had undergone a load test to check her stability. A group of men had been ordered to run back and forth over her deck; indeed after the third run, the boat had reportedly almost capsized. The presiding admiral, however, had this alarming test result hushed up.

Further investigation proved to be complicated, since the original shipbuilder had died a year after beginning construction and had been replaced by another. The replacement also pleaded his innocence, and pointed to the fact that the king himself had ordered the dimensions of the Vasa and had very probably even intervened in the original plans. Consequently, the investigation reached a dead end.

Actually, the cause of the sinking can be found in the inadequacy of theoretical knowledge in the 17th century. According to modern statistical calculations, the ship was by no means seaworthy. The relationships between the height of the hull (19.3 meters) and to the rigging, as well as to the heavy equipment, show the draft of only 4.8 meters to be clearly insufficient. The shipbuilders of the time relied primarily on experience; the experiment using conventional proportions for the construction of such a large vessel was doomed to fail.

Salvage operations began immediately after the Vasa's sinking, however, not until 1664, with the help of a diving bell, had at least most of the valuable cannons been successfully recovered. Afterwards, the Vasa became only a dim memory until the 1950s, when Anders Franzén, an expert in Swedish naval military history, began the search for the now legendary vessel and located it. In 1957, the "Campaign for Preserving the Vasa" was founded. Never before had such a large ship been recovered. Using special nozzles, it took divers two years to dig tunnels under the wreck, working in complete darkness and at a depth of 32 meters. Thick steel cables were drawn under the keel and despite the danger of the ship falling apart, the first recovery attempt was initiated. The attempt proved successful, and the Vasa was transported to shallow water in 16 stages. It took an additional two years to seal and strengthen the hull. Finally, in April 1961, after 333 years of lying on the harbor seabed, the Vasa was fully recovered. Nearly 40 large anchors, remnants of failed salvage attempts of the past, were found stuck in the broken stern.

Conservation of the vessel required a lengthy and complicated process. It took 17 years of constant spraying with polyethylene glycol to extract 580 tons of water from the saturated oak hull and replace it with this solution – which takes on a wax-like consistency after cooling. More than 13,500 loose pieces needed to be put back in place; the seabed of the discovery site was thoroughly combed, and produced six out of the ten original sails, as well as weapons, furniture, dishes, cases of provisions, clothing and personal belongings, magnificent woodcarvings and over 20 skeletons, including even that of the ship's cat.

A mere 100 meters from the location of the tragic sinking, the "Vasamuseet" was established to house the only completely intact 17th-century ship in the world. Officially opened in 1990 with Carl XVI Gustaf presiding, the Vasa Museum is now among one of the most interesting tourist sites in Stockholm.

The Vasa

"Sweden Incorporated": A Welfare State?

The Swedish social system was considered exemplary in Europe for many years. Not only the Social Democrats raved about a model system that the Swedes themselves described as a successful mixture of economic efficiency, the *Aktiebolaget Sverige* (Sweden Corporation), and all-encompassing social insurance coverage, the *folkhem* (welfare state).

Up until the 1970s, the Swedish social system appeared to be the optimal one for its advocates. Second only to Switzerland, Sweden achieved a leading position in Europe in regard to the gross national product per capita. Deep into the 1980s, unemployment was just as insignificant a topic as poverty or even the homeless. Low inflation rates, and a slight national

Above: Sweden's overall childcare program with kindergartens and nurseries is accepted as a shining example for the rest of the world.

debt completed the favorable economic picture.

The basis for this development was summed up in two phrases coined in 1944 by the Swedish Nobel Prize winner Gunnar Myrdal: *Höga skatter – låga räntor* (high taxes – low interest rates). "Low interest rates" do not necessarily represent a policy of lax financial regulation, but for everything necessary to promote the well-being of free enterprise. Above all, this includes low taxation on withheld profits (less than 30% even today), broad-minded regulations regarding tax deductions, and trade union wage policies favoring businesses with the highest productivity. The last point led to a radical restructuring of a society that only a hundred years before was primarily agricultural – over 90% of the population today live in cities or large residential areas, and rural areas have become drastically depopulated.

The government did not interfere with the economic process and especially not with subsidies. Also, with less than a 10%

share of production, the government only nominally takes part in economic activity – only ore mines and a few steelworks in the north, national forests, and the production of electricity are worth mentioning here. Trade unions and company management, both well organized, work together cooperatively to each other's advantage in keeping to the so-called "Spirit of Saltsjöbaden" (cf. p. 201). This was, in fact, an alliance of employee *and* employer, not only exclusively for the employee, which shows why time and again similar attempts in other European companies were met with a deadlock.

So much for the success of the "Sweden Corporation." But what happened to its counterweight – the *folkhem*? This had also been incredibly successful for years. As a social welfare system established by the social democratic prime minister Albin Hansson in 1932 during the worldwide economic depression, the conservative political parties could offer no solution to counter this newly presented concept. The consequences have been that, aside from two short interludes, conservatives are still unable to gain control of the government. At first, the *folkhem* consisted merely of modest, basic insurance covering unemployment, illness and old age. Through taxation, as opposed to individual contributions, every senior citizen had the right to a pension. This meant there would be no special privileges for the self-employed or for the bureaucrats (in Sweden considered only as salaried civil servants). Two additional peculiarities: unemployment insurance is administrated by the trade unions, and continued pay is managed by the state health insurance agencies. The former contributes to the high degree of organization of the trade unions, while the latter relieves the employer.

Since the 1950s, social security benefits have been extended to all-encompassing insurance coverage, limiting social welfare benefits to actual emergencies

only. The payment allowance for dependent children is many times higher here than in the rest of Europe. The abundance of kindergartens and day nurseries, with teacher-children ratios of 1:5 and 1:3 respectively, has remained unmatched. Furthermore, all college and university students receive a grant of twice the children's payment allowance as well as an interest-free student loan (which is relative to the current rate of inflation), that must be repaid only after the individual has reached a certain level of income and which allows for as much as 30 years for repayment. This has led to an immense easing of tension in the "generation gap," since young people are no longer financially dependent upon their parents.

The elderly, however, have not been short-changed either: a so-called years-of-service pension has been added to the universal pension. The amount of the pension is calculated according to the individual's 15 highest income years and, naturally, it is protected from inflation fluctuations. Additionally, there are housing subsidies and financial aid for this, that and the other. In the 1970s, there were even housing subsidies in case home owners were no longer financially able to keep up their bank payments.

All of this was financed not only by the flourishing economy, but also by the extremely high taxes as already mentioned. In addition to proportional municipal taxes averaging of 30% of the income, a federal income tax of 5 to 85% had to be paid on the remaining 70%. Since there are really no deductions worth mentioning, this means a tax burden of at least 33.5% even for low-income earners. In the 1970s, taxpayers in the middle income bracket earning approximately US $2,000 (ca. £1,300) were burdened with taxes exceeding 50%. For some of the self-employed, such as the author Astrid Lindgren, the taxation system led to a burden of over 100%, since she had to pay employer's contributions of 15% in addi-

Sweden, Inc.

tion to the normal 90% rate on her income. This can all be read in her fairy tale *Pomperipossa*, which she dedicated to Gunnar Sträng, the Minister of Finance at the time.

The high taxation led to the acceleration of a process that is generally considered as a fine achievement: the world's largest employment rate for employable women lies at 80% of the female population. Since as early as the 1970s, hardly a single breadwinner could feed a family on his net earnings, and women were simply forced to find jobs – whether emancipated or not. They did find jobs, not in the high-productivity sectors of industry, but in the civil service and mostly in part-time positions. Formerly unpaid family-oriented tasks traditionally performed by women, such as the care and upbringing of children or care of the sick and the elderly, were transformed into modest gross earnings of which at least a third of the income again flows back to the government. The low wages in the government sector, which nevertheless constitute 70% of the gross national product, have also influenced wages in the private sector. Journalists, for example, even working for a prominent newspaper, earn hardly more than half of what they would earn in comparable countries, and that's while paying higher taxes. For this reason, the gross national product per capita has fallen to a middle position in Europe; it lies at up to 25% below that of other EU countries.

As a matter of course, massive resistance developed against the high taxation: lowering taxable income by utilizing all possible legal means and through jobs paid under the table. But since in Sweden all government documents are open to public perusal, including income tax declarations, everyone knows the

Right: To what extent social coverage will remain to this Swedish child in the future remains uncertain.

financial affairs of his neighbor. A citizen only needs to purchase the annually published local *Skattekalendar* (tax calendar) to establish that an ostentatiously living neighbor has failed to pay his taxes. *Nolltaxerare* (zero taxpayer) is a favorite insult, especially trumped up by the media, for the rich or those suspected of being so. In the *folkhem*, therefore, discord prevails.

Just as tax returns can't be held private, bank accounts are also open to scrutiny. It's the duty of banking institutions to voluntarily report anything that could interest the internal revenue service. Although it's true that everyone does his best to decrease his tax burden, at the same time, everyone keeps a close watch to thwart the attempts of others. The *Kungliga svenska avundsjukan* (royal Swedish envy) admitted to by the self-critical, sets limits difficult to understand by a non-Swede. Nevertheless, the internal revenue service, despite their zeal for justice, is completely open to logical arguments. Laws are not necessarily carried out to the letter, but are by no means open to bribery. The ruling principal could be seen as pragmatic judgment being made in view of the complications involved in the individual case.

Real problems in the Swedish system began, however, as the manifold social assistance, despite high taxation (for example, a value added tax of 25%) could no longer be financed. The government fell further into debt, which it in turn imposed upon the banks through emergency measures. The result is that since the 1970s, the inflation rate remains a two-digit figure, with correspondingly high interest rates and a hefty national debt, as well as an ever-weakening krone, devaluated 75% since the 1960s.

Until the crisis of 1991/92, the unemployment rate of no more than 3% could be maintained. Now unemployment has risen to over 10%. Since the national debt exceeded 75% and the budget deficit 12%

over the gross national product, it came to pass in 1994 that the Social Democrats, for only the second time since 1932, lost to the conservative parties. These, in turn – using desperate economic savings programs connected with a reduction of the state's maximum tax rate to 60% – however, created no immediate improvement of the unfavorable economic situation, so that the government fell once again to the Social Democrats.

The Social Democrats, in fact, managed to turn the situation around: the public deficit could be changed to a small surplus causing a debt reduction to 70% and an unemployment decrease to 8%. The same thing occurred to the inflation and interest rates, which today only slightly exceed those of the comparatively low European levels. This is all the result of radical savings measures which for other European social democratic parties would be unthinkable: cuts in children's benefits and pensions, considerable self-contribution to health and child care, and, especially, the adoption of a three-day maximum in fully-paid sick days, the salary being reduced to 75% for additional sick days.

With the destruction of the *folkhem*, however, the Social Democrats expected a bit too much from their followers: in the elections of September 1998, they reached, with only 36% of the vote, their worst results since the 1920s. The winners this time were not the conservative opposition parties that offered promises of tax reduction by lowering government benefits, but the left-wing socialist parties, which managed to double their supporters and, in coalition with the Green Party, achieved over 16% of the vote. They promised the reinstatement of social benefits – if need be through tax increases. They agreed to tolerate the Social Democratic minority rule only under the condition that election promises be held. If through these measures the *folkhem* of the past, the success of which is certainly based on a flourishing economy, can really be reestablished, seems highly doubtful.

Sweden, Inc.

239

METRIC CONVERSION

Metric Unit	US Equivalent
Meter (m)	39.37 in.
Kilometer (km)	0.6241 mi.
Square Meter (sq m)	10.76 sq. ft.
Hectare (ha)	2.471 acres
Square Kilometer (sq km)	0.386 sq. mi.
Kilogram (kg)	2.2 lbs.
Liter (l)	1.05 qt.

TRAVEL PREPARATIONS

Arrival

A valid personal identity card or passport is necessary for inhabitants of the European Union and associated countries to enter Sweden. When entering from another Scandinavian country, there are no longer checks at the border due to the existing customs and passport union. Children under 16 can be noted in the passport of the parents or travel with their own passport.

Pets can be taken into the country, however, only in connection with an allowance procedure taking up to six months. National vehicle documents are valid in Sweden and must always be kept with you. Vaccinations are not necessary unless you have been in an epidemic area prior to entering.

Money

The Swedish currency is the krona (SEK), which is divided into 100 öre. The smallest denomination in circulation is the 5-öre coin; this explains the rounding off at the cash registers. There is no limit on the import or export of cash. Eurochecks have not been accepted since 1999, but cash withdrawals with an EC card are possible at many automatic teller machines. This also goes for the leading credit cards (Visa, Mastercard), which are also accepted in many shops, hotels, gas stations and restaurants.

When changing cash for krona, the banks and exchange offices charge a processing fee of 25 SEK regardless of the amount changed. The Forex exchange offices at the train stations and airports are the cheapest.

Health

The Swedish health care system is efficient and extensive. There are reciprocal agreements with all EU countries and many other European countries. You go to an *Akutmottagningen* in hospitals in the cities, or to the *Vårdcentralen* out in the country. This works best through the nationwide emergency number (tel. 112), which takes care of transportation in case of an emergency.

Further treatment is taken care of by the admission centers, which must be paid for in cash. Since treatment costs are not very high, the your health insurance company at home usually reimburses you for the sum paid up front.

Medication is mainly by prescription in Sweden. The names of medication carried by the pharmacies abroad are often different from those at home. It is therefore recommendable to always carry with you the medication you require for the length of your trip.

Climate / When to go

Sweden's temperate climate is due to the west wind and the close proximity to the Atlantic Ocean, whose influence decreases the farther east and north you go. The summers can be very hot and dry, and the winters very cold. The average amounts of precipitation are significantly below those of central Europe; however, the prevailing west wind sees to it that the weather is quite changeable. Just as morning sunshine is no guarantee that it's going to be a beautiful day, a morning rain shower does not necessarily indicate a rainy day.

Due to the long days in the summer, the average number of sunshine hours is much higher than in central Europe, although temperature variations of 15°C from one day to the next are not uncommon. The water in the south reaches temperatures of 20°C in the summer, as does the water in the shallow bays along the Gulf of Bothnia.

The peak season for travel begins in southwestern Sweden in May, the sunniest month, and ends in September. In northern Sweden there are really only two seasons to speak of: the bright summer, when the sun doesn't set, and the dark winter, when it doesn't rise.

June, July and August are the summer months. It is possible to have a winter vacation with snow north of Dalarna from November to March. The season reaches its peak there at Christmastime.

Clothing

The unpredictable weather requires travelers to plan for any eventuality. Dressing in layers is a tried and tested method. Bring sturdy footwear, as the wilderness often begins directly adjacent to the road. Sweaters and rain gear are also necessary in the summer. The dress code in Sweden is very casual: formal clothing is generally only worn at official events.

Tourist Information

Addresses and phone numbers of information offices found in the *INFO* sections at the end of each regional chapter can prove to be very helpful even before starting your trip. Everything from where to rent boats and bicycles to where to find souvenir bargains and recommendable hotels and restaurants is provided.

GETTING THERE

By Plane

SAS (code sharing with United and Air Canada), Quantas, British Airways and Delta serve Stockholm and Gothenburg from all major airports. Visby and Malmö can also be reached by direct flights from abroad. In addition, a shuttle bus runs between the airport in Copenhagen and the train station in Malmö. Furthermore, many charter and last-minute airlines offer a multitude of connections, many of which, however, can only be booked at short notice.

By Train

All direct rail connections from central Europe are from Germany; they go via the Sassnitz-Trelleborg stretch in the east, and "as the crow flies" in the west with two ferry passages: Puttgarden/Rødby and Helsingør/Helsingborg. The train cars roll onto the ferries, and you don't have to leave your compartment. The trains end in Malmö, Helsingborg or Gothenburg and have connections to Sweden's inland high-speed network.

By Ferry / Ship

The above-mentioned train ferries also transport motor vehicles and passengers without train reservations. In addition, there are other ferries for cars and passengers, whereby the night ferries have no compartments.

Ferries between Germany and Sweden (approximations for the summer season): Sassnitz-Trelleborg (DFO HansaFerry, 4 hours, 5 times daily); Rostock-Trelleborg (DFO, 6 hours, 6-7 times daily); TT-Line Combi-carrier (7 hours, 2-3 times daily; DFO-Catamaran (3 hours, 2-3 times daily); Travemünde-Trelleborg (TT-Line, 7-9 hours, 4-6 times daily); Kiel-Gothenburg (Stena Line, 13-14 hours, once daily).

Ferries between Denmark and Sweden (a selection): Helsingør-Helsingborg (ca. 20 minutes, every 20-30 minutes); Dragør-Limhamn (ca. 1 hour, 17 times daily); Rønne (Bornholm, with connection from Sassnitz)-Ystad (ca. 3 hours, 3 times daily); Grenå-Varberg (ca. 4 hours,

Guidelines

2 times daily); Frederikshavn-Gothen-burg (3 hours, 6 times daily).

Advance reservations and early arrival at the ferry terminal are highly recommended during the high season. All ferries offer discount fares; it is worthwhile to compare. The shortest connection might not be the cheapest, and the fares are usually cheaper on weekdays than on weekends.

By Car

Since there will not be a land connection to Sweden between Copenhagen and Malmö until the Öresund Bridge is finished in 2001, motorists have to take one of the above-mentioned ferries. It's good to remember that day ferries are often faster than those at night, which, in addition to the transportation fare, also sell tickets for a bunk in a compartment. As a rule, one lump sum is charged for a car including all passengers.

By Bus

More than 30 major European cities offer bus connections to Sweden. More information can be obtained from: Eurolines, 52 Grovener Gardens, London SW1, tel. 0990-143219 (from outside the U.K. tel. 0044-1582-404511). Internet: www.eurolines.co.uk.

TRAVELING IN SWEDEN

By Car

Sweden has a fully developed road system and there are very few extreme inclines, which makes almost all roads accessible year round. The Swedish traffic regulations correspond to those of central Europe for the most part. Speed limits in residential areas are 30 kph, in built-up areas 50 kph, on secondary roads 70-90 kph and 90-110 kph on highways. Fines for exceeding the speed limit by 20 kph can be as high as US $130, fines for passing violations are about the same. Ignoring a no-stopping or no-parking

sign will cost you a hefty US $80. It really becomes expensive, though, when the blood alcohol limit of 0.2 ppm has been exceeded, which costs at least one month's salary. Dipped headlights are obligatory day and night – violating this is usually cause for a written warning.

In case of a breakdown, the *Larmtjänst* (breakdown service) can be reached nationwide at the following telephone number: 22341600.

Due to the fact that unofficial camping at rest stops has taken the upper hand in recent years, overnight stays are only permitted at specially designated rest areas. These have waste tank disposal facilities for closed systems available.

By Train

The density of the rail network in Sweden corresponds to the population; it is denser in the south than in the north. Rail travel offers a real alternative to driving due to the long distances. All large cities have connections with the *X2000* high-speed trains, which reach speeds of up to 200 kph. The 480-kilometer trip from Gothenburg to Stockholm takes three hours.

The *Lapplandspilen* is especially interesting; it links Mälmo with Narvik. The *Inlandsbana* is a regularly scheduled "bus on rails" between Mora and Gällivare from midsummer to mid-August. It also runs as a steam train on some stretches. There are rail passes for more extensive train travel; with these you can pay a set price for unlimited travel in the main network within a given time frame.

More information on the Inlandsbana can be found on the Internet at: www.inlandsbanan.se/english/frmain.html.

By Bus

The Swedish bus company Swebus offers good connections for the whole country, even as far as to Oslo and Trysil in Norway. This includes some 1,500 locations with a good 300 of them being express connections. Information can be obtained by Swebus Express, City Terminals, Klarabergsviadukten 72, 11664 Stockholm, tel. 08-231440.

By Ship

The Swedish coastlines, lakes and canals offer a multitude of possibilities for recreational sailors. Citizens of many European countries are not required to register when arriving in Sweden by boat, unless, of course, they have goods on board to declare (see "Customs," p. 244). Your international boating certificate is sufficient for documentation purposes. There are boat rental agencies at practically all inland lake harbors and seaports offering boats of every sort. No boat piloting license is required for boats less than 12 meters long and four meters wide. Information can be obtained from the local tourist information office.

By Ferry

There are only long ferry routes within Sweden on the way to Gotland. The Nynäshamn-Visby and Oskarshamn-Visby links are served by "Destination Gotland." All large Baltic Sea carriers (DFO HansaFerry, TT Line, Stena Line, Silja Line) offer reasonably priced through fares to Gotland. In the summer season, a ferry travels between Öland (Grankullavik) and Gotland (Klintehamn) twice daily.

Smaller ferries between islands without bridges are often free of charge.

By Plane

Mainly SAS and its subsidiary Linjeflyg serve the domestic network, which includes all towns with more than 10,000 inhabitants. In addition, there are regional carriers such as Transwede, which flies between Stockholm and Halland and Nordic, linking Östersund with Malmö, Gothenburg and Stockholm. For reservations on all domestic

flights, the nationwide telephone number is: 020-727727. Local tourist offices can provide you with information concerning round-trip tours and helicopter flights.

Car Rental

Rental car agencies are represented at all larger airports. A minimum age of 21, driver's license and a credit card are required. Major rental car companies allow you to reserve and pay for a car before you even leave on your trip; in doing so you can avoid paying the high value added tax in Sweden. Even so, the local agencies which work together with domestic Swedish airlines are sometimes cheaper. This is especially true for renting trailers. It's best to check with the local tourist office, if you haven't already booked a package deal from home which includes a mobile home or camper.

Boat Tours

It is a good idea to contact a shipping company in advance for trips on the Göta and Dalsland canals (The Göta Canal Steamship Company, Ltd., Gothenburg, tel. 031-803615, and AB Göta Kanalbolag, Motala, tel. 0141-53510; Dalslandia shipping company, Mellerud, tel. 0530-31010).

Reservations are also possible through larger travel agencies.

PRACTICAL TIPS FROM A TO Z

Alcohol

Only *Lättöl* (light beer) with less than 0.5% alcohol and non-alcoholic wine can be sold in supermarkets and at gas stations in Sweden. They are also served in restaurants, which classify themselves as *alkoholfri* (non-alcoholic) or have no liquor license. Otherwise, alcoholic beverages are only sold in the state-run stores of the *Systembolaget*. These can be found in any town with a communal administration; something that is extremely rare in the north.

Nationwide opening hours are 9:30 a.m. to 6 p.m. Monday through Friday, Thursday until 7 p.m. They are closed on weekends and holidays. Prices are high, and customers must be at least 20 years of age.

Swedish *Starköl* (beer with 4.5% alcohol) is comparable to a European beer. Wine is imported, and the classic Swedish potato spirits *Skåne*, which is flavored with herbs, has given way to Absolut Vodka. Swedish mulled wine, *Glögg*, is made from red wine, spirits and sugar; you might want to take an aspirin with it. The import regulations for alcoholic beverages have loosened since Sweden joined the European Union (see "Customs"), this should not, however, entice visitors to sell their surplus. This can not only lead to confiscation, but also a hefty fine. Gifts of alcohol, on the other hand, are allowed.

Banks

Opening hours are from Monday through Friday from 9:30 a.m. to 3 p.m., until 1 p.m. before a holiday. Forex exchange offices are open daily from 8 a.m. to 9 p.m. There is an ATM in practically every town which accepts major credit cards, frequently the EC card as well.

Camping

Around 90 percent of the 750 or so Swedish campgrounds have been rated by the Swedish camping association (SCR) with up to three stars. A membership card, the *Campingkort*, is required and can be ordered from the Sveriges Campingvärdars Riksförbund (SCR, "Addresses," p. 247). The necessary annual season pass is obtainable at the campgrounds themselves. Since camping in unofficial areas is now illegal, many campgrounds offer so-called "quickstops" for one night, which permit staying from 9 p.m. to 9 a.m.

Camping coupons, which offer reasonable standard rates, are available at the

ferry agencies which serve Sweden. They are sold only outside of Sweden.

Customs

European citizens of at least 20 years of age may import duty free: 1 liter of spirits (over 22 percent alcohol) or 3 liters of liqueur (up to 22 percent alcohol), plus 5 liters of wine and 15 liters of beer (non-European citizens: 1 liter of spirits or 3 liters of wine).

Visitors over 18 may import 300 cigarettes or 250 grams of tobacco (non-European citizens: 200 cigarettes or 200 grams of tobacco). Otherwise, presents valuing 1,000 SEK may be taken in, but their weight may not exceed 15 kg. It is prohibited to import potatoes, root vegetables, beans, peas, milk, cream, fresh cheese, eggs and fresh meat, as well as all cured and smoked food items. To import hunting weapons, permission must be applied for by the hosting hunter.

Eating and Drinking

Fortunately, Sweden's cuisine is better than its reputation; however, compared with so-called international specialties and fast food, it is diminishing increasingly. Particularly hotel kitchens are poor examples of this. Instead of *strömming med potatis* (Baltic Sea herring with boiled potatoes) or *sill i kapprock* (herring baked in foil) there are "exotic" specialties, such as Wiener schnitzel with French fries, Chinese eggrolls, and Rheinland-style sauerbraten. This is certainly the fault of those tourists who consistently refused Swedish food for so long. The meals cooked in Sweden fulfill three prerequisites: local and inexpensive ingredients are used; the meals are easy to prepare; and servings are generous.

Meals which dominate the Swedish kitchen are those which can either be easily reheated or used for something else. Let us take *Jul skinka* (Christmas ham) for example; it is cooked on Christmas Eve, breaded and fried on Christmas Day, and the rest is made into a type of goulash the following day. It is always served with puréed peas. Since Swedish gravies are often sweet and sticky, it's a good idea to order a dish consisting of fish – either boiled, fried or smoked.

The pancakes (*plättar*) are especially delicious with berry jam. The assortment of cakes leave nothing to be desired. Bread is generally sweet and very soft. You can resort to crispbread or eat the bread with salted butter. The breakfast buffets are definitely worth it, where there is a spread of hot and cold foods, cornflakes, muesli and fruit. The next step up from the breakfast buffet is the *Smörgåsbord* (literally "bread table"), where there is not only open-faced sandwiches, but a lavish spread of hot and cold food sold at a fixed price. Many hotels offer such a buffet at least once a week.

Electricity

Sweden's electrical current is 220 volts.

Emergency Calls

The following emergency number is free of charge: 112. At the time of this printing, the old emergency number 90000 was also in use.

Everyman's Right

The Everyman's Right rule in Scandinavia governs the right of the individual to feel free to calmly wander about in the countryside. This was established at a time when walking was the main way of getting round. It demands respect for nature and permission from the landowner: When on someone else's land, everyone is to behave in such a way as to disturb no one and damage nothing.

The Everyman's Right rule has been abused so frequently in recent years that they are considering doing away with it – at least for foreigners. It is therefore recommendable to be very careful when taking advantage of it The Everyman's Right rule is not meant for motorists, groups, campers or mobile home drivers, who have often broken this rule due to their ignorance of the inherent responsibility it carries with it.

Festivals and Holidays

The largest Christian festivals are each celebrated with two holidays. In addition, New Years' Day, Epiphany (January 6), Good Friday, International Workers' Day (May 1) and All Saints Day are official public holidays. Ascension Day has a double meaning in Sweden; it is also the day of teetotalers. The biggest secular festival, Midsummer Day, is celebrated on the last weekend of June beginning on Friday. The national holiday on June 6 commemorating Gustavus Vasa ascending the throne is a work day, as is Saint Lucia's Day on December 13, when the "Queen of Lights" illuminates the long winter nights. The festivals with the most convivial drinking are, besides Midsummer, Walpurgis Night (April 30), when spring is celebrated, and the crab festival in the middle of August, marking the close of the season for shellfish. (For regional festivals, please see the *Guidepost* of the regional chapter.)

Fishing

Fishing with a hand-held rod is allowed free of charge in all coastal waters, as well as in the five large lakes (Vänern, Vättern, Mälaren, Hjälmaren, Storsjön). A fishing license (*Fiskekort*) is required for all waters and can be purchased at tourist offices, sporting goods shops and gas stations. There are daily, weekly and monthly licenses.

Contact address: Sportfiskarna, PO Box 2, 16321 Spånga, tel. 08-7953350.

Hotels / Vacation Homes / Youth Hostels

There is neither a uniform classification system nor a complete list of the

Guidelines

many hotels in Sweden. The Swedish Hotels Consortium (SHR) has published a guide which covers only about 60 percent of the country's hotels (available from many Swedish tourism agencies). It also explains the various discount systems of the individual hotel chains: there are, for example, possibilities of getting a reduction of up to 50 percent of the official rates by using card systems, hotel coupon booklets or by just booking any of the special deals which are also offered in the summer months. Also be aware that early booking is rewarded – as a general rule: the earlier you book your room, the cheaper it is.

The *Guideposts* at the end of the travel chapters are a further help in finding a room. Categories here are based on the regular rates and mean: ☺☺☺ (Luxury; more than SEK1,400), ☺☺ (Moderate; SEK 750-1,400; and ☺ (Budget; SEK 350-750).

Those who decide on purchasing a coupon booklet must establish the sequence of their travel stops in advance, and should always confirm the reservation at the hotel or campground two days in advance. The most widespread hotel coupon system in Scandinavia is Pro-Scandinavia. It is affiliated with over 400 hotels in more than 300 cities and towns.

Almost all campgrounds rent simple bungalows. Farmhouses on the roadside also offer overnight accommodations (*Stuga*) at moderate prices. You can also look for the sign *Rum* (room), indicating a Bed & Breakfast.

Located on ships, in lighthouses and in prisons, the more than 230 youth hostels found in Sweden also offer rooms for families with children. Most of them belong to the Swedish Touring Club (*Svenska Turistföreningen*; *STF*), which is affiliated with the International Youth Hostel Association. For further information, contact the STF at: PO Box 25, 10120 Stockholm, tel. 08-4632100, e-mail: info@stfturist.se.

Post Offices

Opening hours are Monday through Friday from 9 a.m. to 6 p.m., Saturdays until noon. Newsstands and souvenir shops sell postage stamps in small amounts. Post offices do not offer telephone services.

Shopping

Stores are generally open Monday through Friday from 9 a.m. to 6 p.m., Saturday until 2 or 4 p.m. Grocery stores are often open until 10 p.m. Foodstuffs are also sold at gas stations, which are usually open around the clock. Popular souvenirs are handicrafts made of wood, straw, glass or textiles, which are frequently very unconventional – and no wonder; Sweden's first design school was founded as long ago as 1845.

All large shopping centers, and many gas stations as well, have souvenir sections where a lot of kitsch is sold alongside quality items. The *hemslöjd* shops are widespread; they sell many original items, but are expensive. Sports equipment, fishing and trekking gear is relatively cheap in Sweden.

Delicacies such as smoked salmon, cloudberry jam (*hjortronsylt*) and candy sticks (*polkagrisar*) are popular. Tax-free shopping is no longer permitted for citizens of European Union countries, so that Swedish products outside of Sweden are often cheaper due to a lower level of Value Added Tax.

Smoking

Smoking is prohibited in all buildings in Sweden, except for in bars and at designated areas in restaurants. This ban includes sport stadiums. Cigarettes are sold at newsstands, 20 cigarettes cost a good US $5.

Taking a Number

Everywhere in Sweden where people are served in turn, there is a machine from which you take a number. When your number appears on the indicator board, it is your turn. Exceptions are not made. Those who stand in line without a number are mercilessly sent to the rear.

Telephones

A telephone card, available at any newsstand (*Pressbyrå*), is necessary for making a call from a public pay-phone. The country code for calling from Sweden to Australia is 00961, to the UK 00944, and to the US and Canada 0091. The country code for Sweden is +46.

ADDRESSES

Embassies

AUSTRALIA: Sergels Torg 12, 11157 Stockholm, tel. 08-6132900.
CANADA: Tegelbacken 4, Box 16129, 10323 Stockholm, tel. 08-4533000.
UK: Skarpögatan 6-8, 11593 Stockholm, tel. 08-6719000.
US: Dag Hammarskjölds Väg 31, 11589 Stockholm, tel. 08-7835300.

Camping

Sveriges Campingvärdars Riksförbund, PO Box 255, 45117 Uddevalla, tel. 0522-39345.

Airlines

SAS: Reservation office, domestic and international flights, Stockholm, Stureplan 8, tel. 020-727727.
BRITISH AIRWAYS: Arlanda Airport, tel. 08-7979720.
DELTA: Stockholm Strandvägen 1, tel. 08-6656480.
SWISSAIR: Arlanda Airport, tel. 08-59361679.

Tourist Information

Stockholm (postal code 10393), Sverigehuset, Hamngatan 27, PO Box 7542, tel. 08-7892790, e-mail: info@stoinfo.se; hotel center at main train station, tel. 08-240880; Arlanda Airport, Terminal 2, tel. 08-7976100. **Göteborg** (postal code

41110), Kungsportsplatsen 2, tel. 031-100740, e-mail: info@gbg.co.se. **Malmö** (postal code 21120) Skeppsbron, tel. 040-300150, e-mail: turism.malmo.com. **Örebro** (postal code 70135) Slottet, PO Box 33000, tel. 019-212121, e-mail: destination@orebro.se.

Swedish Embassies

AUSTRALIA: 5 Turrana Street, A.C.T. 2600, Yarralumla, Canberra, tel. 2-62702700, fax 2-62702755.
CANADA: 377 Dalhousie Street, Ottawa, ON K1N 9N8, tel. (613) 241-8553, fax (613) 241-2277.
UK: 11 Montagu Place, London W1H 2AL, tel. 0171-917 6400.
US: 1501 M. Street, NW, Washington, DC 20005, tel. (202) 467-2600.

Language Guide

Thank you (very much) . . . . . . *Tack (så mycket)*
You're welcome. . . . . *Varsågod*
Good morning . . . . *God morgon*
How do you do . . . . *Goddag*
Good-bye . . . . *Adjö*
Hello . . . . *Hej*
Bye-bye . . . . *Hej då*
Excuse me . . . . *Förlåt*
Yes . . . . *ja, jo*
No; not . . . . *nej; ej, inte*
Old . . . . *gammla*
New. . . . . *ny*
Right . . . . *till höger*
Left . . . . *till vänster*
How much does ... cost? *Vad kostar ...?*

In a Restaurant

Menu . . . . *matsedeln*
The bill, please . . . . *Notan, tack*
Fried . . . . *stekt*
Boiled. . . . . *kokt*
Bread. . . . . *bröd*
Butter . . . . *smör*
Cheese . . . . *ost*
Ham . . . . *skinka*
Sausage. . . . . *korv*

Beef	*oxkött*	Vomiting	*kräkning*
Pork	*fläsk*	Train station	*järnvägsstation*
Goulash	*kalops*	Post office	*postkontor*
Chicken	*kykling*	Postage stamp	*frimärke*
Fish	*fisk*	Single room	*enkelrum*
Perch	*abborre*	Double room	*dubbelrum*
Cod	*torsk*	Key	*nyckel*
Pike	*gädda*		
Herring	*strömming*		
Salmon	*lax*		
Prawns	*räkor*		
Fish dumplings	*fiskbullar*		

Numbers

0	*noll*
1	*ett*
2	*två*
3	*tre, trettio*
4	*fyra*
5	*femtio*
6	*sextio*
7	*sju*
8	*åttio*
9	*nittio*
10	*tio*
11	*elva*
12	*tolv*
13	*tretton*
14	*fjorton*
15	*femton*
16	*sexton*
17	*sjutton*
18	*arton*
19	*nitton*
20	*tjugo*
25	*tjugofem*
30	*trettio*
40	*fyrtio*
50	*femtio*
60	*sextio*
70	*sjuttio*
80	*åttio*
90	*nittio*
100	*hundra*
150	*hundrafemtio*
200	*tvåhundra*
1,000	*tusen*

Vegetables — *grönsaker*
Carrots — *morötter*
Cabbage — *kål*
Pear — *päron*
Blackberry — *björnbär*
Strawberry — *jordgubbe*
Raspberry — *hallon*
Cherry — *körsbär*
Milk — *mjölk*
Coffee — *kaffe*
Tea — *te*
Water — *vaten*
Lemonade — *läsk*
Ice cream — *glass*
Draft beer — *fatöl*

Traffic, Automobile

Stop — *Stopp*
Caution — *Se upp, giv akt*
Construction site — *vägarbete*
One-way street — *enkelriktad*
No through street — *infart förbjuden*
Road closed — *gatan avstängt*
Tow — *ta på släp*
Car — *bil*
Starter — *självstart*
Battery — *batteri*
Breakdown — *sönder*
Flat tire — *punktering*
Gas station — *(bensin)mack*
Garage (workshop) — *bilverkstad*
Oil change — *oljebyte*

Miscellaneous

Doctor — *läkare*
Dentist — *tandläkare*
Diarrhea — *diarré*

The letters å, ä and ö are at the end of the Swedish alphabet. Pronunciation (regional differences): An "o" is often pronounced like oo, and a "u" is very similar to the phonetic y; g before the vowels e, i, y, ä, and ö as well as dj, hj and lj, additionally lg and rg at the end of syllables are pronounced like "y"; k before e, i, y, ä and ö as well as kj, sj, stj and tj sound more or less like a sharp "shh."

AUTHORS

Gerhard Lemmer: Project Editor and main author of this book, Mr. Lemmer is a study-tour guide. Throughout and after his studies of sociology, politics, history and art history, he traveled extensively around the world, until he decided to make his hobby a profession in 1983. He travels to Sweden for visits to cultural landmarks and natural landscapes several times a year.

Birgit Krämer: Ms. Krämer studied Romance languages and literature, as well as art history. The diverse connections of the Vikings with the Romance area aroused her interest in Scandinavia, where she has been a study-tour guide for a number of years. She wrote the articles on the "Vasa" and "Astrid Lindgren," as well as the chapter on Stockholm together with Gerhard Lemmer. She made valuable contributions to all other sections of this book.

Otto Steiger: Dr. Steiger has been a professor of economics at the University of Bremen, Germany, since 1973. After completing his studies of economics and its history in Berlin and Uppsala, he taught at the universities of Uppsala, Stockholm and Umeå. From 1989 to 1992, he was on the nomination committee for the Nobel Prize for Economics at the Swedish Academy of Sciences. He explains the theory of the "Welfare State" in this book.

PHOTOGRAPHERS

Guidelines

INDEX

Explore the World

NELLES GUIDES

NORWAY

GREEK ISLANDS

SPAIN

AVAILABLE TITLES

Australia
Bali / Lombok
Berlin and Potsdam
Brazil
Brittany
Burma → Myanmar
California
  *Las Vegas, Reno,
  Baja California*
Cambodia / Laos
Canada
  *Ontario, Québec,
  Atlantic Provinces*
Canada
  *Pacific Coast, the Rockies,
  Prairie Provinces, and
  the Territories*
Canary Islands
Caribbean
  *The Greater Antilles,
  Bermuda, Bahamas*
Caribbean
  The Lesser Antilles
China – Hong Kong
Corsica
Costa Rica
Crete
Croatia – *Adriatic Coast*
Cyprus
Egypt
Florida

Greece – *The Mainland*
Greek Islands
Hawai'i
Hungary
India
  *Northern, Northeastern
  and Central India*
India – *Southern India*
Indonesia
  *Sumatra, Java, Bali,
  Lombok, Sulawesi*
Ireland
Israel - *with Excursions
  to Jordan*
Kenya
London, England and
  Wales
Malaysia - Singapore
  - Brunei
Maldives
Mexico
Morocco
Moscow / St. Petersburg
Munich
  *Excursions to Castles,
  Lakes & Mountains*
Myanmar (Burma)
Nepal
New York – *City and State*
New Zealand
Norway
Paris
Philippines

Poland
Portugal
Prague / Czech Republic
Provence
Rome
Scotland
South Africa
South Pacific Islands
Spain – *Pyrenees, Atlantic
  Coast, Central Spain*
Spain
  *Mediterranean Coast,
  Southern Spain,
  Balearic Islands*
Sri Lanka
Syria – Lebanon
Sweden
Tanzania
Thailand
Turkey
Tuscany
U.S.A.
  The East, Midwest and South
U.S.A.
  *The West, Rockies and
  Texas*
Vietnam

FORTHCOMING

Cuba
Dominican Republic
Peru

Nelles Guides – authoritative, informed and informative.
Always up-to-date, extensively illustrated, and with first-rate relief maps.
256 pages, approx. 150 color photos, approx. 25 maps.